# THE
# STATLER BROTHERS
# DISCOGRAPHY

**The Statler Brothers**

Phil Balsley, Harold Reid, Jimmy Fortune, and Don Reid—from the cover of the 1996 Showbook. Photo courtesy of The Statler Brothers.

# THE
# STATLER BROTHERS
# DISCOGRAPHY

*Compiled by*
## Alice Y. Holtin

Forewords by Johnny Cash
and Jerry Kennedy

Discographies, Number 71

**GREENWOOD PRESS**
Westport, Connecticut • London

**Library of Congress Cataloging-in-Publication Data**

Holtin, Alice Y.
    The Statler Brothers discography / compiled by Alice Y. Holtin ;
foreworks by Johnny Cash and Jerry Kennedy.
        p.   cm. — (Discographies, ISSN 0192-334X ; no.71)
    Includes bibliographical references and index.
    ISBN 0-313-29663-4 (alk. paper)
    1. Statler Brothers—Discography.  I. Title.  II. Series.
ML156.7.S785H65   1997
016.782421642′092′2—dc21        97-5301

British Library Cataloguing in Publication Data is available.

Library of Congress Catalog Card Number: 97-5301
ISBN: 0-313-29663-4
ISSN: 0192-334X

First published in 1997

Greenwood Press, Post Road West, Westport, CT 06881
An imprint of Greenwood Publishing Group, Inc.

Printed in the United States of America

10 9 8 7 6 5 4 3 2 1

# Copyright Acknowledgments

The editor and publisher gratefully acknowledge permission for use of the following material:

Excerpts from **The Johnny Cash Discography** by John L. Smith. Copyright ©1985 by John L. Smith. Reprinted with permission of Greenwood Publishing Group, Inc., Westport, Connecticut.

Excerpts from **The Statler Brothers 30ᵗʰ Anniversary Celebration Scrapbook**, by Colin Escott. Copyright © 1994 Mercury Nashville. All rights reserved. Used by permission.

Lyrics from "We" by Don Reid. Copyright © 1970, published by House of Cash, Inc. Used by permission of the House of Cash, Inc.

Lyrics from songs by the Statler Brothers, published by American Cowboy Music Co., Inc. All rights assigned to All Nations Publishing Co., Inc., Beverly Hills, California. Used by permission of All Nations Publishing Co., Inc.
     "You've Been Like A Mother To Me," Don Reid, ©1974.
     "Together," Carroll "Bull" Durham, ©1974.
     "Some I Wrote," Don Reid, Harold Reid, ©1977.
     "We Got Paid By Cash," Harold Reid, Don Reid, ©1980.

Individual lines of lyrics by the Statler Brothers, published by the American Cowboy Music Co., Inc. All rights assigned to All Nations Publishing Co., Inc., Beverly Hills, California. Used by permission of All Nations Publishing Co., Inc.

Lyrics from "The Rest of My Life," by Don Reid. Copyright © 1992, published by Statler Brothers Music, Inc. All rights assigned to All Nations Publishing Co., Inc., Beverly Hills, California. Used by permission of All Nations Publishing Co., Inc.

Lyrics from "What We Love To Do," by Wil Reid and Langdon Reid. Copyright ©1994, published by Beverly Manor Music, Inc./Admin. by Copyright Management Inc. All rights reserved. Used by permission.

Individual lines of lyrics by the Statler Brothers, published by Beverly Manor Music, Inc./Admin. by Copyright Management, Inc. Used by permission.

# Dedication

To Harold, Phil, Jimmy & Don --

And to the memory of Lew --


Thank you for being there and for your sacrifices,
and for sharing your life and your love of music
with your fans.

And a very special "Thank You" to your families.
Their sacrifice may have been greater than yours.

# Contents

"There is a friend that sticks closer than a brother."

My extended family in the music business have always been as precious to me as blood on blood. The Statler Brothers are a prime example. From that day in the early sixties, when I first heard them sing, at Watermelon Park, in Virginia, until today, I've loved them as my own. This discography of their fabulous journey, record wise, is precious to me. It's like a family document.

With the release of this discography, now we can all share in the information that has bonded these four guys to our hearts and souls through music.

Long ago I was bonded to them through love. The Statler Brothers Discography is a treasure of so many things that are precious, and if you're just lookin' for the fact's ma'am, you'll find them all here.

Share with me this loving, lasting legacy of my brothers, The Statlers.

*John Cash*

# Foreword by Jerry Kennedy

I first met the Statlers when I played guitar on some of their Columbia sessions in the late '60s. If my memory is any good at all, we did a gospel album the first time I was called. Naturally I was aware of "Flowers on the Wall," and I remember looking forward to the sessions so I could meet the group. I wasn't disappointed -- I enjoyed the music, and I really did like the guys. I was called back to do more sessions later.

Working as a session guitarist was not my only job in the '60s. I was also the head of Mercury Records office in Nashville. It was my job to find talent and produce records for the label. Sometime during the summer of 1970, I received a call from Harold Reid. He informed me of the Statlers' desire to leave Columbia Records, and he wanted to know if we would be willing to talk to them about the possibility of signing with Mercury. Thank God I agreed to the meeting and as they say, "the rest is history."

Harold, Phil, Don and Lew became very successful artists on Mercury, but they became much more than that -- they became my good friends. Maybe that's why the artist-producer relationship has lasted for over twenty-six years. That translates into a lot of music. We've had fun all the way -- that's one of the great things about workin' with talented friends. They've really made my job easy. We've also been through some trying situations together. When Lew had to leave the group, he left some big shoes to be filled. This could have been a real disaster, but the guys found Jimmy (who showed up with some real big shoes of his own) and the beat went on -- no lookin' back. They did what they had to do and did it well and I got a new friend in the deal. There was a new Statler sound that was just as good as before. The stylistic group sound was still there with a touch of freshness that really complimented what was already a very successful act, and they became even more successful.

This well researched and factual book is the work of a real Statler fan -- Alice Holtin. She has done a fantastic job of gathering all the information pertaining to the Statler Brothers' career. She's taken me on a walk through a lot of great memories . . . dates, titles, times, musicians, etc. I'm really thankful and proud to have been a small part of their career, because like Alice, I'm a real Statler fan, too.

# Preface

I was 12 years old, and home from school with the flu. I remember I had a high fever and slept almost all the time. My mom had left the radio on and every time I woke up the same song was playing -- and that song was *"Flowers on the Wall."* I had never heard a song played so many times in one day before; the DJs, and America, had discovered the Statler Brothers. By the end of the day I was much improved, and so was the world of Country Music.

Over the years, their music has become a very personal thing to many of their fans. They have covered so many types of music, such varied aspects of life, and have touched all of us. That's why they became, and have remained, extremely popular (second only to Ol' Blue Eyes [Frank Sinatra], himself) -- it was easy for everyone to relate to their music.

Different sections of this work are preceded by their song lyrics. This is the avenue they have chosen to share with us their lives (some are very biographical). These lyrics relate directly to the material that follows in each section. We, their fans, can find lyrics that apply to the way we feel about them, too. There is one song that comes to my mind, lines from which are applicable to this book.

> *"If I could just be a part of your memory,*
> *You would carry the rest of your life . . . ."*

The Statlers have given unselfishly of themselves through the years, and have become an important part of the memories of many of us. We would all like to do something for them, to show our appreciation for the sacrifices they've had to make -- they and their families.

> *"If I could just do something for you,*
> *That has never been done for you before;*

*If I could leave something behind me, . . .*
*Then I'd be gone like a wild wind in winter*
*Knowing I had done one thing right.*
*If I could just make you happy for a moment,*
*I'd be happy the rest of my life."*

THE REST OF MY LIFE
(Don Reid)

To Don, Harold, Phil, & Jimmy -- I hope this is one thing I've done right, and you are happy with the results, at least for a moment.

-- A.H.

# Acknowledgments

There are many who have encouraged me in this project. My family -- my husband, Rodger; my daughter, Monica; and my sons, Jim, Andy, Brian, and Peter -- have been patient and long-suffering when Mom would go into what they call *"Statler-mode."* Their assistance in researching, tolerance of my long hours in the library, and late nights at the computer made all this possible.

Our long-time friend and fellow record collector, David J. Diehl of Harlingen, Texas, was the first to convince me I could do this book, and he provided me with leads and pointed me in the right direction.

Ms. Kira Florita and Ms. Claudia Mize at Mercury Records, Nashville. Their assistance with the in-depth material I needed, their willingness to help, and their hospitality made me feel very welcome.

Mrs. Ann Peters, and the staff members at the Statler Brothers offices in Staunton, Virginia. I appreciate very much all their help, and the information they provided for me.

Mr. Jerry Kennedy -- Don Reid referred to him as "a great guy and a great friend. Without him, there never would have been a Statler Brothers hit record." Now I know what Don meant. Jerry is one-of-a-kind. Without his interest and his contributions, this book would be worthless.

To my friend and mentor, John L. Smith -- I couldn't have done it without him. It was his interest in my efforts, and his guiding hand when I got stuck, that made possible the work you see here. His experience was more than I had hoped to be able to draw from when I began this. Thanks, John.

A special thanks to Johnny Cash for his contribution to this work. He first recognized the Statler Brothers' talents and abilities. He liked what he saw and heard, and he brought them to the attention of the American public. This book shows the result of his farsightedness.

My thanks to those who helped provide me with copies of documents necessary to this work, and their recollections of specific events: Mayo Taylor at the Center for Popular Music in Murfreesboro, Tennessee; Bob Pinson and Ron Pugh at the Country Music Foundation in Nashville, Tennessee; Carol Hardin at the Nashville Association of Musicians; Nick Shaffran, Sony Music Special Products, New York, NY; and Ms. Pam Repp, Jim Owens Productions, Nashville, Tennessee.

# Introduction

The quartet known as *The Statler Brothers* was originally made up of four young men from Staunton, Virginia: Harold Reid, bass; Phil Balsley, baritone; Don Reid, lead; and Lew DeWitt, tenor. When Lew was forced to retire in 1982 for health reasons, Jimmy Fortune was chosen to sing the tenor part. The Statler Brothers are unique in country music, not just because they are a group in a genre of single performers, but because of their musical style. They all grew up together in the hills and valleys of Virginia, with the same values and ideals. (Jimmy didn't grow up with the others, but his background is strikingly similar.) Those values and ideals are reflected in the songs they write and in their performance. Those values and ideals touch a lot of people's hearts, and make them very easy to identify with -- the ups and downs of life that we all experience. But they have the talent to put it to music.

They were born in the Shenandoah Valley of Virginia. It is also the birthplace of gospel music.[1] Learning to sing in harmony of their faith and love of God, and His for mankind, they learned a musical style that has carried them through life doing what they love to do. The Statlers learned to carry over this type of singing into other types of music. Beginning with their third album, it has been their policy to always include a gospel song on every album, and on every television show. (Even the Roadhog included a gospel song in his program.) Their concerts always include a gospel segment. This also sets them apart in the world of music today. Many country singers have come from a similar background, but few require one gospel song on **every** album.

Barbara Mandrell said it best in the liner notes she wrote for the album, **The Legend goes on . . . .** She used the term "Statlerized" to describe a song after the

---

[1] **I'll Fly Away, The Life Story of Albert Brumley**, p. 130.

Statler Brothers have sung it. It will never sound the same again. Every title listed in chapters two through four have been "Statlerized."

This publication is not intended to be a biography or an in-depth scholarly analysis of the lives of the Statlers. This started out as an effort to get my own collection in order. But I wanted to know more about the music I love so much, and this is the result.

One person who has been a great source of encouragement to me is John L. Smith, author of the **Johnny Cash Discography, Vols. I & II; The Johnny Cash Record Catalog**, and the award-winning **Waylon Jennings Discography**, both published by Greenwood Press. I was concerned that the Statlers' years with Johnny Cash were going to be the hardest for me to document. Mr. Smith has been more than gracious in allowing me to use the material from his book as it relates to the Statlers' participation in Johnny Cash's recording career. Mr. Smith also wrote some introductory notes to the **Johnny Cash Discography, Vol. I**, regarding discographies in general which are applicable to this work, and I could not phrase them any better. With his permission, they follow here.

A discography can be defined as "simply a work of reference to all the known recordings by a given performer or group of performers or by those coming within certain limits of style, category, period, or composition" (Rust/1980:3). Or, discography can be further detailed and divided into such categories as scientific, analytical, historical, and systematic as Gordon Stevenson points out in his 1972 article in *Library Trends* (Stevenson/1972). I would, however, take exception with the definition of a discography given only as "a catalogue of phonograph records; especially, a comprehensive list of the recordings made by a particular performer or of a particular composer's work" (Connor/1971:1). While it is true that many listings of recordings over the years have appeared as "discographies," more information needs to be included than merely singles and albums alone.

In order to properly study the recording career of any artist, more must be known than just their release credits. These must be supplemented by session information, giving location of the session, session musicians, master numbers and, where possible, even the times during which the sessions took place. Composer credits should be included to show how heavily an artist relies on his own compositions [*Or how much his audience prefers his own compositions.-AH*] and the material of others to fill his catalog. Producer credits, as well, should be given in order to study how the artist's repertory and style are changed and what effect producers have on the music of a given artist.

The obvious fact that they remain "continuing" artists means that further updates of the subjects will be necessary in the future.

The scope of this book is to give a recording history of the Statler Brothers using a listing of over 187 sessions, covering a period from April, 1964, through May, 1995. These sessions have produced over 498 masters. The finished product is shown in the Index of Releases, which is not a complete catalog of the releases.

The recording career of the Statler Brothers is marked by four distinctive factors. Those factors automatically divide their career into four different sections, determined by career status and recording company. Chapter One is the sessions as background vocals for Johnny Cash on the Columbia label (their name may or may not appear on the label). Chapter Two is sessions released under their name on Columbia. Chapter Three is the beginning of the Mercury years, sessions with Lew DeWitt, and more of their own compositions. Chapter Four is the sessions with Jimmy Fortune, and compositions written by more of their children -- The Second Generation. Keys to abbreviations appear at the beginning of each chapter. Because some of these chapters overlap, i.e., one and two, and one and three, they are not a strict chronological listing, but are grouped as mentioned above. A Chronological Session Listing is given in Appendix I.

The Statlers made some recordings in Virginia in the early 1960s. They were known as "The Kingsmen" then, and were background vocalists for local artists. More information on these recordings is found in Appendix II.

They began to work for Johnny Cash on March 9, 1964, in Canton, Ohio. It was their first national exposure. Cash was recording for Columbia Records at the time, and he took them to the studio. The first contract the Statlers entered into with Columbia was actually signed by Cash, for the Statlers' services. The Statlers first recording session with Columbia was April 3, 1964. Their first session with Johnny Cash was December 18, 1964.

**Master Numbers** -- For the last century, standard practice has been that any title by an artist was assigned a number when recorded. If it required more than one try ("take"), at the same recording session, to get a recording satisfactory to all concerned, those repeated "takes" were assigned Take Numbers as a suffix to the same master number (i.e., 52359-3). Generally, a take that was issued, or ultimately rejected and not issued, had an individual master number. At Columbia and Mercury studios, any future recording of this same title was given a new master number. This was to locate a title in the master vaults as they were needed for release, or reissue at a future date. [These are not to be confused with issue (or catalog) numbers. About 1986, Mercury Records discontinued the use of master numbers and went to File ID numbers.]

**File ID Numbers** -- When Mercury ceased the use of master numbers, about 1986, they began to use File ID numbers. This number identifies the box in the vault files that contains the tape on which this title is found. That tape may contain an entire album, or as many recording sessions as they could get on one tape. More than one title will have the same ID number, and a title may have several ID numbers if it has been reissued. For the purpose of this work, I have included all the File ID numbers that could be documented.

**Issue (or Catalog) Numbers** -- Each disc (45 rpm singles and LP's), tape (single or album, cassette or 8-track), or compact disc is given a number when released to the public. These are referred to as issue numbers. These issue numbers are also used for the product in industry catalogs, and therefore are also the catalog number.

**Overdub sessions** -- The advancements in recording technology have brought us amazing sound quality. They also have changed the recording methods used by the studios. In the early days, every singer and musician gathered in one room and worked together to achieve a satisfactory take. With the advent of multi-track magnetic recording tape and the ability to record on each track **separately**, everyone did not have to present at the same time. Some could record at a later date, even in a different studio, and all of it be mixed together electronically into one final product.

These sessions are given in detail on each title, except string overdubs. Because of the number of musicians involved, they are listed in detail (date, time, and personnel) only on the first master number they appear. On succeeding masters, it refers back to the first master for details ("OD -- 4/26/71, Strings, see 48461"). The overdub session was recorded in the same studio as the original session, unless otherwise noted. For the period in which Mercury ceased to use master numbers, complete string overdub session details are given on the first title they appear. Other titles will refer the reader back to the first listing by the session date and name of the first title, and the overdub date ("OD -- see 1/12/88, MAKING MEMORIES, overdub of 6/8/88").

**Licensing** -- Recording companies can release a title made by another recording company through what is known as licensing. Columbia Records (now Sony Music) has sold to Mercury Records on separate occasions, the license to reissue one or more of the Columbia recordings on the Mercury label.

**Musicians** -- I have made a diligent effort to identify what instruments are played by which musicians. These men and women are extremely talented and most play more than one instrument. Some explanation is necessary.

Jerry Kennedy has played guitar, dobro, and even electric sitar on these recordings. What he played at a particular session depended on what other musicians were present and what type of sound he was looking for. On overdub sessions, the same situation existed. He may have played guitar on the regular session and again on the overdub to give it a richer sound. The same procedure also for the dobro. Or he may have played one at the session and the other at the overdub. Since he has been present on all 366 Mercury sessions (and numerous overdub sessions) and few records exist as to exactly what he played when, both instruments are given. When the musician listing on an album gave him credit for only one instrument, that is the one I have used. On regular session entries, the entry is "Jerry Kennedy (g,db)." Overdub sessions are usually given as "Jerry Kennedy (g/db)."

Charlie McCoy has at various times played vibes, organ, and/or harmonica on these sessions. Where identifiable, it is so noted. Otherwise, the entry is "Charlie McCoy (org,hm,vb)."

**Composer Credits** -- The composer credits are given when known. There are several titles the Statlers have recorded over the years which have outlasted the original composer's copyright, and have become known as "Traditional" or "Public Domain." I have included the original composer's name (when known) and the date of the work in brackets, in an effort to keep from permanently losing the composer's identity.

# Documentation

I have made a concentrated effort to obtain documented source material for everything included here. My sources are listed here for your reference.

**Chapter One** -- Reprinted from the discography of Johnny Cash, compiled by John L. Smith, with some minor changes by Mr. Smith as concerned the participation of the Statlers in Johnny Cash's recording career.

**Chapter Two** -- Columbia Records' Artist Job Sheets, Artist Contract Cards, Label Mastering Instructions, musician's appointment books archived at the Country Music Foundation, the musicians themselves, conversation with the Statlers 10/7/96. Musicians' contracts for this time period could not be located.

**Chapter Three** - Contracts, Nashville Association of Musicians; Mercury Records Nashville Production Reports, Record Information Sheets, Label Copy sheets; album copy, conversations with Jerry Kennedy and the Statler Brothers.

**Chapter Four** -- Contracts, Nashville Association of Musicians; Mercury Records Nashville Production Reports, Record Information Sheets, Label Copy sheets; album copy, conversations with Jerry Kennedy and the Statler Brothers.

**Chapter Five** -- The albums themselves; Mercury Nashville Production Reports, Record Information Sheets, Label Copy sheets.

**Chapter Six** -- Album copy.

**Chapter Seven** - Research of the back issues of *Billboard* magazine, 1965-1995; microfilm, microfiche, and hard copy bound volumes.

**Chapter Eight** - My own work, taken from songs written by members of the Statler Brothers.

**Chapter Nine** -- The Statler Brothers Office, Staunton, Virginia.

**Chapter Ten** -- The Statler Brothers Office, Staunton, Virginia; the Office of the Program Director, The Nashville Network, Nashville, Tennessee.

**Chapter Eleven** - The Statler Brothers Office, Staunton, Virginia.

Every discographer's greatest fear is the loss or destruction of vital files.  In this instance, the files I found to be the most valuable are the musicians union contracts. There are some scattered dates throughout this work for which these documents are not available.  For these dates, I was able to find master numbers in the Mercury files, including production reports, copies of notes on tape master boxes, studio notes, label copy and mastering instructions.  The information given regarding musicians for these same dates is taken from the album covers, and is so noted.  For names I recognized, I assigned an instrument based on what my information showed they played at other sessions; therefore they are marked "instrumentation in brackets my assumption."  Included here is what information I could find.  [I did the best I could with what I had; at least it's not totally lost to us.]

My final comment -- I take full responsibility for the accuracy of the information contained within these pages and would hope that any mistakes discovered by readers would be brought to my attention for correction.

> "If we had known you were going to come along and write a book, we would have written it all down!"

> --Jerry Kennedy

# THE
# STATLER BROTHERS
# DISCOGRAPHY

# WE GOT PAID BY CASH

It started March of '64, many years ago
We were hired by Johnny Cash to open up his show
Four boys, a worn-out Cadillac with a roadmap on the dash
For the next eight and one-half years, we got paid by Cash.

He took us down to Nashville to Columbia Studios.
Not knowing where we came from, they told us where to go.
But Johnny said, "I like 'em -- don't you give them no trash."
You see, we were Johnny's Little Boys, and we got paid by Cash.

Chorus:
We were there when June became Johnny's lovin' bride,
And we sang to him that morning our buddy Luther died,
And we were there when the son was born that filled them both with pride,
And we were there when John remembered God was on his side.

We watched him on the concert stage and watched him write his songs,
And saw the things we had to do and the things that could go wrong.
And if we had to start again, we'd do it in a flash --
'Cause we learned more than we earned when we got paid by Cash.

Then came the time when our career demanded that we go,
And through some tears we all shook hands that last and final show.
All those years we never had a contract or a clash,
Whatever we may be today, we owe it all to Cash.

Now John will tell you there were years when times were good and bad
But we can tell you they were some of the best we ever had.
Carl Perkins and the Carters and the Tennessee Three --
We were one big happy family, and would have done it all for free!

*Harold Reid/Don Reid*, April 30, 1980
American Cowboy Music Co., Inc.
Used by permission of
    All Nations Publishing Co., Inc.

# CHAPTER 1

# We Got Paid by Cash:
# The Cash Years

Many fans will remember that the Statlers toured with Johnny Cash, but may not be aware of the many background vocals they provided for Johnny Cash recordings during this period. Because their job with Cash represented their first big break, and a lot of their earliest records were Cash backgrounds, it is appropriate that we begin here with Mr. Cash. This chapter covers only those sessions with Cash. (See Appendix I for a Chronological Session Listing.) The album covers may or may not give the Statlers credit as appearing on the record.

The remaining material in this chapter is an abridgement of material from **The Johnny Cash Discography** (1985), a compilation by John L. Smith. If you wish more information about the recording career of Johnny Cash, please see the above referenced work which covers the years 1954 through 1984, as well as **The Johnny Cash Discography, 1984-1994**, and **The Johnny Cash Record Catalog**, both compiled by John L. Smith and published by Greenwood Press in 1994.

KEY TO ABBREVIATIONS and PREFIXES
"4-xxxxx" - 5-digit numbers preceded by "4-" are 45 rpm singles
"CL" - monaural long-plays.
"CS" - stereo long-plays.
"no cc" - no composer credits are known.
"V" - anthology albums; include a number of different artists.
"Mer" - Mercury release

============================================================

Columbia Studios, Nashville                    December 18/19, 1964
                                                      (10:00-01:00)
Johnny Cash, vocal, guitar; Carter Family, vocals; Marshall Grant, bass; W.S. Holland, drums; Charlie McCoy, harmonica; Luther Perkins, electric guitar; Bill Pursell, piano; Boots Randolph, saxophone. Prod. Don Law and Frank Jones.

NCO-80925  **AMEN**  (Hairston)
           CL-2309/CS-9109 -- *Orange Blossom Special*

**Note:**     Male vocals on AMEN sounds like **Statler Brothers** but Columbia ledger
sheets make no mention of them.  *(In a letter to the author dated 10/12/95, Don
Reid confirmed that the Statlers are indeed on this recording.--A.H.)*
======================================================================

Columbia Studios, Nashville                                    March 12, 1965
Johnny Cash, vocal, guitar; Marshall Grant, bass; W.S. Holland, drums; Bob
Johnson, five-string banjo -1, mando-cello -2; Luther Perkins, electric guitar;
**Statler Brothers, vocals**; Unknown saxophone -5 (possibly Boots Randolph).
Prod: Don Law and Frank Jones.

NCO-82646  **A LETTER FROM HOME**  (M.Carter, D.Dean) -1
           C2L38/C2S838 -- *Ballads of the True West*
           CL-2446/CS-9246 -- *Mean As Hell*

NCO-82648  **TWENTY-FIVE MINUTES TO GO**  (Shel Silverstein) -2
           C2L38/C2S838 -- *Ballads of the True West*
           CL-2446/CS-9246 -- *Mean As Hell*
======================================================================

Columbia Studios, Nashville                                    March 13 1965
Johnny Cash, vocal, guitar; Maybelle Carter, autoharp -1; Carter Family, vocals -2;
Marshall Grant, bass; W.S. Holland, drums; Bob Johnson, guitar; Luther Perkins,
electric guitar; **Statler Brothers, vocals**.  Prod: Don Law and Frank Jones.

NCO-82650  **RODEO HAND**  (Peter LaFarge)
           BFX-15033 -- *Tall Man*

NCO-82652  **STAMPEDE**  (Peter LaFarge) -1,2
           C2L38/C2S838 -- *Ballads of the True West*
           CL-2446/CS-9246, *Mean As Hell*
======================================================================

Columbia Studios, Nashville                                    May 12, 1965
Johnny Cash, vocal, guitar; Carter Family, vocals; Marshall Grant, bass; W.S.
Holland, drums; Luther Perkins, electric guitar; **Statler Brothers, vocals**; Unknown
trumpets -1 (possibly Karl Garvin & William McElhiney).  Prod: Don Law and
Frank Jones.

NCO-82744  **THUNDERBALL**  (Johnny Cash) -1
           BFX-15030 -- *Johnny & June*

NCO-82745  **MISTER GARFIELD**  (Jack Elliott)
           4-43313 -- backed w/STREETS OF LAREDO

NCO-82746   **THE STREETS OF LAREDO**   (arr by Johnny Cash)
                   4-43313 -- backed w/MISTER GARFIELD

**Note:**   Columbia ledger sheet information for this session gives the notation
"edited version" for both MISTER GARFIELD and THE STREETS OF LAREDO. Despite
the assigning of new master numbers for this session, MISTER GARFIELD appears
to be the same as cut on March 11, 1965, except for the absence of a narrative
introduction while the single version of THE STREETS OF LAREDO still appears to be
the same as the March 10, 1965, recording.

================================================================

Columbia Studios, Nashville                                        June 11, 1965
Johnny Cash, vocal, guitar; Carter Family, vocals; Marshall Grant, bass; **Lew
DeWitt (of Statler Brothers) whistler -1**; W.S. Holland, drums; Luther Perkins,
electric guitar; **Statler Brothers, vocals**; Unknown trumpet -2 (possibly Karl
Garvin or William McElhiney); Unknown piano -3. Prod: Don Law and Frank
Jones.

NCO-82775   **THE SONS OF KATIE ELDER**   (E.Sheldon, E.Bernstein) -2
                   4-43342 -- backed w/A CERTAIN KINDA HURTIN'
                   OL-6420/OS2820 -- movie soundtrack, *The Sons of Katie Elder*
                   STS2004 -- *The Heart of Johnny Cash*

NCO-82776   **A CERTAIN KINDA HURTIN'**   (Johnny Cash) -1,3
                   4-43342 -- backed w/THE SONS OF KATIE ELDER
                   KH-30916 -- *Understand Your Man*
                   STS2004 -- *The Heart of Johnny Cash*

**Note:**   THE SONS OF KATIE ELDER appears on the soundtrack album of the
Paramount motion picture of the same name starring John Wayne. However, it was
not included in the actual picture soundtrack.

================================================================

Columbia Studios, Nashville                                        July 28, 1965
Johnny Cash, vocal, guitar; Marshall Grant, bass; W.S. Holland, drums; Luther
Perkins, electric guitar; **Statler Brothers, vocals**; Unknown female chorus;
Unknown organ - possibly Bill Pursell. Prod: Don Law and Frank Jones.

NCO-82817   **HAPPY TO BE WITH YOU**
                   (June Carter, Johnny Cash, Merle Kilgore)
                   4-43420 -- backed w/PICKIN' TIME
                   CL-2537/CS-9337 -- *Happiness Is You*

================================================================

Columbia Studios, Nashville                                     November 29, 1965
Johnny Cash, vocal, guitar; Carter Family,  vocals; Marshall Grant, bass; W.S.
Holland, drums; Bob Johnson, guitar; Luther Perkins, electric guitar; **Statler
Brothers, vocals**. Prod: Don Law and Frank Jones.

NCO-83011   **SHE CAME FROM THE MOUNTAINS**   (Peter LaFarge)
                CL-2537/CS-9337 -- *Happiness Is You*

=================================================================

Columbia Studios, Nashville                                  December 1, 1965
Johnny Cash, vocal, guitar; Carter Family, vocals; Marshall Grant, bass; W.S.
Holland, drums; Luther Perkins, electric guitar; **Statler Brothers, vocals**; Unknown
vibes or organ -1, possibly Bill Pursell.  Prod: Don Law and Frank Jones.

NCO-83024   **GUESS THINGS HAPPEN THAT WAY**   (Jack Clement)
                Knox Music
                CL-2537/CS-9337 -- *Happiness Is You*
                KC-30887 -- *The Johnny Cash Collection*
                KH-30138 -- *The Walls of a Prison*

NCO-83025   **HAPPINESS IS YOU**   (Johnny Cash, June Carter)  -1
                CL-2536/CS-9337 -- *Happiness Is You*
                STS2004 -- *The Heart of Johnny Cash*

=================================================================

Columbia Studios, Nashville                                  January 11, 1967
Johnny Cash, vocal, guitar; **Phil Balsley (of the Statler Brothers)**, vocal; Norman
Blake, dobro; June Carter, vocal; Marshall Grant, bass; W.S. Holland, drums;
Luther Perkins, electric guitar.  Prod:  Don Law and Frank Jones.

NCO-120349 **PACK UP YOUR SORROWS**   (R.Farina, P.Marden)
                4-44011 -- backed w/JACKSON
                CL-2728/CS-9528 -- *Carryin' on with Cash & Carter*
                KH-31256 -- *Give My Love to Rose*

=================================================================

Columbia Studios, Nashville                                  January 12, 1967
Johnny Cash, vocal, guitar; Carter Family, vocals; Marshall Grant, bass; W.S.
Holland, drums; Bob Johnson, mando-cello; Carl Perkins, electric guitar; Luther
Perkins, electric guitar; **Statler Brothers, vocal**.  Prod:  Don Law and Frank Jones.

NCO-120355 **THE WIND CHANGES**   (Johnny Cash)
                4-44288 -- backed w/RED VELVET

=================================================================

Folsom Prison, California                                    January 13, 1968
Johnny Cash, vocal, guitar; June Carter, vocal -1; Carter Family, vocals; Marshall
Grant, bass; W.S. Holland, drums; Carl Perkins, electric guitar; Luther Perkins,
electric guitar; **Statler Brothers, vocals**.  Prod:  Bob Johnston.

NCO-98435-A     **FOLSOM PRISON BLUES**   (Johnny Cash)

NCO-98436       **BUSTED**   (Harlan Howard)

| | |
|---|---|
| NCO-98437-A | DARK AS A DUNGEON  (Merle Travis) |
| NCO-98438-A | I STILL MISS SOMEONE  (Johnny Cash, Roy Cash, Jr.) |
| NCO-98439-A | COCAINE BLUES  (T.J. Arnell) |
| NCO-98440-A | TWENTY-FIVE MINUTES TO GO  (Shel Silverstein) |
| NCO-98441 | I'M NOT IN YOUR TOWN TO STAY  (no cc) |
| NCO-98442-A | ORANGE BLOSSOM SPECIAL  (E.T. Rouse) |
| NCO-98443-A | LONG BLACK VEIL  (M.Wilken, D.Danny) |
| NCO-98444-A | SEND A PICTURE OF MOTHER  (Johnny Cash) |
| NCO-98445-A | THE WALL  (Harlan Howard) |
| NCO-98446-A | DIRTY OLD EGG SUCKING DOG  (Jack Clement) |
| NCO-98447-A | FLUSHED FROM THE BATHROOM OF YOUR HEART  (Jack Clement) |
| NCO-98448 | JOE BEAN  (J.R. Hall) |
| NCO-98449-A | JACKSON  (G.Rodgers, B.Wheeler) |
| NCO-98450 | I'VE GOT A WOMAN  (Ray Charles) -1 |
| NCO-98451 | JOHN HENRY  (Johnny Cash) |
| NCO-98452-A | GREEN, GREEN GRASS OF HOME  (Curly Putnam) |
| NCO-98453 | GREYSTONE CHAPEL  (Glen Sherley) |
| NCO-98454-A | GREYSTONE CHAPEL  (Glen Sherley) |
| NCO-98455-B | GIVE MY LOVE TO ROSE  (Johnny Cash) |
| NCO-98456-B | LONG-LEGGED GUITAR PICKIN' MAN  (Marshall Grant) -1 |
| NCO-98457-B | I GOT STRIPES  (C.Williams, Johnny Cash) |

**Note:**   Even though the **Statler Brothers** were present at this concert, and did perform with others on the program, none of the tunes on which they appear were released on the **Folsom Prison** album.

Columbia Studios, Nashville                                                July 29, 1968
Johnny Cash, vocal, guitar; Carter Family, vocals; Marshall Grant, bass; W.S.
Holland, drums; Carl Perkins, electric guitar; Luther Perkins, electric guitar; **Statler
Brothers, vocals**; Unknown strings -1. Prod: Bob Johnston.

NCO-98315    **LAND OF ISRAEL**    (Johnny Cash)   -1
             KCS-9726 -- *The Holy Land*

NCO-98316    **NAZARENE**    (Johnny Cash) -1
             KCS-9726 -- *The Holy Land*

Columbia Studios, Nashville                                                July 30, 1968
Johnny Cash, vocal, guitar; Carter Family, vocals; Marshall Grant, bass; W.S.
Holland, drums; Jan Howard, vocal; Carl Perkins, electric guitar; Luther Perkins,
electric guitar; **Statler Brothers, vocals**. Prod: Bob Johnston.

NCO-98318    **TOWN OF CANA**    (Johnny Cash)
             KCS-9726 -- *The Holy Land*

NCO-98319    **THE FOURTH MAN**    (Arthur Smith)
             KCS-9726 -- *The Holy Land*

NCO-98320    **BEAUTIFUL WORDS**    (Johnny Cash)
             KCS-9726 -- *The Holy Land*

NCO-98321    **DADDY SANG BASS**    (Carl Perkins)
             4-44689 -- backed w/HE TURNED THE WATER INTO WINE
             4-33153 -- backed w/FOLSOM PRISON BLUES (live)
             KCS-9726 -- *The Holy Land*
             KC-30887 -- *The Johnny Cash Collection*

**Note:**   The narrative tracks of TOWN OF CANA and BEAUTIFUL WORDS were
recorded on location in the Holy Land.  BEAUTIFUL WORDS was recorded on the
site of the Sermon on the Mount.

Columbia Studios, Nashville                                                July 31, 1968
Johnny Cash, vocal, guitar; Carter Family, vocals; Marshall Grant, bass; W.S.
Holland, drums; Carl Perkins, electric guitar; Luther Perkins, electric guitar; **Statler
Brothers, vocals**. Prod: Bob Johnston.

NCO-98322    **HE TURNED THE WATER INTO WINE**    (Johnny Cash)
             4-44689 -- backed w/DADDY SANG BASS
             KCS-9726 -- *The Holy Land*

NCO-98323   **COME TO THE WAILING WALL**   (Johnny Cash)
            KCS-9726 -- *The Holy Land*

**Note:**  This is the last studio session for Luther Perkins before his death on August 5, 1968. Carl Perkins filled in on lead guitar until Bob Wootton was hired in September, 1968.

====================================================================

Columbia Studios, Nashville                            August 29, 1968
Johnny Cash, vocal, guitar; Carter Family, vocals; Marshall Grant, bass; W.S. Holland, drums; Carl Perkins, electric guitar; **Statler Brothers, vocals**; Unknown strings -1. Prod: Bob Johnston.

NCO-98331   **THE TEN COMMANDMENTS**   (Lew DeWitt) -1
            KCS-9726 -- *The Holy Land*

NCO-98332   **WASN'T THAT A TERRIBLE THING**   (no cc)

NCO-98333   **THE KING OF LOVE**   (Harold Reid)
            -- unissued --

====================================================================

San Quentin Prison, California                        February 24, 1969
Johnny Cash, vocal, guitar; June Carter Cash, vocal -1; Carter Family, vocals; Marshall Grant, bass; W.S. Holland, drums; Carl Perkins, electric guitar; **Statler Brothers, vocals**; Bob Wootton, electric guitar. Prod: Bob Johnston.

NCO-99102   **WRECK OF THE OLD '97**   [sic]
            (arr by Johnny Cash, Bob Johnson, Norman Blake)

NCO-99103   **I WALK THE LINE**   (Johnny Cash)

NCO-99104   **DARLIN' COMPANION**   (John Sebastion) -1

NCO-99105   **STARKVILLE CITY JAIL**   (Johnny Cash)

NCO-99106   **SAN QUENTIN #1**   (Johnny Cash)

NCO-99107   **SAN QUENTIN #2**   (Johnny Cash)

NCO-99108   **WANTED MAN**   (Bob Dylan)

NCO-99109   **A BOY NAMED SUE**   (Shel Silverstein)

NCO-99110   **PEACE IN THE VALLEY**   (arr by Johnny Cash)

NCO-91111  **FOLSOM PRISON BLUES**  (Johnny Cash)

NCO-91112  **I WALK THE LINE**  (Johnny Cash)

NCO-91113  **DRUM SOLO**  (W.S. Holland)

NCO-91114  **RING OF FIRE**  (June Carter, Merle Kilgore)

NCO-91115  **FOLSOM PRISON BLUES**  (Johnny Cash)

NCO-91116  **FOLSOM PRISON BLUES**  (Johnny Cash)

**Note:**  For a time Cash traditionally ended his shows by having different performers in his touring group sing a line or two from the closing numbers. In this instance June Carter is featured on NCO-99111, The Carter Family on NCO-99112, W.S. Holland on NCO-99113, the **Statler Brothers** are featured on NCO-99114, and Carl Perkins on NCO-99115. None of these cuts were used on the San Quentin album. This concert was filmed by Granada TV of Europe. {*The Statlers do not appear on any selection released on the* Live from San Quentin *album. -AH*}

========================================================================

Ryman Auditorium, Nashville                                    July 10, 1970
Johnny Cash, vocal; Carter Family with Arlene Hardin, vocals; Marshall Grant, bass; W.S. Holland, drums; **Statler Brothers, vocals**; Bob Wootton, electric guitar; Bill Walker Orchestra consisting of: Byron Bach, Brenton Banks, violin; Glenn Baxter, Marvin Chantry viola; John Darnall, guitar; William Fitzpatrick, Solie Fott, viola; William Harris, Lillian Hunt, Sheldon Kurland, violin; Rex Peer, Jerry Shook, guitar; Gary Vanosdale, viola; Gary Williams, John Williams, Stephanie Woolf, viola; William Wright, Unknown instrument; unknown brass instruments. Prod: Bob Johnston.

NCO-104589  **I'M GONNA TRY TO BE THAT WAY**  (Johnny Cash)
          45211 -- backed w/SUNDAY MORNING COMING DOWN
          C-30100 -- *The Johnny Cash Show*
          KH-31602 -- *The Johnny Cash Songbook*
          C-32240 -- *Sunday Morning Coming Down*

NCO-108546  **THERE AIN'T NO EASY RUN**  (Dave Dudley, Tom T. Hall)
          C-30100 -- *The Johnny Cash Show*

NCO-108548  **THESE HANDS**  (Eddy Noack)
          C-30100 -- *The Johnny Cash Show*

NCO-108550  **DETROIT CITY**  (Mel Tillis, Bobby Bare)
          C-30100 -- *The Johnny Cash Show*

**Note:** The masters for this session were actually taken from the soundtrack of the ABC-TV series <u>The Johnny Cash Show</u> during the January to June, 1970, season. However, they were not given master numbers until later in the year. The exceptions include I'M GONNA TRY TO BE THAT WAY, which was taken from a later show and given a current number. All masters were recorded live at the Ryman Auditorium, home of the old Grand Ole Opry. Masters NCO-108548 is from the February 4, 1970, show; NCO-108550 from the February 11, 1970, show; NCO-108546 from the April 8, 1970, show.

===============================================================

*Note:   By this time, the Statler Brothers had signed a contract with Mercury Records. They appear on the following sessions courtesy of Mercury.*

Sessions With Mercury -- See Chapter Three.

Sept. 11, 1970; Oct. 19, 1970; Nov. 10, 1970; Apr. 14-16, 1971; Nov. 16-18, 1971; Jan. 14, 1972; Apr. 11-13, 1972.

===============================================================

House of Cash Studios, Hendersonville, Tenn.                          May 15, 1972
Johnny Cash, vocal, guitar; Larry Butler, keyboard; Carter Family, vocals -1; Charlie Cochran, piano; Ray Edenton, Larry Gatlin, guitars; Marshall Grant, bass; W.S. Holland, drums; Red Lane, guitar; Mark Morris, percussion; Carl Perkins, electric guitar; **Statler Brothers, vocals**; Don Tweedy, saxophone; Bob Wootton, electric guitar; Unknown strings -2. Prod: Larry Butler.

NCO-108379 **I SEE MEN AS TREES WALKING**   (Johnny Cash) -1
       KG-32253 -- *The Gospel Road*

NCO-104845 **THE LAST SUPPER**   (Larry Gatlin) -1,2
       4-45786 -- backed w/CHILDREN
       KG-32253 -- *The Gospel Road*

NCO-104846 **LORD, IS IT I?**   (Harold Reid, Don Reid)
       KG-32253 -- *The Gospel Road*

===============================================================

House of Cash Studios, Hendersonville                                 May 17, 1972
Johnny Cash, vocal, guitar; Carter Family, **Statler Brothers, vocals**; First Session: Byron Bach, cello; Brenton Banks, George Brinkley, violin; Larry Butler, keyboard; Marvin Chantry, viola; Stephen Clapp, violin; Charlie Cochran, piano; Solie Fott, viola; Martin Katahn, Sheldon Kurland, violin; Martha McCrory, cello; Ann Migliore, bass; Mark Morris, percussion; James Stephany, guitar; Ernest Szugy, bass; Sam Terranova, violin; George Tidwell, trumpet; Don Tweedy, saxophone; Stephanie Wolfe, viola. Second Session: Larry Butler, Keyboard; Charlie Cochran, piano; Ray Edenton, Red Lane, guitars; Mark Morris, drums; Don Tweedy, saxophone. Prod: Larry Butler.

NCO-114833 **ASCENSION** and **AMEN CHORUS**   (Johnny Cash, L. Murray)
            KG-32253 -- *The Gospel Road*

NCO-114847 **THE LORD'S PRAYER** and **AMEN CHORUS**
            (Johnny Cash, L. Murray)
            KG-32253 -- *The Gospel Road*

NCO-114872 **BLESSED ARE**  (Johnny Cash, L. Murray)
            KG-32253 -- *The Gospel Road*

=================================================================
House of Cash Studios, Hendersonville                              May 30, 1972
Johnny Cash, narration.  Prod: Larry Butler.

NCO-114893 **FEAST OF THE PASSOVER**  (Johnny Cash, L. Murray)
            KG-32253 -- *The Gospel Road*

**Note:**  All background music, orchestra and vocals were apparently overdubbed.
The **Statler Brothers** appear only on this master at this session.
=================================================================
Dallas, Texas                                                        June, 1972
Johnny Cash, vocal, guitar; Carter Family, vocals; Marshall Grant, bass; W.S.
Holland, drums; Statler Brothers, vocals; Bob Wootton, electric guitar.

            **I SEE MEN AS TREES WALKING**  (Johnny Cash)
            EXPLO 72 -- *Jesus Sound Explosion*

**Note:**  This song was recorded at a live performance at "Explo '72" in Dallas,
Texas, sponsored by the Campus Crusade for Christ International, Arrowhead
Springs, San Bernadino, California.
=================================================================

House of Cash Studios, Hendersonville                              July 27, 1972
Johnny Cash, vocal, guitar; Larry Butler, keyboard; Carter Family, vocals -1;
Charlie Cochran, piano; **Lew DeWitt, vocal solo -2**; Ray Edenton, guitar;; Marshall
Grant, bass; Wayne Gray, mandolin; Gary L. Grossett, drums; Jerry Hensley,
guitar; W.S. Holland, drums; Mark Morris, percussion; Carl Perkins, electric guitar;
**Statler Brothers, vocals -3**; Jimmy Young, guitar; Bob Wootton, electric guitar.
Prod: Larry Butler.

NCO-114522 **KING OF LOVE**  (Harold Reid) -1,3
            KC-31754 -- *Johnny Cash Family Christmas*

NCO-114530 **OLD FASHIONED TREE**  (A.Becker, C.Williams) -2
            KC-31754 -- *Johnny Cash Family Christmas*
=================================================================

House of Cash Studios, Hendersonville                                    July 28, 1972
Johnny Cash, vocal, guitar;; Norman Blake, guitar; Larry Butler, keyboard; Charlie
Cochran, piano; Ray Edenton, guitar; Marshall Grant, bass; W.S. Holland, drums;
Mark Morris, percussion; Carl Perkins, electric guitar; Bob Wootton, electric guitar.
Prod: Larry Butler.

NCO-114535 **MERRY CHRISTMAS MARY** (M.S.Tubb, R.Hancock)
            KC-31754 -- *Johnny Cash Family Christmas*

NCO-114536 **WELCOME BACK JESUS** (Johnny Cash)

**Note:** Even though Columbia ledger sheets and House of Cash **do not list** the
Carter Family and **Statler Brothers** for this session, they both **do appear** on
MERRY CHRISTMAS MARY and WELCOME BACK JESUS. *[Emphasis mine. AH]*
===============================================================

## INDEX OF BOOTLEG RELEASES

MIB-80201   FOREIGN RECORDINGS & OTHERS
            THE BOY FROM ARKANSAS
            Hammers and Nails

MIB-80301   TV SHOW OF FEBRUARY 11, 1970
            I'm Just One Song Away

MIB-80601   TV SHOW OF FEBRUARY 4, 1970
            This Old [sic] House

**Note:**   There were six of the MIB albums. All had the same jackets which
            included an album number and the contents for the entire series on the
            back of each cover. The disc labels, themselves, carried no information
            and were color coded with each record having a different color.

---

## INDEX OF ABC TELEVISION SERIES
Dates are original air dates.

JUNE 7, 1969
    Daddy Sang Bass
        (JC & Carter Family)

JUNE 14, 1969
    Swing Low, Sweet Chariot
        (JC & Carter Family)

JUNE 21, 1969
    He's Got the Whole World in His
        Hands    (JC & Carter Family)

JULY 5, 1969
    Lead Me Gently Home
        (JC & Carter Family)

JULY 12, 1969
    These Hands
        (JC & Carter Family)

JULY 19, 1969
    Lead Me, Father
        (JC & Carter Family)

JULY 26, 1969
    Billy Christian (JC)
    He Turned the Water into Wine
        (JC & Carter Family)

AUGUST 2, 1969
    Walk with Your Neighbor
        (JC & Carter Family)

AUGUST 9, 1969
    Steal Away
        (JC & Carter Family)

AUGUST 16, 1969
    The Old Account
        (JC, June Carter Cash, Carl Perkins, &
        Carter Family)

AUGUST 23, 1969
    Rollin' in My Sweet Baby's Arms
    I Saw a Man  (JC & Carter Family)

AUGUST 30, 1969
    How Great Thou Art
        (JC & Carter Family)

SEPTEMBER 6, 1969
The Ten Commandments
(JC & Carter Family)

SEPTEMBER 20, 1969
Were You There
(JC & Carter Family)

SEPTEMBER 27, 1969
Battle Hymn of the Republic
(JC & Carter Family)

JANUARY 21, 1970
Lonesome Valley (JC)

JANUARY 28, 1970
Daddy Sang Bass
(JC & Carter Family)
Peace in the Valley
(JC & Carter Family)

FEBRUARY 4, 1970
This Old House (JC)

FEBRUARY 11, 1970
Rollin' in My Sweet Baby's Arms
(JC, Carter Family, Carl Perkins)
He Turned the Water into Wine
(JC, Carter Family, Carl Perkins)

FEBRUARY 18, 1970
The Old Account
(JC & Carter Family)

FEBRUARY 25, 1970
Keep on the Sunnyside
(JC & Carter Family)

MARCH 4, 1970
Preachin', Prayin', Singin'
(JC & Carter Family)
Greystone Chapel
(JC, Carter Family, Carl Perkins)
Were You There
(JC, Carter Family, Carl Perkins)

MARCH 11, 1970
Jesus Was a Soul Man
(JC, Carl Perkins, Carter Family, &
Lawrence Reynolds)

MARCH 18, 1970
Mister Garfield
(JC, Carter Family, Carl Perkins, &
Tommy Cash)

MARCH 25, 1970
Seeing Nellie Home
(JC, Carter Family, Carl Perkins)

APRIL 1, 1970
Billy Christian (JC)
How Great Thou Art
(JC, Carter Family, Carl Perkins)

APRIL 8, 1970
Smile on Your Brother
(Entire Cast)
Ten Commandments
(Entire Cast)

APRIL 22, 1970
Children, Go How I Send Thee
(Entire Cast)

MAY 6, 1970
Life Is Like a Mountain Railroad
(JC & Carter Family)

MAY 13, 1970
Keep on the Sunnyside
(JC & Carter Family)

SEPTEMBER 30, 1970
Daddy Was an Old-Time Preacher
Man   (JC & Carter Family)

OCTOBER 7, 1970
Everybody Loves a Nut (JC)
Wings of a Dove
(JC & Carter Family)

**OCTOBER 28, 1970**
Children, Go How I Send Thee
(JC & Carter Family)
I'll Have a New Life
(JC, Carter Family, & Tennessee Ernie
Ford)

**NOVEMBER 4, 1970**
Suppertime
(JC & Carter Family)

**NOVEMBER 11, 1970**
I Got Stripes
(JC & Carter Family)

**NOVEMBER 18, 1970**
Everybody Loves a Nut
(JC & Cass Elliott)
I'll Be Satisfied
(JC, Maybelle & Sara Carter, & Carter
Family)

**DECEMBER 2, 1970**
Daddy Sang Bass
(JC & Carter Family)
Put Your Hand in the Hand
(JC, Carter Family, Homer & Jethro,
Merle Haggard, Bonnie Owens & Anne
Murray)

**DECEMBER 16, 1970**
Old Time Religion
(JC, Carter Family, Carl Perkins)

**DECEMBER 23, 1970**
Twelve Days of Christmas
(JC & Carter Family)
Do What You Do Do Well
(JC, Carter Family, Everly Brothers, Ike
Everly, Tommy Cash, Mr. & Mrs. Ray
Cash & Roy Orbison)
Silent Night
(Entire Cast w/Carrie Cash at piano)

**JANUARY 13, 1971**
In the Sweet Bye and Bye
(JC & Carter Family)
Are You Washed in the Blood
(JC & Carter Family)

One More Ride
(JC, Carter Family, Jane Morgan, Bill
Anderson, Jan Howard, Gordon Lightfoot
& Homer & Jethro)

**JANUARY 27, 1971**
The Fourth Man
(JC, Carter Family & Carl Perkins)

**FEBRUARY 10, 1971**
May the Bird of Paradise Fly Up
Your Nose
(JC, Carter Family, Jim Nabors, Archie
Campbell, Junior Samples, Stringbean,
George Lindsey, Homer & Jethro, &
Ferlin Husky)

**FEBRUARY 17, 1971**
Mama Don't Allow
(JC, Carter Family, Carl Perkins, James
Taylor, Linda Ronstadt, Neil Young,
Tony Joe White, Albert Brooks & Earl
Scruggs)

**FEBRUARY 24, 1971**
Everybody Is Going to Have
Religion in Glory
(JC & Carter Family)
Praise the Lord
(JC, Blackwood Brothers & Oak Ridge
Boys)
Salvation Has Been Brought Down
(JC, Blackwood Brothers & Oak Ridge
Boys)
When the Saints Go Marchin' In
(JC, Carter Family, Blackwood Brothers,
Oak Ridge Boys, Edwin Hawkins, Staple
Singers, Stuart Hamblen & Billy Graham)

**MARCH 3, 1971**
Jesus Loves Me
(JC & Carter Family)

**MARCH 10, 1971**
I'll Fly Away
(JC & Carter Family)

MARCH 17, 1971
   June Makes the Flowers Grow
      (JC & Carter Family)
   Belshazah
      (JC & Carter Family)

MARCH 24, 1971
   May the Good Lord Bless
      and Keep You
      (JC, Carter Family, & Maybelle Carter)

MARCH 31, 1971
   I'll Take You Home Again
      Kathleen   (JC)
   He'll Understand and Say Well
      Done   (JC & Carter Family)

**Note:**   During the above listed television shows the music was provided by the Tennessee Three: Marshall Grant, electric bass; W.S. Holland, drums; Bob Wootton, electric guitar; The "new" Carter Family: Maybelle, Anita, Helen and June with the later addition of Arlene Hardin*; The Statler Brothers: Phil Balsley, Lew DeWitt, Don Reid, Harold Reid; Norman Blake, guitar, dobro, banjo; Carl Perkins, electric guitar; The Bill Walker Orchestra.

*Note from Don Reid -- Robbie Hardin, not Arlene.

# WE

We walked the warm streets of Florida
    with sand in our pockets lots of times.
Worked the cold streets of New York with
    four guitars, a tin cup just for dimes.
We spent one winter in Winnipeg
    and a summer in Mississippi sun.
Had some trouble once in Fargo,
    some bad times in Encino, but we had fun.

We made the papers once in Phoenix
    when we stopped and tried to break up a fight.
We made keno in Reno
    and lost it all in Vegas the very next night.
We hopped a train in Chicago,
    and skinny-dipped in San Francisco's bay.
We checked in all the big hotels,
    and used the fire escape to get away.

And we wouldn't trade it all for the world and all its gold.
    It's the past that makes the future worth living.
Mother Luck's been good to us,
    and we will praise her in our songs.
For the good times and the good things she has given.

We flew into Kansas City early
    April 24th without a plane.
We got stranded in a snowstorm
    with some girls from Salt Lake City on a train.
We spent a week one night in LA
    looking for a doctor's daughter on the strip.
Then we ended up somewhere near Nashville
    pitching songs and waiting tables for a tip.

*Don Reid*
October 19, 1970
House of Cash, Inc.
Used by permission of
    the House of Cash, Inc.

# CHAPTER 2

# Flowers on the Wall: On Their Own

This chapter covers the recording sessions made with Columbia on their own, and released under their name, between 1964 and 1969. Their first recording session is actually in this chapter, and many of these fall in between sessions in Chapter One. (A Chronological Session Listing appears in the Appendix.)

Unfortunately, musicians union contracts were not preserved in archival form before 1970. From the recollections of persons present (including the Statlers), it has been determined that the following musicians participated throughout this period: Marshall Grant (bass), Ray Edenton (guitar), Grady Martin (guitar), Luther Perkins (guitar); Jerry Kennedy (guitar), Carl Perkins (guitar), Buddy Harman (drums), Chip Young (guitar), Fred Carter (dobro), Pete Wade (guitar), Bill Pursell (piano), Jerry Reed (bjo).

The Country Music Foundation has several session appointment books that were kept by some musicians. By comparing the session dates (which were obtained from Columbia Artist Job Sheets) with these appointment books, it was possible to determine on which sessions these musicians appear.

## KEY TO ABBREVIATIONS & PREFIXES

"CL" - monaural long-plays, Columbia series.
"CS" - stereo long-plays, Columbia series.
"4-xxxxx" - 5-digit numbers preceded by "4-" are 45 rpm releases.
"no cc" - no composer credits are known.
"Prod:" - Produced by:
"arr" - arrangement/arranger
"TL" - Time-Life release.
"BMI" - Broadcast Music, Inc.
"ASCAP" - American Society of Composers, Authors & Publishers
"CSP" - Columbia Special Products
"CMT" - Columbia Musical Treasury

"Mer" - Mercury Records
"A" - Anthology albums; various artists

INSTRUMENT ABBREVIATIONS
    g - guitar         el g - electric guitar     d - dobro
    b - bass          st g - steel guitar       p - piano
    dm - drums       hm - harmonica

All sessions were at Columbia Studios, Nashville, Tennessee.

================================================================

April 3, 1964
(14:00-17:00)

Norman Blake (g,db); Ray Edenton, Grady Martin (g); Buddy Harman (dm); Joe Zinkan (b); Johnny Cash (train whistle). Remaining musicians unknown. Prod: Don Law and Frank Jones.

NCO-80253    **WRECK OF THE OLD 97**  Traditional
                    (arr. Johnny Cash, Bob Johnson, Norman Blake)
                    House of Cash, Inc.; BMI -- Take #9
                    4-43069 -- backed w/HAMMERS AND NAILS
                    TLCW-14 -- *The Statler Brothers* (TL)
                    CK64764 -- *The Essential Statler Bros., 1964-1969*

**Note:** The WRECK OF THE OLD 97 is significant in two aspects. The setting of the story is the Shenandoah Valley of Virginia, the home of these four gentlemen. As recorded by Vernon Dalhart in 1924, it introduced the record-buying public to country music. This time, it introduced the record-buying public to the Statler Brothers.

    The Artist Job Sheet shows the title as "WRECK OF THE OLD '97," as does the label on the original single release. It has been reissued twice, and both use the apostrophe. An apostrophe used before a number usually indicates it is a year, i.e., '57 for 1957. The number in this title is not a year, it is the number assigned to the engine by the railroad company. Review of copyright listings and original sheet music shows this title without an apostrophe.

================================================================

April 3, 1964
(17:15-20:00)

Johnny Cash (recitation); Ray Edenton, Grady Martin (g); Marshall Grant (b); W.S. Holland (dm); Luther Perkins (el g); Norman Blake (db). Remaining musicians unknown. Prod: Don Law and Frank Jones.

NCO-80254    **HAMMERS AND NAILS**  (Lucille Crough)
                    Moss Rose Publishing, Inc.; BMI -- Take #9
                    4-43069 -- backed w/WRECK OF THE OLD 97
                    KH-32256 -- *Do You Love Me Tonight & Other Favorites*

BT-24276 -- *How Great Thou Art*
CL2231/CS9031 -- *Kentucky Derby Day* (A)
HS-11214 -- *America's Greatest Country Stars Live & in Person*
CK64764 -- *The Essential Statler Bros., 1964-1969*

==========================================================

July 28, 1964
( )

Session musicians unknown. Prod: Don Law and Frank Jones.

NCO-50664    **YOUR FOOLISH GAME** (Don Reid, Harold Reid)
House of Cash, Inc.; BMI -- Take #6
4-43146 -- backed w/I STILL MISS SOMEONE

NCO-80665    **I STILL MISS SOMEONE** (Johnny Cash, Roy Cash, Jr.)
House of Cash, Inc.; BMI -- Take #7
4-43146 -- backed w/YOUR FOOLISH GAME
CL2449/CS9249 -- *Flowers on the Wall*
CG-31557 -- *The World of the Statler Brothers*
CK64764 -- *The Essential Statler Bros., 1964-1969*

**Note:** YOUR FOOLISH GAME is the first song issued which was written by members of the quartet.

==========================================================

March 13, 1965
(15:00-17:00)

Session musicians unknown. Prod: Don Law and Frank Jones.

NCO-82653    **FLOWERS ON THE WALL** (Lew DeWitt)
Southwind Music, Inc.; BMI -- Take #1
4-43315 -- backed w/BILLY CHRISTIAN
4-33134 -- backed w/RUTHLESS
CL2449/CS9249 -- *Flowers on the Wall*
H30610 -- *Big Country Hits*
CG31557 -- *The World of the Statler Brothers*
AE2-1018 -- *Hall of Fame, Vol. 3* (A)
SM3008 -- *History of Country Music* (A)
TLCW-14 -- *The Statler Brothers* (TL)
518-945 -- *30th Anniversary Celebration* (Mer)
A18491 -- *Oh Happy Day* (CD)
BT16554 -- *Always Here*
BT16745 -- *Best of the Statler Bros.*
CK64764 -- *The Essential Statler Bros., 1964-1969*

NCO-82654   **BILLY CHRISTIAN**   (Tom T. Hall)
            New Keys Music, Inc.; BMI -- Take #1
            4-43315 -- backed w/FLOWERS ON THE WALL
            CL2449/CS9249 -- *Flowers on the Wall*
            H-31325 -- *Roy Acuff, Johnny Horton, Statler Bros., &*
                        *Lil' Jimmy Dickens Together* (A)
            CG31557 -- *The World of the Statler Brothers*
            TLCW-14 -- *The Statler Brothers* (TL)

**Note:**   FLOWERS ON THE WALL found the land where pop, folk, and country meet.
It sounded enough like a pop record to get played on Top 40 stations, enough like
a country record to get played on country stations, and it became a top five record
on both charts toward the end of 1965.[1]  (See Chapter 7, Chart History.)

===========================================================

November 30, 1965
(18:00-21:00)

Ray Edenton (g).  Remaining musicians unknown.  Prod: Don Law and Frank
Jones.

NCO-83013   **MY DARLING HILDEGARDE**   (Don Reid)
            Acclaim Music, Inc.; BMI
            -- rejected --

NCO-83014   **KING OF THE ROAD**   (Roger Miller)
            Tree Publishing Co., Inc.; BMI -- Take #8
            CL2449/CS9249 -- *Flowers on the Wall*
            H30610 -- *Big Country Hits*
            CG31557 -- *The World of the Statler Brothers*
            BT16745 -- *Best of the Statler Brothers* (CD)
            A18491 -- *Oh Happy Day* (CD)

NCO-83015   **MEMPHIS**   (Chuck Berry)
            Arc Music Corp.; BMI -- Take #5
            CL2449/CS9249 -- *Flowers on the Wall*
            H-31325 -- *Roy Acuff, Johnny Horton, Statler Bros., &*
                        *Lil' Jimmy Dickens Together* (A)
            BT16554 -- *Always Here*

**Note:**   MY DARLING HILDEGARDE was remade on 1/12/66, master #83086.

===========================================================

--------------------

[1]From *The Statler Brothers 30th Anniversary Celebration* by Colin Escott,
page 7.  Used by permission of Mercury Nashville.

December 1, 1965
(18:00-21:00)
Ray Edenton (g); remaining musicians unknown.  Prod: Don Law and Frank Jones.

NCO-83021   **I'M NOT QUITE THROUGH CRYING**  (Lew DeWitt)
Southwind Music, Inc.; BMI -- Take #3
CL2449/CS9249 -- *Flowers on the Wall*
CG31557 -- *The World of the Statler Brothers*
BT16745 -- *Best of the Statler Brothers* (CD)
A18491 -- *Oh Happy Day* (CD)

NCO-83022   **MY REWARD**  (Allan Roberts)
Robert Music Corp.; ASCAP -- Take #4
CL2449/CS9249 -- *Flowers on the Wall*
CG31557 -- *The World of the Statler Brothers*

NCO-83023   **THE DOODLIN' SONG**   (Harold Reid)
Southwind Music, Inc.; BMI -- Take #7
4043526 -- backed w/MY DARLING HILDEGARDE
CL2449/CS9249 -- *Flowers on the Wall*
CG31557 -- *The World of the Statler Brothers*

========================================================

December 2, 1965
(18:00-21:00)
Ray Edenton (g); remaining musicians unknown.  Prod: Don Law and Frank Jones.

NCO-83026   **QUITE A LONG, LONG TIME**  (Lew DeWitt)
Southwind Music, Inc.; BMI -- Take #6
CL2449/CS9249 -- *Flowers on the Wall*
CG31557 -- *The World of the Statler Brothers*
BT16554 -- *Always Here*

NCO-83027   **THIS OLE HOUSE**  (Stuart Hamblen)
Hamblen Music Co., Inc.; BMI -- Take #5
CL2449/CS9249 -- *Flowers on the Wall*
CG31557 -- *The World of the Statler Brothers*
BT16554 -- *Always Here*
A18491 -- *Oh Happy Day* (CD)
A24362 -- *The Statler Bros./The Oak Ridge Boys* (CD)
BT24276 -- *How Great Thou Art*
CK64764 -- *The Essential Statler Bros., 1964-1969*

NCO-83028   **THE WHIFFENPOOF SONG**
(M.Minnigerode, G.S. Pomeroy, T.B. Galloway, Rudy Vallee)
Miller Music Corp.; ASCAP -- Take #7

CL2449/CS9249 -- *Flowers on the Wall*
CG31557 -- *The World of the Statler Brothers*

==================================================================

January 12, 1966
(                    )

Ray Edenton (g); remaining musicians unknown.
Prod: Don Law and Frank Jones.

NCO-83086    **MY DARLING HILDEGARDE** (Don Reid)    --Remake--
Acclaim Music, Inc.; BMI -- Take #8
4-43526 -- backed w/THE DOODLIN' SONG
CL2449/CS9249 -- *Flowers on the Wall*
BT16554 -- *Always Here*
CK64764 -- *The Essential Statler Bros., 1964-1969*

**Note:**   First tune **issued** which was written solely by Don Reid, the most prolific writer of the group.

==================================================================

April 1, 1966
(22:00-01:00)
Grady Martin (g); remaining musicians unknown.  Prod: Don Law and Frank Jones.

NCO-83388    **GREEN GRASS** (R. Greenaway, R. Cook)
Mills Music, Inc.; ASCAP -- Take #13
KH-32256 -- *Do You Love Me Tonight & Other Favorites*
CK64764 -- *The Essential Statler Bros., 1964-1969*

NCO-83389    **IS THAT WHAT YOU'D HAVE ME DO** (Lew DeWitt)
Southwind Music, Inc.; BMI -- Take #4
4-43624 -- backed w/THE RIGHT ONE
KH-32256 -- *Do You Love Me Tonight & Other Favorites*

**Note:**   #83388 is NOT GREEN, GREEN GRASS OF HOME.  That was recorded on 5/25/67.  In a letter to the author, dated 10/12/95, Don Reid related the story of GREEN GRASS.  "This is the song recorded by Gary Lewis & the Playboys.  We recorded and released it three weeks before he did but the publisher had our label pull our record off the market as a favor to Gary's label."

==================================================================

April 29, 1966
(                    )

Marshall Grant (b); Luther Perkins (g); Carl Perkins (g); remaining musicians unknown.  Prod: Don Law and Frank Jones.

NCO-83427    **THE RIGHT ONE** (Jack Clement)
Jack Music, Inc.; BMI

4-43624 -- backed w/Is THAT WHAT YOU'D HAVE ME DO
KH-32256 -- *Do You Love Me Tonight & Other Favorites*
TLCW-14 -- *The Statler Brothers* (TL)
CK64764 -- *The Essential Statler Bros., 1964-1969*

NCO-83427   **THAT'LL BE THE DAY**   (Don Reid)
Hill & Range Songs, Inc.; BMI
4-43868 -- backed w/MAKIN' ROUNDS
KH-32256 -- *Do You Love Me Tonight & Other Favorites*
TLCW-14 -- *The Statler Brothers* (TL)
A18491 -- *Oh Happy Day* (CD)
CK64764 -- *The Essential Statler Bros., 1964-1969*

NCO-83489   **MAKIN' ROUNDS**   (Don Reid)
Acclaim Music, Inc.; BMI
4-43868 -- backed w/THAT'LL BE THE DAY
KH-32256 -- *Do You Love Me Tonight & Other Favorites*

======================================================

February 13, 1967
(_____)

Jerry Reed (bjo-1); remaining musicians unknown.  Prod:  Don Law and Frank Jones.

NCO-120410   **HALF A MAN**   (J. Bazzell) -1
Window Music Co., Inc.; BMI
KH-32256 -- *Do You Love Me Tonight & Other Favorites*
CK64764 -- *The Essential Statler Bros., 1964-1969*

NCO-120411   **DO YOU LOVE ME TONIGHT**   (Lew DeWitt)
Hill & Range Songs, Inc.; BMI
4-44070 -- backed w/RUTHLESS
KH-32256 -- *Do You Love Me Tonight & Other Favorites*
BT16745 -- *Best of the Statler Bros.* (CD)

======================================================

March 14, 1967
(_____)

Jerry Kennedy (g,db); remaining musicians unknown.  Prod: Bob Johnston.

NCO-120452   **'SCUSE ME MISS ROSE**   (no cc)
Hill & Range Music, Inc.; BMI
-- unissued --

NCO-120453   **RUTHLESS**   (Bobby Braddock)
Tree Publishing Co., Inc.; BMI
4-44070 -- backed w/DO YOU LOVE ME TONIGHT

4-33134 -- backed w/FLOWERS ON THE WALL
CL2719/CS9510; PCT9519 -- *Statler Bros. Sing the Big Hits*
CG31557 -- *The World of the Statler Brothers*
CWS2 -- *Welcome to Columbia Country* (A)
BT16745 -- *Best of the Statler Bros.* (CD)
TLCW-14 -- *The Statler Brothers* (TL)
518-945 -- *30th Anniversary Celebration* (Mer)
CK64764 -- *The Essential Statler Bros., 1964-1969*

NCO-120454   **SHENANDOAH**   Traditional
                 (arr - Lew DeWitt, Harold Reid, Don Reid, Phil Balsley)
             Southwind Music, Inc.; BMI
             CL2719/CS9519; PCT9519 -- *Statler Bros. Sing the Big Hits*
             CG31557 -- *The World of the Statler Brothers*
             CK64764 -- *The Essential Statler Bros., 1964-1969*

==============================================================

Columbia Studio A                                      May 25, 1967
                        (14:00-17:00; 18:00-22:00; 22:00-01:00)
Lew DeWitt (whistle-1); session musicians unknown. Prod: Bob Johnston.

NCO-120098   **THERE GOES MY EVERYTHING**   (Dallas Frazier)
             Blue Crest & Husky Music, BMI
             CL2719/CS9519; PCT9519 -- *Statler Bros. Sing the Big Hits*
             CG31557 -- *The World of the Statler Brothers*
             BT16745 -- *Best of the Statler Brothers* (CD)
             A1849 -- *Oh Happy Day* (CD)

NCO-120099   **GREEN, GREEN GRASS OF HOME**   (Curly Putnam)
             Tree Publishing Co., Inc.; BMI
             CL2719/CS9519; PCT9519 -- *Statler Bros. Sing the Big Hits*
             H30610 -- *Big Country Hits*
             CG31557 -- *The World of the Statler Brothers*
             DS365 -- *Thirty Great Hits* (CMT)
             BT16745 -- *Oh Happy Day* (CD)

NCO-120100   **RELEASE ME (AND LET ME LOVE AGAIN)**
                 (E. Miller, W.S. Stevenson, R. Yount)
             Four Star Music Co., Inc.; BMI
             CL2719/CS9519; PCT9519 -- *Statler Bros. Sing the Big Hits*
             CG31557 -- *The World of the Statler Brothers*
             BT16745 -- *Best of the Statler Brothers* (CD)
             DS365 -- *Thirty Great Hits* (A)

NCO-120101   **FUNNY, FAMILIAR, FORGOTTEN FEELINGS**   (Mickey Newbury)
             Acuff-Rose Publishing, Inc.; BMI

CL2719/CS9519; PCT9519 -- *Statler Bros. Sing the Big Hits*
CG31557 -- *World of the Statler Brothers*
BT16745 -- *Best of the Statler Brothers* (CD)

NCO-120102 **RUBY, DON'T TAKE YOUR LOVE TO TOWN** (Mel Tillis)
Cedarwood Publishing Co., Inc.; BMI
CL2719/CS9519; PCT9519 -- *Statler Bros. Sing the Big Hits*
H30610 -- *Big Country Hits*
CG31557 -- *The World of the Statler Brothers*
BT16745 -- *Best of the Statler Brothers* (CD)
A1849 -- *Oh Happy Day* (CD)

NCO-120103 **ALMOST PERSUADED** (G. Sutton, B. Sherrill)
Al Gallico Music Corp.; BMI
CL2719/CS9519; PCT9519 -- *Statler Bros. Sing the Big Hits*
H30610 -- *The World of the Statler Brothers*
BT16745 -- *Best of the Statler Brothers* (CD)

NCO-120104 **WALKING IN THE SUNSHINE** (Roger Miller)  -1
Tree Publishing Co., Inc.; BMI
4-44245 -- backed w/YOU CAN'T HAVE YOUR KATE & EDITH TOO
CL2719/CS9519; PCT9519 -- *Statler Bros. Sing the Big Hits*
H30610 -- *Big Country Hits*
CG31557 -- *The World of the Statler Brothers*
BT16745 -- *Best of the Statler Brothers* (CD)

===========================================================

June 22, 1967
(_____)

Jerry Kennedy (g,db); remaining musicians unknown.  Prod: Bob Johnston.

NCO-120123 **YOU CAN'T HAVE YOUR KATE & EDITH TOO**
(Bobby Braddock, Curly Putnam)
Tree Publishing Co., Inc.; BMI
4-44245 -- backed w/WALKING IN THE SUNSHINE
CL2719/CS9519; PCT9519 -- *Statler Bros. Sing the Big Hits*
CG31557 -- *The World of the Statler Brothers*
BT16745 -- *Best of the Statler Brothers* (CD)
TLCW-14 -- *The Statler Brothers* (TL)
518-945 -- *30th Anniversary Celebration* (Mer)
CK64764 -- *The Essential Statler Bros., 1964-1969*

NCO-120124 **I CAN'T HELP IT (IF I'M STILL IN LOVE WITH YOU)**
(Hank Williams)
Fred Rose Music, Inc.; BMI
CL2719/CS9519; PCT9519 -- *Statler Bros. Sing the Big Hits*

H30610 -- *Big Country Hits*
CG31557 -- *The World of the Statler Brothers*
BT16745 -- *Best of the Statler Brothers* (CD)

==================================================================

August 28, 1967
(                    )

Session musicians unknown.  Prod: unknown, but probably Bob Johnston.

NCO-120165   **CHURCH IN THE WILDWOOD**  (W. Pitts)
             Public Domain
             C-30324/CA-30324 -- *Country Hymns* (A)
             P2-13429 -- *Gospel's Top 20* (A)

NCO-120166   **HE**  (no cc)
             Avas Music
             -- unissued --

NCO-120167   **HOW GREAT THOU ART**  (Carl Boberg, 1886.  Translated from the
             original Swedish by Stuart K. Hine, 1949.)
             Manna Music, Inc.; BMI
             -- rejected --   Remade, see #100792, 4/22/69; and #100823, 5/7/69.

NCO-120168   **WHAT A FRIEND WE HAVE IN JESUS** - Traditional
                      [Joseph Scriven, 1855; Charles C. Converse, 1868]
             Public Domain
             -- unissued --

NCO-120169   **JUST IN TIME**  (Lew DeWitt)
             Southwind Music, Inc.; BMI
             -- rejected --    Remade, see #100816, 4/25/69.

NCO-120170   **KING OF LOVE**  (Harold Reid)
             Southwind Music, Inc.; BMI
             -- rejected --    Remade, see #100820, 4/25/69.

NCO-120171   **JUST A LITTLE TALK WITH JESUS**  (Cleavant Derricks)
             Public Domain
             -- unissued --

NCO-120172   **THINGS GOD GAVE ME**  (Don Reid)
             Southwind Music, Inc.; BMI
             -- rejected --  Remade, see #100824, 5/7/69.

NCO-120173   **PASS ME NOT** - Traditional
                      [Fanny J. Crosby, William H. Doane, 1868]

Public Domain   (arr - Statler Brothers)
-- rejected --   Remade, see #100818, 4/25/69.

NCO-120174   **A BEAUTIFUL LIFE** Traditional [William M. Golden, 1918]
Public Domain
-- unissued --

NCO-120175   **PRECIOUS MEMORIES** Traditional [J.B.F. Wright, 1938]
Public Domain
-- unissued --

====================================================================

Columbia Studio A                                            January 11, 1968
                                                      (14:00-18:00; 18:00-21:30)
Session musicians unknown. Prod: Bob Johnston.

NCO-98256   **STELLA MALONE** (H. Mills)
Moss Rose Publications, Inc.; BMI
-- unissued --

NCO-98257   **TAKE A BOW, RUFUS HUMFRY** (W. Meshel)
Meager Music, BMI
4-44480 -- backed w/JUMP FOR JOY

NCO-98258   **JUMP FOR JOY** (Bobby Braddock)
Tree Publishing Co., Inc.; BMI
4-44480 -- backed w/TAKE A BOW, RUFUS HUMFRY
TLCW-14 -- *The Statler Brothers* (TL)
CK64764 -- *The Essential Statler Bros., 1964-1969*

NCO-98259   **DON'T THINK TWICE IT'S ALRIGHT** (Bob Dylan)
M. Witmark & Sons, ASCAP
-- unissued --

====================================================================

Columbia Studio B                                              June 3, 1968
                                                              (16:00-17:00)
Session musicians unknown. Prod: Frank Jones.

NCO-98556   **I'M THE BOY** (Lew DeWitt)
Southwind Music, Inc.; BMI
4-44608 -- backed w/SISSY
KH-32256 -- *Do You Love Me Tonight & Other Favorites*
CK64764 -- *The Essential Statler Bros., 1964-1969*

NCO-98557   **STAUNTON, VA** (Carl Perkins)
Cedarwood Publishing Co., Inc.; BMI
-- unissued --   Remade, see #98560, 6/4/68.

NCO-98558    **CONFUSED**  (no cc)
             Blue Echo
             -- unissued --

NCO-98559    **THAT CERTAIN ONE**  (Don Reid)
             Southwind Music, Inc.; BMI
             -- unissued --

===============================================================

Columbia Studio B                                    June 4, 1968
                                                     (18:00-21:30)

Ray Edenton (g); remaining musicians unknown.  Prod:  Frank Jones.

NCO-98560    **STAUNTON, VA**  (Carl Perkins)    --Remake--
             Cedarwood Publishing Co., Inc.; BMI
             KH-32256 -- *Do You Love Me Tonight & Other Favorites*
             TLCW-14 -- *C&W Classics: The Statler Brothers* (TL)

NCO-98561    **SISSY**  (Don Reid)
             House of Cash, BMI
             4-44608 -- backed w/I'M THE BOY
             CK64764 -- *The Essential Statler Bros., 1964-1969*

===============================================================

Columbia Studio B                                    April 22, 1969
                                                     (14:00-17:00)

Session musicians unknown.  Prod:  George Richey

NCO-100792   **HOW GREAT THOU ART**  (Carl Boberg, 1886. Translated from the
                 original Swedish by Stuart K. Hine, 1949.)
             Manna Music, Inc.; BMI
             -- rejected --   Remade, see #100823, 5/7/69.

NCO-100794   **THE FOURTH MAN**  (Arthur Smith)
             Lynn Music Corp.; BMI
             CS-9878 -- *Oh Happy Day*
             KH-31560 -- *How Great Thou Art*

===============================================================

Columbia Studio B                                    April 25, 1969
                                                     (18:00-21:30)

Ray Edenton, Grady Martin (g); Jerry Kennedy (g,db); remaining musicians
unknown. Prod:  George Richey.

NCO-100814   **DADDY SANG BASS**  (Carl Perkins)
             Cedarwood Publishing Co., Inc.; & House of Cash, BMI
             CS9878 -- *Oh Happy Day*
             H-30610 -- *Big Country Hits*

K-31325 -- *Roy Acuff, Johnny Horton, Statler Bros., &
        Lil' Jimmy Dickens Together* (A)
A18491 -- *Oh Happy Day* (CD)
A24362 -- *The Statler Bros./The Oak Ridge Boys* (CD)

NCO-100815  **ARE YOU WASHED IN THE BLOOD** - Traditional
            [Elisha A. Hoffman, 1878]  arr - Statler Brothers
            House of Cash, BMI
            CS-9878 -- *Oh Happy Day*
            KH-31560 -- *How Great Thou Art*
            C 10779 -- *Hymns of Gold* (CSP)

NCO-100816  **JUST IN TIME** (Lew DeWitt)   -- Remake--
            House of Cash, BMI
            CS-9878 -- *Oh Happy Day*
            KH-31560 -- *How Great Thou Art*

NCO-100817  **LESS OF ME** (Glen Campbell)
            Beechwood Music Corp.; BMI
            KH-31560 -- *How Great Thou Art*
            CK64764 -- *The Essential Statler Bros., 1964-1969*

=============================================================

Columbia Studio B                                    April 25-26, 1969
                                                     (22:00-01:30)
Ray Edenton, Grady Martin (g); Jerry Kennedy (g,db); remaining musicians
unknown.  Prod: George Richey.

NCO-100818  **PASS ME NOT** - Traditional  (arr Statler Brothers)
            Public Domain
            CS-9878 -- *Oh Happy Day*

NCO-100819  **LED OUT OF BONDAGE**  (R.L. Prather)
            Peer International Corp.; BMI
            CS-9878 -- *Oh Happy Day*

NCO-100820  **KING OF LOVE**  (Harold Reid)
            House of Cash, Inc.; BMI
            CS-9878 -- *Oh Happy Day*

=============================================================

Columbia Studio B                                        May 7, 1969
                                                     (18:00-21:00)
Jerry Kennedy (g,db); remaining musicians unknown.  Prod:  George Richey.

NCO-100823  **HOW GREAT THOU ART**  (Carl Boberg, 1886. Translated from the
            original Swedish by Stuart K. Hine, 1949.)

Manna Music, Inc.; BMI
4-44899 -- backed w/OH HAPPY DAY
CS-9878 -- *Oh Happy Day*
C-32246 -- *Do You Love Me Tonight & Other Favorites*
KH-31560 -- *How Great Thou Art*
A24362 -- *The Statler Bros./The Oak Ridge Boys* (CD)
BT24276 -- *How Great Thou Art* (CD)

NCO-100824  **THINGS GOD GAVE ME** (Don Reid)     --Remake--
House of Cash; BMI
CS9878 -- *Oh Happy Day*
KH-31560 -- *How Great Thou Art*

NCO-100825  **OH HAPPY DAY**  Traditional - arr. Statler Brothers
            [Philip Doddridge, 1755; attr. Edward F. Rimbault, 1854]
House of Cash; BMI
4-44899 -- backed w/HOW GREAT THOU ART
CS9878 -- *Oh Happy Day*
KH-31560 -- *How Great Thou Art*
H30610 -- *Big Country Hits*
A18491 -- *Oh Happy Day* (CD)
A24362 -- *The Statler Bros./The Oak Ridge Boys* (CD)
P 12620 -- *Hymns of Gold, Vol. II* (A)
CK64674 -- *The Essential Statler Bros., 1964-1969*

At this time, the Statler Brothers' contract with Columbia Records expired. The Brothers chose not to renew.

They had met Jerry Kennedy when recording their *Oh Happy Day* album. Jerry was then head of Mercury Records' Nashville office. Harold gave Jerry a call. The Statlers were cold on records then, but Jerry was interested. He told them he didn't have time to find material for them, they'd have to find their own. That was the opportunity they had waited for -- they were about to leave their mark on country music. Their future had just become a "bed of roses."

**Johnny Cash & Company**

A previously unpublished photograph taken in 1966. Back row—Luther Perkins, W.S. Holland, Marshall Grant (The Tennessee Three); Johnny Cash; and Don Reid, Phil Balsley, Harold Reid, Lew DeWitt (The Statler Brothers). Front row—Helen Carter, Maybelle Carter, June Carter, Anita Carter (The Carter Family). Photo courtesy of The Statler Brothers.

# TOGETHER

The snow was bad in Winnipeg when brother fell and hurt his leg
Our luck was bad up in Green Bay, the bus broke down, we lost a day
We blew a tire in Washington, and bought us one in Oregon
And through it all we sang together.

We paid a fine in Idaho, but made enough in Lake Tahoe
To take us on to Hollywood, where it was warm and things were good.
We met our favorite movie star and talked of him to Wichita
And through it all we sang together.

The nights were cold in Saginaw, the days too hot in Arkansas
And still we sang our songs in harmony.
Every night we think of home when we were in our rooms alone
And wonder, "Is it worth the agony?"

We've traveled every road I know from Canada to Mexico
And never have we had a fight that we can't laugh and make things right
And tho' sometimes we don't agree, I'll stand beside the other three and
Through it all we'll sing together.

Carroll "Bull" Durham
October 8, 1974
American Cowboy Music Co., Inc.
Used by permission of
    All Nations Publishing Co., Inc..

# CHAPTER 3

# Bed of Roses: The Beginning of the Statler Brothers' Era

In 1970, the Statler Brothers began recording on the Mercury label, and their career was about to become a proverbial "bed of roses" -- hence this chapter title. The first song they recorded (BED OF ROSE'S) was a play on this phrase. (See note on page 36.) They were encouraged to record more of the material they wrote themselves, and their fans loved it. What appears to be taking advantage of a nostalgia theme is actually just four boys writing about growing up -- and they grew up at the same time a lot of other people did. Shared experiences create a common ground of understanding, and a friendship between the artists and the fans that continues today.

All Mercury masters are preceded by a number, signifying whether the master is a monophonic or stereophonic recording: 1-mono; 2-stereo.

KEY TO ABBREVIATIONS and SYMBOL
"DJ" -   45 rpm singles issued only to radio stations for disc jockey use, usually with the same title on both sides.
"SR" and "SRM" - stereo LP albums.
(6 digit numbers) - later stereo LP releases, change of numbering system; i.e., 518-945
"SRD" - stereo promotional LP issued only to radio stations.
"CC" - 45 rpm released in the "Celebrity Country" series
"MEPL" - a DJ only issue of a 7-inch LP (untitled)
70,000 and 50,000 numbers - a 45 rpm release, i.e., 73141
"TLCW" - Time-Life Country & Western series
"HM" - Heartland Music
"K" - K-tel
"RD" - Reader's Digest
"TL" - Time-Life
"OD" - overdub session
"PD" - public domain

"arr" - arrangement/arranger
"BMI" - Broadcast Music, Inc.
"ASCAP" - American Society of Composers, Authors & Publishers
"SESAC" - Selected Editions of Standard American Catalogues
▶ (VCR "Play" button) - Available on video.

## INSTRUMENT ABBREVIATIONS

| | | |
|---|---|---|
| g - guitar | dm - drums | el g - electric guitar |
| hm - harmonica | f - fiddle | p - piano |
| vb - vibes | b - bass | db - dobro |
| kb - keyboard | org - organ | bjo - banjo |
| uke - ukelele | st g - steel guitar | el b - electric bass |
| sax - saxophone | man - mandolin | vo - vocals |

All releases are Mercury Records unless otherwise noted.
All Mercury releases were produced by Jerry Kennedy.
======================================================================

Mercury Custom Recording Studio                     September 11,1970
                                                       (14-00-17:00)
Hargus "Pig" Robbins (p); Harold Bradley, Ray Edenton, Chip Young (g); Jerry
Kennedy (g,db); Bob Moore (b); Buddy Harman (dm), Roy Dea (el b).

2-47182  **BED OF ROSE'S**  (Harold Reid)
            House of Cash, Inc.; BMI
            73141 -- backed w/THE LAST GOODBYE
            CC-34030 -- backed w/PICTURES
            DJ-292 -- DJ release
            SR6-1317 -- *Bed of Rose's*
            PTV1003 -- *Memories . . . Now and Forever* (Canadian Rel)
            SRM1-1037 -- *The Best of the Statler Brothers*
            RB6-112 -- *Statler Brothers' Greatest Hits* (RD)
            TLCW-14 -- *C&W Classics: The Statler Brothers* (TL)
            RD7A-235 --*Best of SB, Their Greatest Hits & Finest Performances* (RD)
            NC 568 -- *The Statler Brothers Country* (K)
            518-945 -- *30th Anniversary Celebration*
            8077-V1 -- *The Very Best of the Statler Brothers* (Realm)

**Note from Mercury files:** "In the title 'BED OF ROSE'S' the apostrophe indicates
possessive form . . . it is not a mistake!" (Here, "Rose" is a girl's name.) Where this
title has appeared without the apostrophe, it is noted as [sic].

2-47183  **THE LAST GOODBYE**
            (Harold Reid, Don Reid, Phil Balsley, Lew DeWitt)
            House of Cash, Inc.; BMI
            73141 -- backed w/BED OF ROSE'S
            SR6-1317 -- *Bed of Rose's*

2-47184  **THE JUNKIE'S PRAYER**  (Lew DeWitt)
Southwind Music, Inc./Caretta Music, Inc.; BMI
SR6-1317 -- *Bed of Rose's*

===================================================================

Mercury Custom Recording Studio                    October 19, 1970
                                                      (14:00-17:00)
Charlie McCoy (hm-1,vb,org-2); Hargus "Pig" Robbins (p); Harold Bradley, Ray
Edenton, Chip Young (g); Jerry Kennedy (g,db-3), Bob Moore (b), Buddy Harman
(dm).

2-47209  **TOMORROW NEVER COMES**  (Ernest Tubb, Johnny Bond) -2
Noma Music, Inc.; BMI
SR6-1317 -- *Bed of Rose's*

2-47210  **THIS PART OF THE WORLD**  (Lew DeWitt) -3
House of Cash, Inc.; BMI
OD -- Pete Drake (st g), date unknown.
73194 -- backed w/NEW YORK CITY
SR6-1317 -- *Bed of Rose's*

2-47211  **ME AND BOBBY MCGEE**  (Kris Kristofferson, Fred Foster) -1,-3
Combine Music Corp.; BMI
SR6-1317 -- *Bed of Rose's*
TLCW-14 -- *C&W Classics: The Statler Brothers* (TL)
RD7A-235 --*Best of SB, Their Greatest Hits & Finest Performances* (RD)

===================================================================

Mercury Custom Recording Studio                    October 20, 1970
                                                      (14:00-17:00)
Charlie McCoy (hm-1); Hargus "Pig" Robbins (p); Harold Bradley, Ray Edenton,
Chip Young (g); Jerry Kennedy (g,db-2); Bobby Thompson (bjo-3); Bob Moore
(b); Buddy Harman (dm).

2-47212  **NEIGHBORHOOD GIRL**  (Harold Reid, Don Reid) -2,.3
House of Cash, Inc.; BMI
SR6-1317 -- *Bed of Rose's*

2-47213  **WE**  (Don Reid) -1,-2
House of Cash, Inc.; BMI
SR6-1317 -- *Bed of Rose's*

2-47214  **ALL I HAVE TO OFFER YOU IS ME**
         (Dallas Frazier, A.L. "Doodles" Owens)
Hill & Range Songs, Inc./Blue Crest Music, Inc.; BMI
OD -- Pete Drake (st g), date unknown.
SR6-1317 -- *Bed of Rose's*
RD7A-235 --*Best of SB, Their Greatest Hits & Finest Performances* (RD)

===================================================================

Mercury Custom Recording Studio                              November 10, 1970
                                                               (14:00-17:00)
Charlie McCoy (hm-1,vb,org); Hargus "Pig" Robbins (p); Harold Bradley, Ray
Edenton, Chip Young (g); Jerry Kennedy (g,db-2); Bob Moore (b); Buddy Harman
(dm).

2-47232  **FIFTEEN YEARS AGO**  (Raymond A. Smith) -1
         Hello Darlin' Music, Inc.; SESAC
         OD -- Pete Drake (st g), date unknown.
         SR6-1317 -- *Bed of Rose's*

2-47233  **PICTURES**  (Don Reid, Lew DeWitt)
         House of Cash, Inc.; BMI
         -- rejected -- Remade on 4/15/71, #48464.

2-47234  **NEW YORK CITY**  (Don Reid) -1,-2
         House of Cash, Inc.; BMI -- two takes, used #1
         73194 -- backed w/THIS PART OF THE WORLD
         SR6-1317 -- *Bed of Rose's*
         SRM1-1037 -- *Best of the Statler Brothers*
         TLCW-14 -- *C&W Classics: The Statler Brothers* (TL)
         RD7A-235 --*Best of SB, Their Greatest Hits & Finest Performances* (RD)
         8077-V2 -- *The Very Best of the Statler Brothers* (Realm)

Mercury Custom Recording Studio                                April 14, 1971
                                                               (14:00-17:00)
Charlie McCoy (org-1,hm-2,vb-3); Hargus "Pig" Robbins (p); Harold Bradley, Ray
Edenton, Chip Young (g); Jerry Kennedy (g,db); Bob Moore (b); Buddy Harman
(dm); string arr Cam Mullins -4.

2-48461  **MOMENTS TO REMEMBER**  (Robert Allen, Al Stillman) -3,-4
         Larry Spier, Inc.; ASCAP
         OD -- 4/26/71, 10:00-12:00, Lillian Hunt, Carl Gorodetzky, Solie Fott,
             Jerzy Kosmala, David Vanderkooi, Stephanie Woolf, Sheldon
             Kurland, Brenton Banks, Marvin Chantry, Sam Terranova,
             George Binkley, Byron Bach.
         OD -- 5/6/71, 10:00-12:00, Jerry Kennedy (g/db), Pete Drake (st g),
             Hargus Robbins (p).
         SR6-1349 -- *Pictures of Moments to Remember*

2-48462  **JUST SOMEONE I USED TO KNOW**  (Jack Clement) -1,-3
         Glad Music Co./Jack Music, Inc.; BMI
         OD -- 4/26/71,Strings, see 48461.
         SR6-1349 -- *Pictures of Moments to Remember*

2-48463  **WHEN YOU AND I WERE YOUNG, MAGGIE**  (PD) [J.A. Butterfield] -2
         (arr - Don Reid, Harold Reid, Lew DeWitt, Phil Balsley)
         House of Cash, Inc.; BMI
         SR6-1349 -- *Pictures of Moments to Remember*

========================================================

Mercury Custom Recording Studio                                    April 15, 1971
                                                                   (14:00-17:00)
Charlie McCoy (org-1,hm-2,vb-3); Hargus "Pig" Robbins (p); Harold Bradley, Ray
Edenton, Chip Young (g); Jerry Kennedy (g,db-4); Bob Moore (b); Buddy
Harman (dm).

2-48464  **PICTURES**  (Don Reid, Lew DeWitt) -1,-3
         House of Cash, Inc.; BMI
         OD -- 4/28/71, 10:00-12:30, Jerry Kennedy (g/db), Pete Drake (st g),
              Hargus Robbins (p).
         73229 -- backed w/MAKING MEMORIES
         CC-34030 -- backed w/BED OF ROSE'S
         SR6-1349 -- *Pictures of Moments to Remember*
         SRM1-1037 -- *Best of the Statler Brothers*
         PTV1003 -- *Memories . . . Now and Forever* (Canadian Rel)
         TLCW-14 -- *C&W Classics: The Statler Brothers* (TL)
         RD7A-235 --*Best of SB, Their Greatest Hits & Finest Performances* (RD)
         8077-V2 -- *The Very Best of the Statler Brothers* (Realm)

2-48465  **SECOND THOUGHTS**  (Don Reid, Harold Reid) -2,-4
         House of Cash, Inc.; BMI
         73253 -- backed w/YOU CAN'T GO HOME
         SR6-1349 -- *Pictures of Moments to Remember*

2-48466  **THINGS**  (Lew DeWitt) -2
         House of Cash, Inc.; BMI
         SR6-1349 -- *Pictures of Moments to Remember*

**Note:**  #48464 is a remake of #47233, 11/10/70.

========================================================

Mercury Custom Recording Studio                                    April 16, 1971
                                                                   (10:00-13:00)
Charlie McCoy (hm-1); Floyd Cramer (p); Earl Scruggs (bjo-2); Harold Bradley,
Ray Edenton, Chip Young (g); Jerry Kennedy (g,db); Bob Moore (b); Buddy
Harman (dm); string arr Cam Mullins -3.

2-48467  **I WONDER HOW THE OLD FOLKS ARE AT HOME**  -1,-2
         (F.W. Vandersloot, Herbert S. Lambet)
         Jerry Vogel Music, Inc.; ASCAP
         SR6-1349 -- *Pictures of Moments to Remember*

2-48468  **YOU CAN'T GO HOME**  (Don Reid)  -3
House of Cash, Inc.; BMI
OD -- 4/26/71, Strings, see 48461.
OD -- 4/28/71, 10:00-12:30, Jerry Kennedy (g/db), Pete Drake (st g),
     Hargus Robbins (p).
73253 -- backed w/SECOND THOUGHTS
SR6-1349 -- *Pictures of Moments to Remember*
RD7A-235 --*Best of SB, Their Greatest Hits & Finest Performances* (RD)
8077-V1 -- *The Very Best of the Statler Brothers* (Realm)

2-48469  **FADED LOVE**  (Johnny Wills, Bob Wills)  -3
Hill & Range Music, Inc.; BMI
OD -- 4/26/71, Strings, see 48461.
SR6-1349 -- *Pictures of Moments to Remember*
RD7A-235 --*Best of SB, Their Greatest Hits & Finest Performances* (RD)

===============================================================

Mercury Custom Recording Studio                          April 16, 1971
                                                         (14:00-17:00)
Charlie McCoy (org-1,vb-2); Hargus Robbins (p); Harold Bradley (g,uke-3); Ray
Edenton, Chip Young (g); Jerry Kennedy (g,db); Bob Moore (b); Buddy Harman
(dm).

2-48470  **WHEN YOU ARE SIXTY-FIVE**  (Don Reid)  -1,-2
American Cowboy Music Co., Inc.; BMI
OD -- Weldon Myrick (st g), date unknown.
Final mix date - 1/31/78.
SRM1-5007 -- *Entertainers . . . On & Off the Record*

2-48471  **TENDER YEARS**  (Darrel Edwards)
Glad Music Co., BMI
OD -- Pete Drake (st g), date unknown.
SR6-1349 -- *Pictures of Moments to Remember*
RD7A-235 --*Best of SB, Their Greatest Hits & Finest Performances* (RD)

2-48472  **MAKING MEMORIES**  (Don Reid, Harold Reid)  -1,-3
House of Cash, Inc.; BMI
OD -- 5/6/71, 10:00-12:00, Pete Drake (st g); Hargus Robbins (p).
73229 -- backed w/PICTURES
SR6-1349 -- *Pictures of Moments to Remember*

===============================================================

Mercury Custom Recording Studio                      November 16, 1971
                                                         (14:00-17:00)
Jerry Kennedy (g,db); Harold Bradley, Jerry Shook, Chip Young (g); Bob Moore
(b); Buddy Harman (dm); Hargus Robbins (p); Charlie McCoy (hm-1,org-2).

2-48577  **TAKE ME HOME COUNTRY ROADS**  -1
(Bill Danoff, Taffy Nivert, John Denver)  arr - Statler Brothers
Cherry Lane Music Co.; ASCAP
OD -- 11/29/71, 14:00-16:00, Jerry Kennedy (db), Pete Drake (st g),
Buddy Spicher (f).
SR6-1358 -- *Innerview*
RD7A-235 --*Best of SB, Their Greatest Hits & Finest Performances* (RD)

2-48578  **DADDY**   (Don Reid, Harold Reid) -2
House of Cash, Inc.; BMI
OD -- 11/29/71, 14:00-16:00, Jerry Kennedy (db), Pete Drake (st g),
Buddy Spicher (f).
SR6-1358 -- *Innerview*

2-48579  **A DIFFERENT SONG**  (Don Reid) -1
House of Cash, Inc.; BMI
SR6-1358 -- *Innerview*

==============================================================

Mercury Custom Recording Studio                    November 17, 1971
                                                        (10:00-13:00)
Jerry Kennedy (g,db); Bob Moore (b); Chip Young, Jerry Shook (g); Harold
Bradley (g,uke-1); Hargus  Robbins (p); Buddy Harman (dm); Roy Dea (el b);
Charlie McCoy (vb-2); string arr Cam Mullins -3.

2-48580  **NEVER ENDING SONG OF LOVE**  (Delaney Bramlett)
Metric Music; BMI
OD -- 11/29/71, 14:00-16:00, Jerry Kennedy (db), Pete Drake (st g),
Buddy Spicher (f).
SR6-1358 -- *Innerview*
RD7A-235 --*Best of SB, Their Greatest Hits & Finest Performances* (RD)

2-48581  **SINCE THEN**  (Lew DeWitt) -1,-2
House of Cash, Inc.; BMI
73275 -- backed w/DO YOU REMEMBER THESE
MEPL-11 -- DJ release, also included I'LL TAKE CARE OF YOU, and Open
End Interview
SR6-1358 -- *Innerview*

2-48582  **I'LL TAKE CARE OF YOU**  (Don Reid) -3
House of Cash, Inc.; BMI
OD -- 11/29/71, 10:00-12:00, Jerry Kennedy (db), Pete Drake (st g),
Hargus Robbins (p).
OD -- 12/20/71, 10:00-12:00, Jerry Kennedy (g), Lillian Hunt, George
Binkley, Martin Katahn, Stephen Clapp, Byron Bach, Sheldon

Kurland, Martha McCrory, Sam Terranova, Stephanie Woolf, Marvin Chantry, Solie Fott, Brenton Banks.
MEPL-11 -- DJ release, also included SINCE THEN & Open End Interview
SR6-1358 -- *Innerview*

=================================================================

Mercury Custom Recording Studio                          November 17, 1971
                                                             (14:00-17:00)
Jerry Kennedy (g,db); Bob Moore (b); Buddy Harman (dm); Hargus Robbins (p); Chip Young, Jerry Shook, Harold Bradley (g); Charlie McCoy (vb-1); string arr Cam Mullins -2.

2-48583   **DO YOU REMEMBER THESE**   (Harold Reid, Don Reid, Larry Lee)  -2
          House of Cash, Inc.; BMI
          OD -- 12/20/71, Strings, see 48582.
          OD -- 12/29/71, 10:00-11:30,
                Jerry Kennedy (g/db), Steve Sefsik (clarinet).
          73275 -- backed w/SINCE THEN
          CC-35035 -- backed w/THE CLASS OF '57
          SR6-1358 -- *Innerview*
          SRM1-1037 -- *Best of the Statler Brothers*
          PTV1003 -- *Memories . . . Now and Forever* (Canadian Rel)
          RB6-112 -- *Statler Brothers' Greatest Hits* (RD)
          TLCW-14 -- *C&W Classics: The Statler Brothers* (TL)
          RD7A-235 --*Best of SB, Their Greatest Hits & Finest Performances* (RD)
          NC 568 -- *The Statler Brothers Country* (K)
          518-945 -- *30th Anniversary Celebration*
          8077-V1 -- *The Very Best of the Statler Brothers* (Realm)

2-48584   **SHE THINKS I STILL CARE**   (Dickey Lee)  -1,-2
          Jack Music, Inc.; BMI
          OD -- 11/29/71, 10:00-12:00, Jerry Kennedy (db), Pete Drake (st g),
                Hargus Robbins (p).
          OD -- 12/20/71, Strings, see 48582.
          SR6-1358 -- Innerview
          RD7A-235 --*Best of SB, Their Greatest Hits & Finest Performances* (RD)

2-48585   **EVERYDAY WILL BE SUNDAY BYE AND BYE**   (PD)  arr - Bob Miller
          MCA, Inc.; ASCAP
          SR6-1358 -- *Innerview*

=================================================================

Mercury Custom Recording Studio                          November 18, 1971
                                                             (14:00-17:00)
Jerry Kennedy (g,db-1); Bob Moore (b); Buddy Harman (dm); Hargus Robbins (p, celeste-2); Jerry Shook, Harold Bradley, Chip Young (g); Charlie McCoy (hm-3); string arr Cam Mullins -4.

2-48586 **GOT LEAVIN' ON HER MIND** (Jack Clement) -1,-3,-4
Jack Music, Inc.; BMI
OD -- 11/29/71, 14:00-16:00, Jerry Kennedy (db), Pete Drake (st g),
Buddy Spicher (f).
SR6-1358 -- *Innerview*

2-48587 **I'D RATHER BE SORRY** (Kris Kristofferson)
Buckhorn Music Publishing Co., Inc.; BMI
OD -- 11/29/71, 14:00-16:00, Jerry Kennedy (db), Pete Drake (st g),
Buddy Spicher (f).
SR6-1358 -- *Innerview*

2-48588 **TOMORROW IS YOUR FRIEND** (Don Reid) -2,-3
American Cowboy Music Co., Inc.; BMI
OD -- 12/20/71, Strings, see 48582.
Final mix date -- 1/31/78.
SRM1-5007 -- *Entertainers . . . On & Off the Record*

**Note:** #48588 is the only lullaby recorded by the Statlers.
===========================================================

January 14, 1972
2-49750 Open End Interview with the Statler Brothers
MEPL-11 -- DJ release, also included SINCE THEN and I'LL TAKE CARE
OF YOU
Released 2/1/72.

**Note:** An "Open End Interview" was a recording where an artist was interviewed
and only the responses to the questions were recorded. The questions were printed
on the album cover so the local DJ could read the questions, then play the answers
-- thus "interviewing" said artist.
===========================================================

Mercury Custom Recording Studio                     April 11, 1972
(14:00-17:00)
Jerry Kennedy (g,db); Bob Moore (b); Harold Bradley, Chip Young, Ray Edenton
(g); Hargus Robbins (p); Charlie McCoy (hm-1,vb-2); Buddy Harman (dm); string
arr Cam Mullins -3.

2-49788 **WHEN MY BLUE MOON TURNS TO GOLD** -2,-3
(Wiley Walker, Gene Sullivan)
Peer International Corp.; BMI
OD -- 5/30/72, 10:00-12:30, Jerry Kennedy (g/db), Martha McCrory,
Byron Bach, Lillian Hunt, Gary Vanosdale, Marvin Chantry,
Martin Katahn, Stephanie Woolf, George Binkley, Sam
Terranova, Sheldon Kurland, Brenton Banks, Carl Gorodetzky.
OD -- 6/6/72, 14:00-17:00, Jerry Kennedy (g/db), Pete Drake (st g).

Final mix -- 6/14/72
MELP-25 -- DJ release, also included THE SATURDAY MORNING RADIO
    SHOW (Roadhog) and 1953-DEAR JOHN-HONKY-TONK BLUES
SR6-1367 -- *Country Music Then & Now*
RD7A-235 --*Best of SB, Their Greatest Hits & Finest Performances* (RD)

2-49789  **NO ONE WILL EVER KNOW** (Mel Foree, Fred Rose) -2,-3
    Milene Music, Inc.; ASCAP
    OD -- 5/30/72, Strings, see 49788.
    OD -- 6/6/72, 14:00-17:00, Jerry Kennedy (g/db), Pete Drake (st g).
    Final mix -- 6/14/72
    SR6-1367 -- *Country Music Then & Now*

2-49790  **EVERY TIME I TRUST A GAL** (Lew DeWitt) -1
    House of Cash, Inc.; BMI
    Final mix -- 6/14/72
    73315 -- backed w/THE CLASS OF '57
    SR6-1367 -- *Country Music Then & Now*

Mercury Custom Recording Studio            April 12, 1972
            (10:00-13:00)
Bob Moore (b); Harold Bradley, Chip Young, Ray Edenton (g); Hargus Robbins
(p); Buddy Harman (dm); Charlie McCoy (hm-1); Jerry Kennedy (g,db); Roy Dea
(el b); string arr Cam Mullins -2.

2-49791  **UNDER IT ALL** (Lew DeWitt) -1
    House of Cash, Inc.; BMI
    OD -- 6/6/72, 14:00-17:00, Jerry Kennedy (g/db), Pete Drake (st g).
    OD -- 6/8/72, 10:00-12:00, Hargus Robbins (p).
    Final mix -- 6/14/72
    SR6-1367 -- *Country Music Then & Now*

2-49792  **A STRANGER IN MY PLACE** (Kenny Rogers, Kim Vassey) -2
    Devon Music, Inc./Amos Productions/Flea Show Music, Inc.; BMI
    OD -- 5/30/72, Strings, see 49788.
    OD -- 6/6/72, 14:00-17:00, Jerry Kennedy (g/db), Pete Drake (st g).
    Final mix -- 6/14/72
    SR6-1367 -- *Country Music Then & Now*

2-49793  **1953-DEAR JOHN-HONKY-TONK BLUES** (Don Reid, Harold Reid) -1
    House of Cash, Inc.; BMI
    OD -- 6/7/72, 10:00-12:00,
            Jerry Kennedy (g/db), George Tidwell (trumpet).
    Final mix -- 6/14/72

MEPL-25 -- DJ release, also included SINCE THEN and THE SATURDAY MORNING RADIO SHOW (Roadhog)
SR6-1367 -- *Country Music Then & Now*

===============================================================

Mercury Custom Recording Studio                    April 13, 1972
                                                    (14:00-17:00)
Jerry Kennedy (g,db); Bob Moore (b); Buddy Harman (dm); Harold Bradley, Chip Young, Ray Edenton (g); Hargus Robbins (p); string arr Cam Mullins -1.

2-49794  THE CLASS OF '57  (Don Reid, Harold Reid) -1
         House of Cash, Inc.; BMI
         OD -- 5/30/72, Strings, see 49788.
         Final mix -- 6/14//72
         73315 -- backed w/EVERY TIME I TRUST A GAL
         CC-35035 -- backed w/DO YOU REMEMBER THESE
         814 881-7 --backed w/ELIZABETH
         SR6-1367 -- *Country Music Then & Now*
         SRM1-1037 -- *Best of the Statler Brothers*
         RD7A-235 --*Best of SB, Their Greatest Hits & Finest Performances* (RD)
         NC 568 -- *The Statler Brothers Country* (K)
         518-945 -- *30th Anniversary Celebration*

2-49795  JESUS, TAKE ANOTHER LOOK AT ME  (Don Reid)
         House of Cash, Inc.; BMI
         OD -- 6/6/72, 14:00-17:00, Jerry Kennedy (g/db), Pete Drake (st g).
         OD -- 6/8/72, 10:00-12:00, Hargus Robbins (p).
         Final mix -- 6/14/72
         SR6-1367 -- *Country Music Then & Now*
         RD7A-235 --*Best of SB, Their Greatest Hits & Finest Performances* (RD)

2-49796  NO LETTER TODAY  (Frankie Brown)
         Peer International Corp.; BMI
         -- rejected --

===============================================================

Mercury Custom Recording Studio                    April 13, 1972
                                                    (18:00-21:00)
Jerry Kennedy (g,db); Bob Moore (b); Buddy Harman (dm); Buddy Spicher (f); Harold Bradley, Chip Young, Ray Edenton (g); Hargus Robbins (p).

2-49797  THE SATURDAY MORNING RADIO SHOW  (Monologue)  [No. 1]
         (Phil Balsley, Lew DeWitt, Don Reid, Harold Reid)
             Little Liza Jane (PD) -- theme; Honky Tonk Girl (Hank Thompson, Chuck Harding) Brazos Valley Music, Inc., BMI; Why Baby Why, (George Jones, Darrell Edwards) Starday Music, BMI; Folsom

Prison (Johnny R. Cash) Hi-Le Music, Inc., BMI; Angel Band (Pearl
D. Jones) Cedarwood Publishing Co., Inc., BMI
American Cowboy Music Co., Inc.; BMI
Final mix -- 6/14/72
MEPL-25 -- DJ release, also included 1953-DEAR JOHN-HONKY-TONK
BLUES and SINCE THEN
SR6-1367 -- *Country Music Then & Now*
518-944 -- *30th Anniversary Celebration* package

2-49798  **THE TEN COMMANDMENTS**  (Lew DeWitt)
House of Cash, Inc.; BMI
Final mix -- 9/16/75
SRM1-1051 -- *The Holy Bible, Old Testament*
SRM2-101 -- *The Holy Bible, Old & New Testaments* (double)

**Note:**      2-49797 credited as Lester "Roadhog" Moran & the Cadillac Cowboys.
See also 10/8/73.

====================================================================

*Sessions with Johnny Cash -- See Chapter One*

May 15, 1972; May 17, 1972; June, 1972; July 27, 1972; July 28, 1972

====================================================================

Mercury Custom Recording Studio                              November 1, 1972
                                                              (14:00-17:00)
Jerry Kennedy (g,db, el sitar-1);Bob Moore (b); Hargus Robbins (p); Chip Young,
Ray Edenton, Harold Bradley (g); Charlie McCoy (org-2, hm-3,vb-4); Buddy
Harman (dm).

2-49882  **WEDDING BELLS**  (Claude Boone) -2,-4
Edwin H. Morris & Co., Inc.; ASCAP
OD -- 12/4/72, 10:00-12:30, Jerry Kennedy (g/db), Bobby Thompson
(bjo), Pete Drake (st g), Hargus Robbins (p).
Final mix -- 12/6/72
SR6-1374 -- *Statler Bros. Sing Country Symphonies in E Major*

2-49883  **A SPECIAL SONG FOR WANDA**  (Harold Reid, Don Reid)
American Cowboy Music Co., Inc.; BMI
OD -- 12/4/72, 10:00-12:30, Jerry Kennedy (g/db), Pete Drake (st g),
Hargus Robbins (p).
Final mix -- 12/8/72
SR6-1374 -- *Statler Bros. Sing Country Symphonies in E Major*

2-49884  **TOO MANY RIVERS**  (Harlan Howard)  -1,-3,-4
Combine Music Corp.; BMI
Final mix -- 12/11/72
SR6-1374 -- *Statler Bros. Sing Country Symphonies in E Major*

2-49885  **BURNING BRIDGES**  (Walter Scott)
Sage & Sand Music, Inc.; SESAC
OD -- 12/4/72, 10:00-12:30, Jerry Kennedy (db), Pete Drake (st g),
    Hargus Robbins (p).
Final mix -- 12/8/72
SR6-1374 -- *Statler Bros. Sing Country Symphonies in E Major*

=====================================================================

Mercury Custom Recording Studio                    November 2, 1972
                                                        (10:00-13:00)
Jerry Kennedy (g,db); Bob Moore (b); Buddy Harman (dm); Hargus Robbins (p);
Ray Edenton, Chip Young, Harold Bradley (g); Charlie McCoy (vb-1,hm-2); string
arr Cam Mullins -3.

2-49886  **DELTA DAWN**  (Alex Harvey, Larry Collins Reid)  -2
UA Music Co., Inc./Big Ax Music, ASCAP
OD -- 12/4/72, 14:00-16:00, Jerry Kennedy (g), Pete Drake (st g),
    Hargus Robbins (p).
Final mix -- 12/8/72
SR6-1374 -- *Statler Bros. Sing Country Symphonies in E Major*
RD7A-235 --*Best of SB, Their Greatest Hits & Finest Performances* (RD)

2-49887  **I BELIEVE IN MUSIC**  (Mac Davis)  -3
Screen Gems-Columbia Music, Inc./Songpainter Music, BMI
OD -- 11/15/72, 18:00-20:15, Columbia Recording Studios, Brenton
    Banks, Gary Vanosdale, Marvin Chantry, Byron Bach, Martha
    McCrory, Stephanie Woolf, Chris Teal, Martin Katahn, Solie Fott,
    Sheldon Kurland, George Binkley, Steven Smith, Jerry Kennedy
    (g/db).
OD -- 12/4/72, 10:00-12:30, Jerry Kennedy (g/db), Bobby Thompson
    (bjo), Pete Drake (st g), Hargus Robbins (p).
Final mix -- 12/6/72
SR6-1374 -- *Statler Bros. Sing Country Symphonies in E Major*
RD7A-235 --*Best of SB, Their Greatest Hits & Finest Performances* (RD)

2-49888  **I'LL BE YOUR BABY TONIGHT**  (Bob Dylan)  -1,-2
Dwarf Music; ASCAP
OD -- 12/4/72, 10:00-12:30, Jerry Kennedy (fretted db),
    Pete Drake (sl db), Hargus Robbins (p).
Final mix -- 12/6/72
SR6-1374 -- *Statler Bros. Sing Country Symphonies in E Major*

=====================================================================

Mercury Custom Recording Studio                                    November 2, 1972
                                                                        (14:00-17:00)
Jerry Kennedy (g,db-1); Bob Moore (b); Buddy Harman (dm); Hargus Robbins (p);
Ray Edenton, Harold Bradley, Chip Young (g); Charlie McCoy (vb-2,hm-3); string
arr Cam Mullins -4.

2-49889    MONDAY MORNING SECRETARY   (Don Reid) -1,-2,-4
           American Cowboy Music Co., Inc.; BMI
           OD -- 11/15/72, Strings, see 49887.
           Final mix -- 12/6/72
           73360 -- backed w/A SPECIAL SONG FOR WANDA
           SR6-1374 -- *Statler Bros. Sing Country Symphonies in E Major*
           TLCW-14 -- *C&W Classics: The Statler Brothers* (TL)
           RD7A-235 --*Best of SB, Their Greatest Hits & Finest Performances* (RD)
           8077-V1 -- *The Very Best of the Statler Brothers* (Realm)

2-49890    WOMAN WITHOUT A HOME   (Don Reid) -2,-4
           American Cowboy Music Co., Inc.; BMI
           OD -- 11/15/72, Strings, see 49887.
           Final mix -- 12/5/72
           73392 -- backed w/I'LL BE YOUR BABY TONIGHT
           SR6-1374 -- *Statler Bros. Sing Country Symphonies in E Major*
           RD7A-235 --*Best of SB, Their Greatest Hits & Finest Performances* (RD)
           518-945 -- *30th Anniversary Celebration*
           8077-V2 -- *The Very Best of the Statler Brothers* (Realm)

2-49891    THEY CAN'T TAKE YOU OUT OF ME   (Harold Reid, Don Reid) -1,-3
           American Cowboy Music Co., Inc.; BMI
           OD -- 12/4/72, 10:00-12:30, Jerry Kennedy (g/db), Pete Drake (st g),
                   Hargus Robbins (p).
           Final mix -- 12/5/72
           SR6-1374 -- *Statler Bros. Sing Country Symphonies in E Major*

=====================================================================

Mercury Custom Recording Studio                                    November 3, 1972
                                                                        (10:00-13:00)
Jerry Kennedy (g,db); Bob Moore (b); Buddy Harman (dm); Hargus Robbins (p);
Chip Young, Harold Bradley, Ray Edenton (g); Charlie McCoy (hm-1,vb-2), Bobby
Thompson (bjo-3), Buddy Spicher (f-4).

2-49892    YOU CAN'T JUDGE A BOOK BY ITS COVER   (Claude Boone) -1,-3,-4
           Gallatin Music Corp., BMI
           Final mix -- 11/8/74
           SRM1-1019 -- *Sons of the Motherland*

2-49893  **(I WANT TO CARRY YOUR) SWEET MEMORIES**  (Lew DeWitt) -3,-4
American Cowboy Music Co., Inc.; BMI
Final mix -- 12/4/72
SR6-1374 -- *Statler Bros. Sing Country Symphonies in E Major*

2-49894  **TAKE GOOD CARE OF HER**  (Arthur Kent, Edward C. Warren) -2
George Paxton Corp., ASCAP
OD -- 12/4/72, 10:00-12:30, Jerry Kennedy (g/db), Pete Drake (st g),
        Hargus Robbins (p).
Final mix -- 7/3/73
SRM1-676 -- *Carry Me Back*
RD7A-235 --*Best of SB, Their Greatest Hits & Finest Performances* (RD)

===========================================================

Mercury Custom Recording Studio                          May 21, 1973
                                                           (14:00-17:00)
Hargus Robbins (kb); Charlie McCoy (hm-1,vb-2); Harold Bradley, Ray Edenton,
Jerry Shook, Chip Young (g); Jerry Kennedy (g,db-3); Bob Moore (b); Buddy
Harman (dm); string arr Cam Mullins -4.

2-50215  **WHAT DO I CARE**  (Johnny Cash) -2,-3
Southwind Music, Inc.; BMI
OD -- Pete Drake (st g), date unknown.
Final mix -- 7/3/73
SRM1-676 -- *Carry Me Back*
TLCW-14 -- *C&W Classics: The Statler Brothers* (TL)

2-50216  **THE STRAND**  (Lew DeWitt) -1,-4
American Cowboy Music Co., Inc.; BMI
OD -- 7/6/73, 10:00-13:00, Jerry Kennedy (g/db), Brenton Banks, Gary
        Vanosdale, Marvin Chantry, Byron Bach, David Vanderkooi, Sam
        Terranova, Solie Fott, George Binkley, Chris Teal, Stephanie
        Woolf, Carl Gorodetzky, Steve Smith, Sheldon Kurland.
Final mix -- 8/2/73
73448 -- backed w/WHATEVER HAPPENED TO RANDOLPH SCOTT
SRM1-676 -- *Carry Me Back*

2-50217  **THE WOMAN I STILL LOVE**  (Don Reid) -4
American Cowboy Music Co., Inc.; BMI
OD -- 7/6/73, Strings, see 50216.
Final mix -- 8/2/73
SRM1-676 -- *Carry Me Back*

===========================================================

Mercury Custom Recording Studio                                        May 22, 1973
                                                                      (14:00-17:00)
Hargus Robbins (kb); Charlie McCoy (hm-1,vb-2); Harold Bradley, Ray Edenton,
Jerry Shook, Chip Young (g); Jerry Kennedy (g,db); Bob Moore (b); Buddy
Harman (dm); string arr Cam Mullins -3.

2-50218   WHATEVER HAPPENED TO RANDOLPH SCOTT   -1
            (Harold Reid, Don Reid)
            American Cowboy Music Co., Inc.; BMI
            Final mix -- 7/3/73
            73448 -- backed w/THE STRAND
            SRM1-676 -- *Carry Me Back*
            PTV1003 -- *Memories . . . Now and Forever* (Canadian Rel)
            SRM1-1037 -- *Best of the Statler Brothers*
            RB6-112 -- *Statler Brothers' Greatest Hits* (RD)
            TLCW-14 -- *C&W Classics: The Statler Brothers* (TL)
            RD7A-235 --*Best of SB, Their Greatest Hits & Finest Performances* (RD)
            518-945 -- *30th Anniversary Celebration*
            8077-V2 -- *The Very Best of the Statler Brothers* (Realm)

2-50219   CARRY ME BACK   (Harold Reid, Don Reid)  -3
            American Cowboy Music Co., Inc.; BMI
            OD -- 7/6/73, Strings, see 50216.
            Final mix -- 8/2/73
            73415 -- backed w/I WISH I COULD BE
            SRM1-676 -- *Carry Me Back*
            PTV1003 -- *Memories . . . Now and Forever* (Canadian Rel)
            SRM1-1037 -- *Best of the Statler Brothers*
            TLCW-14 -- *C&W Classics: The Statler Brothers* (TL)
            RD7A-235 --*Best of SB, Their Greatest Hits & Finest Performances* (RD)
            518-945 -- *30th Anniversary Celebration*

2-50220   WE OWE IT ALL TO YESTERDAY   (Harold Reid, Don Reid)  -3
            American Cowboy Music Co., Inc.; BMI
            OD -- 7/6/73, Strings, see 50216.
            Final mix -- 8/2/73
            SRM1-676 -- *Carry Me Back*
            TLCW-14 -- *C&W Classics: The Statler Brothers* (TL)

2-50221   I WISH I COULD BE   (Don Reid)  -2
            American Cowboy Music Co., Inc.; BMI
            OD -- Pete Drake (st g), date unknown.
            Final mix -- 7/3/73
            73415 -- backed w/CARRY ME BACK
            SRM1-676 -- *Carry Me Back*

Mercury Custom Recording Studio                              May 23, 1973
                                                            (14:00-17:00)
Hargus Robbins (kb); Charlie McCoy (vb-1); Harold Bradley, Ray Edenton, Jerry
Shook, Chip Young (g); Jerry Kennedy (g,db); Bob Moore (b); Buddy Harman
(dm); string arr Cam Mullins -2.

2-50222   **BLUE EYES CRYIN' IN THE RAIN**   (Fred Rose) -2
          Milene Music, Inc.; ASCAP
          OD -- 7/6/73, Strings, see 50216.
          OD -- 7/6/73, Pete Drake (st g).
          Final mix -- 12/7/76
          SRM1-1125 -- *The Country America Loves*
          RD7A-235 --*Best of SB, Their Greatest Hits & Finest Performances* (RD)

2-50223   **SUSAN WHEN SHE TRIED**   (Don Reid)
          American Cowboy Music Co., Inc.; BMI
          Final mix -- 6/28/73 (2-track stereo)
          Final mix -- 9/9/74 (mono - for radio station use only)
          73625 -- backed w/SHE'S TOO GOOD
          DJ-407 -- DJ release (mono mix)
          SRM1-1019 -- *Sons of the Motherland*
          PTV1003 -- *Memories . . . Now and Forever* (Canadian Rel)
          SRM1-1037 -- *Best of the Statler Brothers*
          TLCW-14 -- *C&W Classics: The Statler Brothers* (TL)
          RD7A-235 --*Best of SB, Their Greatest Hits & Finest Performances* (RD)
          518-945 -- *30th Anniversary Celebration*
          8077-V2 -- *The Very Best of the Statler Brothers* (Realm)

2-50224   **THE STREETS OF SAN FRANCISCO**   (Don Reid) -1,-2
          American Cowboy Music Co., Inc.; BMI
          OD -- 7/6/73, Strings, see 50216.
          Final mix -- 8/2/73
          SRM1-676 -- *Carry Me Back*

=================================================================

Mercury Custom Recording Studio                              May 24, 1973
                                                            (10:00-12:30)
Hargus Robbins (kb); Harold Bradley, Pete Wade, Ray Edenton, Chip Young (g);
Jerry Kennedy (g,db); Bob Moore (b); Buddy Harman (dm).

2-50225   **WHEN I STOP DREAMING**   (Ira Louvin, Charles Louvin)
          Acuff-Rose Publications, Inc.; BMI
          OD -- Pete Drake (st g), date unknown.
          Final mix -- 6/28/73
          SRM1-676 -- *Carry Me Back*

2-50226  **THANK YOU WORLD**  (Don Reid, Lew DeWitt)
American Cowboy Music Co., Inc.; BMI
Final mix -- 6/26/73
73485 -- backed w/THE BLACKWOOD BROS. BY THE STATLER BROS.
SRM1-707 -- *Thank You World*
PTV1003 -- *Memories . . . Now and Forever* (Canadian Rel)
SRM1-1037 -- *Best of the Statler Brothers*
TLCW-14 -- *C&W Classics: The Statler Brothers* (TL)
RD7A-235 --*Best of SB, Their Greatest Hits & Finest Performances* (RD)
518-945 -- *30th Anniversary Celebration*
8077-V2 -- *The Very Best of the Statler Brothers* (Realm)

2-50227  **IF WE NEVER HAD**  (Don Reid)
American Cowboy Music Co., Inc.; BMI
OD -- Pete Drake (st g), date unknown.
Final mix -- 7/3/73
SRM1-676 -- *Carry Me Back*

===============================================================

Mercury Custom Recording Studio                             October 8, 1973
                                                            (10:00-13:00)
Lester "Roadhog" Moran and his Cadillac Cowboys (monologues); Jerry Kennedy
(g,db); Buddy Spicher (f); Wichita (el g); Ray Edenton (g); Bob Moore (b); Thomas
Sparkman.**

2-50298  **THE SATURDAY MORNING RADIO SHOW NO. 2**
          (Harold Reid, Don Reid, Phil Balsley, Lew DeWitt)
American Cowboy Music Co., Inc.; BMI
     Little Liza Jane (PD) -- theme; *Woman Sensuous Woman (Gary S.
     Paxton) Acoustic Music, Inc., BMI; Freight Train (Paul James, Fred
     Williams) Peter Maurice Music Co., Ltd., ASCAP; He'll Have to Go
     (Joe Allison, Audrey Allison) Central Songs, Inc., BMI; Medley --
     Hello Darlin' (Conway Twitty) Twitty Bird Music Publishing Co.,
     BMI; Hello Walls (Willie Nelson) Tree Publishing Co., Inc., BMI;
     Funny How Time Slips Away (Willie Nelson) Tree Publishing Co.,
     Inc., BMI; Church in the Wildwood (PD, arr - H.Reid, D.Reid,
     P.Balsley, L. DeWitt) American Cowboy Music Co., Inc., BMI
Final mix -- 2/5/74

2-50299  **ALIVE AT THE JOHNNY MACK BROWN HIGH SCHOOL**
          (Harold Reid, Don Reid, Phil Balsley, Lew DeWitt)
American Cowboy Music Co., Inc.; BMI
     Little Liza Jane (PD) -- theme; Hey Joe (Boudleaux Bryant) Acuff-
     Rose Publications, Inc., BMI; Filipino Baby (Billy Cox, Clarke Van
     Ness) Shapiro Bernstein & Co., Inc., ASCAP; Sixteen Tons (Merle
     Travis) American Music Inc., BMI; Rubber Dolly (PD,  arr - H.Reid,

D.Reid, P.Balsley, L.DeWitt) American Cowboy Music Co., Inc.; BMI; Wildwood Flower (PD, arr - H.Reid, D.Reid, P.Balsley, L.DeWitt) American Cowboy Music Co., Inc.; BMI; Medley -- Keep On the Sunny Side (A.P. Carter, Gary Garett) Peer International Corp., BMI; Waterloo (Marijohn Wilkin, John D. Loudermilk) Cedarwood Publishing Co., Inc., BMI

Final mix -- 2/5/74

2-50300 **RAINBOW VALLEY CONFIDENTIAL AUDITION TAPE**
(Harold Reid, Don Reid, Phil Balsley, Lew DeWitt)
American Cowboy Music Co., Inc.; BMI
Final mix -- 2/5/74

All titles issued on SRM1-708; reissued on 518-944. "Roadhog" - Harold Reid; "Wichita" - Lew DeWitt; "Wesley" - Don Reid; "Red" - Phil Balsley.
*On 50298, Woman Sensuous Woman, was recorded but was not included in the release because the publisher would not give rights.
**Note:** Although Thomas Sparkman is listed on the album cover as a musician, he was the engineer. For a time, the American Federation of Musicians (AFM) allowed engineers to sign the same time card as the musicians. This time card was the source of information for the album copy.

Mercury Custom Recording Studio                    November 13, 1973
                                                              (14:00-17:00)
Jerry Kennedy **[artist]** (g,db); Jerry Carrigan (dm); Charlie McCoy (hm,vb,org); Ray Edenton, Chip Young, Harold Bradley (g); Hargus Robbins (p); Tommy Cogbill (b). **Statler Brothers, vocals.**

2-50310 **ROLLIN' IN MY SWEET BABY'S ARMS** [Lester Flatt]
Public Domain
OD -- 11/13/73, 17:00-18:00, Boots Randolph (sax).
SRM1-692 -- *Jerry Kennedy and Friends*

**Nore:** According to Jerry Kennedy, the Statlers asked if they could be creative. They sang the first chorus straight, but they wrote the second chorus! This is the only time they appeared as guests on another artist's release.

Mercury Custom Recording Studio                    November 27, 1973
                                                              (10:00-13:00)
Hargus Robbins (p, org-1); Charlie McCoy (hm-2); Harold Bradley, Ray Edenton, Chip Young (g); Jerry Kennedy (g,db); Bob Moore (b); Buddy Harman (dm); Thomas Sparkman.**

2-50315 **THE BAPTISM OF JESSE TAYLOR** (Dallas Frazier, Sanger D. Shafer) -1
Blue Crest Music, Inc.; BMI

SRM1-707 -- *Thank You World*
TLCW-14 -- *C&W Classics: The Statler Brothers* (TL)

2-50316   **THE BLACKWOOD BROTHERS BY THE STATLER BROTHERS**   -1,-2
              (Don Reid)
          American Cowboy Music Co., Inc.; BMI
          OD -- 2/28/74, 10:00-12:00, Jerry Kennedy (g,db), Larry Butler (p).
          73485 -- backed w/THANK YOU WORLD
          SRM1-707 -- *Thank You World*
          TLCW-14 -- *C&W Classics: The Statler Brothers* (TL)

2-59317   **COWBOY BUCKAROO**   (Mason Williams)  -2
          Irving Music, Inc.; BMI
          OD -- 2/28/74, 10:00-12:00, Jerry Kennedy (g,db), Larry Butler (p).
          OD -- Pete Drake (st g), date unknown.
          SRM1-707 -- *Thank You World*

**Note:**   See note on Thomas Sparkman at master #2-50298, Oct. 8, 1973.

==================================================================

Mercury Custom Recording Studio                                    November 28, 1973
                                                                      (10:00-13:00)
Hargus Robbins (org,p); Charlie McCoy (hm-1,vb-2); Harold Bradley, Ray
Edenton, Chip Young (g); Jerry Kennedy (g,db); Bob Moore (b); Buddy Harman
(dm); string arr Cam Mullins -3.

2-50318   **CITY LIGHTS**   (Bill Anderson)  -3
          TNT Music, Inc.; BMI
          OD -- Strings, date and musicians unknown.
          OD -- Pete Drake (st G), date unknown.
          Final mix -- 2/12/74
          SRM1-707 -- *Thank You World*

2-50319   **STREETS OF BALTIMORE**   (Tompall Glaser, Harlan Howard)  -3
          Glaser Brothers Music, Inc.; BMI
          OD -- Strings, date and musicians unknown.
          OD -- Pete Drake (st G), date unknown.
          Final mix -- 3/12/74
          SRM1-707 -- *Thank You World*

2-50320   **LEFT-HANDED WOMAN**   (Don Reid, Harold Reid)  -1
          American Cowboy Music Co., Inc.; BMI
          Final mix -- 3/12/74
          SRM1-707 -- *Thank You World*

2-50321 **MARGIE'S AT THE LINCOLN PARK INN** (Tom T. Hall) -2
Newkeys Music, Inc.; BMI
OD -- Pete Drake (st g), date unknown.
Final mix -- 2/28/74
SRM1-707 -- *Thank You World*

====================================================

Mercury Custom Recording Studio                 November 28, 1973
                                                       (18:00-21:00)
Hargus Robbins (p,org-1); Charlie McCoy (hm,vb-2); Harold Bradley, Ray
Edenton, Chip Young (g); Jerry Kennedy (g,db-3); Bob Moore (b); Buddy Harman
(dm); string arr Cam Mullins -4. Thomas Sparkman**

2-50322 **THE BOY INSIDE OF ME** (Lew DeWitt) -2,-4
American Cowboy Music Co., Inc.; BMI
OD -- Strings, date and musicians unknown.
Final mix -- 2/27/74
SRM1-707 -- *Thank You World*

2-50323 **SHE'S TOO GOOD** (Don Reid, Harold Reid) -3
American Cowboy Music Co., Inc.; BMI
OD -- Pete Drake (st g), date unknown.
73625 -- backed w/SUSAN WHEN SHE TRIED
SRM1-707 -- *Thank You World*

2-50324 **EVE** (Don Reid, Harold Reid) -1
American Cowboy Music Co., Inc.; BMI
SRM1-1051 -- *The Holy Bible, Old Testament*
SRM2-101 -- *The Holy Bible, Old & New Testaments* (double)

**Note:** See note on Thomas Sparkman at master #2-50298, Oct. 8, 1973.

====================================================

Mercury Custom Recording Studio                 November 29, 1973
                                                       (10:00-13:00)
Hargus Robbins (org,p); Charlie McCoy (vb-1); Ray Edenton, Harold Bradley,
Chip Young (g); Jerry Kennedy (g,db-2); Bob Moore (b); Buddy Harman (dm);
string arr Cam Mullins -3.

2-50325 **SAMSON** (Lew DeWitt) -1,-2
American Cowboy Music Co., Inc.; BMI
Final mix -- 9/2/75
SRM1-1051 -- *The Holy Bible, Old Testament*
SRM2-101 -- *The Holy Bible, Old & New Testaments* (double)
TLCW-14 -- *C&W Classics: The Statler Brothers* (TL)

2-50326  **NOAH FOUND GRACE IN THE EYES OF THE LORD**  (Richard Schmertz)
Ludlow Music, Inc.; BMI
Final mix -- 8/28/75
73732 -- backed w/HOW GREAT THOU ART
SRM1-1051 -- *The Holy Bible, Old Testament*
SRM2-101 -- *The Holy Bible, Old & New Testaments* (double)

2-50327  **SWEET CHARLOTTE ANN**  (Don Reid) -1
American Cowboy Music Co., Inc.; BMI
OD -- Strings, date and musicians unknown.
Final mix -- 3/12/74
SRM1-707 -- *Thank You World*

=============================================================

Mercury Custom Recording Studio                              May 15, 1974
                                                            (14:00-17:00)
Jerry Kennedy (g,db); Bob Moore (b); Buddy Harman (dm); Hargus Robbins (p);
Ray Edenton, Pete Wade, Chip Young, Harold Bradley (g); Charlie McCoy
(hm-1,vb); Thomas Sparkman.**

2-50377  **THE DREAMER**  (Lew DeWitt)
American Cowboy Music Co., Inc.; BMI
Final mix -- 9/3/75
SRM1-1051 -- *The Holy Bible, Old Testament*
SRM2-101 -- *The Holy Bible, Old & New Testaments* (double)

2-50378  **I'LL GO TO MY GRAVE LOVING YOU**  (Don Reid) -1
American Cowboy Music Co., Inc.; BMI
Final mix -- 11/8/74
73687 -- backed w/YOU'VE BEEN LIKE A MOTHER TO ME
CC-35038 -- backed w/YOUR PICTURE IN THE PAPER
SRM1-1037 -- *Best of the Statler Brothers*
PTV1003 -- *Memories . . . Now and Forever* (Canadian Rel)
TLCW-14 -- *C&W Classics: The Statler Brothers* (TL)
RD7A-235 --*Best of SB, Their Greatest Hits & Finest Performances* (RD)
NC 568 -- *The Statler Brothers Country* (K)
518-945 -- *30th Anniversary Celebration*
8077-V1 -- *The Very Best of the Statler Brothers* (Realm)

2-50379  **HE WENT TO THE CROSS LOVING YOU**  (Don Reid, Harold Reid) -1
American Cowboy Music Co., Inc.; BMI
OD -- 9/10/75, 10:00-12:30, Jerry Kennedy (g/db), Pete Drake (st g),.
Final mix -- 9/10/75
SRM1-1173/SRM1-5001 -- *Short Stories*
SRM1-5001 -- *Entertainers . . . On & Off the Record*
RD7A-235 --*Best of SB, Their Greatest Hits & Finest Performances* (RD)

**\*\*Note:** See note on Thomas Sparkman at master #2-50298, Oct. 8, 1973.

═══════════════════════════════════════════════════════════════

Mercury Custom Recording Studio                              September 30, 1974
                                                                   (10:00-13:00)
Jerry Kennedy (db); Bob Moore (b); Chip Young, Ray Edenton, Pete Wade, Harold
Bradley (g); Hargus Robbins (p); Buddy Harman (dm); string arr Cam Mullins -2.

2-51472  **SO MARY COULD MAKE IT HOME**  (Don Reid) -1
         American Cowboy Music Co., Inc.; BMI
         Final mix -- 11/7/74
         SRM1-1019 -- *Sons of the Motherland*

2-51473  **YOU'VE BEEN LIKE A MOTHER TO ME**  (Don Reid) -2
         American Cowboy Music Co., Inc.; BMI
         OD -- 10/16/74, 11:00-13:00, Jerry Kennedy (g/db), Pete Drake (st g).
         OD -- 10/25/74, 10:00-13:00, Sheldon Kurland, Brenton Banks, Carl
              Gorodetzky, Virginia Christensen, Roy Christensen, Steve Smith,
              Lennie Haight, Marvin Chantry, Byron Bach, George Binkley,
              Stephanie Woolf, Gary Vanosdale, Mary Ann Mullins (tuba).
         Final mix -- 10/31/74
         73687 -- backed w/I'LL GO TO MY GRAVE LOVING YOU
         SRM1-1019 -- *Sons of the Motherland*

═══════════════════════════════════════════════════════════════

Mercury Custom Recording Studio                                 October 1, 1974
                                                                   (10:00-13:00)
Jerry Kennedy (db); Bob Moore (b); Hargus Robbins (p); Harold Bradley, Chip
Young, Ray Edenton, Pete Wade (g); Charlie McCoy (hm,vb-1); Buddy Harman
(dm); string arr Cam Mullins -2.

2-51475  **A LETTER FROM SHIRLEY MILLER**  (Don Reid, Harold Reid)
         American Cowboy Music Co., Inc.; BMI
         OD -- 10/16/74, 11:00-13:00, Jerry Kennedy (g/db), Pete Drake (st g).
         Final mix -- 11/4/74
         SRM1-1019 -- *Sons of the Motherland*

2-51476  **ALL AMERICAN GIRL**  (Don Reid, Harold Reid) -1,-2
         American Cowboy Music Co., Inc.; BMI
         OD -- 10/25/74, Strings, see 51473.
         Final mix -- 11/7/74
         73665 -- backed w/A FEW OLD MEMORIES
         DJ-425 -- DJ release
         SRM1-1019 -- *Sons of the Motherland*
         TLCW-14 -- *C&W Classics: The Statler Brothers* (TL)
         RD7A-235 --*Best of SB, Their Greatest Hits & Finest Performances* (RD)
         8077-V1 -- *The Very Best of the Statler Brothers*

2-51477  **I'LL BE HERE**  (Don Reid) -1
American Cowboy Music Co., Inc.; BMI
OD -- 10/16/74, 11:00-13:00, Jerry Kennedy (g/db), Pete Drake (st g).
Final mix -- 11/7/74
SRM1-1019 -- *Sons of the Motherland*

**Note:**     As related by Phil Balsley, #51476 was their most long-drawn out
composition. From conception to completion was about five years.

Mercury Custom Recording Studio                         October 8, 1974
                                                        (10:00-13:00)
Jerry Kennedy (db); Bob Moore (b); Harold Bradley, Ray Edenton, Chip Young,
Pete Wade (g); Buddy Harman (dm); Charlie McCoy (hm-1, vb-2); Bobby Wood
(p); string arr Cam Mullins - 3.

2-51492  **TOGETHER**  (Carroll "Bull" Durham) -2,-3
American Cowboy Music Co., Inc.; BMI
OD -- 10/25/74, Strings, see 51473.
Final mix -- 11/7/74
SRM1-1019 -- *Sons of the Motherland*

2-51493  **EIGHT MORE MILES TO LOUISVILLE**  (Louis M. "Grandpa" Jones) -1
Hill & Range Songs, Inc.; BMI
OD -- 11/11/74, 15:00-16:00, Louis M. "Grandpa" Jones (bjo).
Final mix -- 11/11/74
SRM1-1019 -- *Sons of the Motherland*

2-51494  **ONE MORE SUMMER IN VIRGINIA**  (Don Reid) -2,-3
American Cowboy Music Co., Inc.; BMI
OD -- 10/25/74, Strings, see 51473.
Final mix -- 11/7/74
SRM1-1019 -- *Sons of the Motherland*

Mercury Custom Recording Studio                       November 19, 1974
                                                        (10:00-13:00)
Bob Moore (b); Jerry Shook, Harold Bradley, Ray Edenton, Pete Wade (g); Hargus
Robbins (p); Buddy Harman (dm); Jerry Kennedy (g,db-1).

2-51519  **HAVE A LITTLE FAITH**  (Don Reid) -1
American Cowboy Music Co., Inc.; BMI
Final mix -- 9/10/75
SRM1-1051 -- *The Holy Bible, Old Testament*
SRM2-101 -- *The Holy Bible, Old & New Testaments* (double)

2-51520  **IN THE BEGINNING**
        (Dorcas Cochran, Fred Wise, Kay Twomey, Ben Weisman)
        Intersong Music, Inc.; ASCAP/Belinda Music, BMI
        Final mix -- 9/10/75
        SRM1-1051 -- *The Holy Bible, Old Testament*
        SRM2-101 -- *The Holy Bible, Old & New Testaments* (double)

2-51521  **THE FOURTH MAN**  (Arthur Smith)
        Clay Music Corp.; BMI
        Final mix -- 9/10/75
        SRM1-1051 -- *The Holy Bible, Old Testament*
        SRM2-101 -- *The Holy Bible, Old & New Testaments* (double)

2-51522  **LED OUT OF BONDAGE**  (Robert L. Prather)
        Peer International Corp.; BMI
        Final mix -- 9/17/75
        SRM1-1051 -- *The Holy Bible, Old Testament*
        SRM2-101 -- *The Holy Bible, Old & New Testaments* (double)

=================================================================

Mercury Custom Recording Studio         <u>November 20, 1974</u>
        (10:00-13:00)
Jerry Kennedy (g,db); Bob Moore (b); Harold Bradley, Jerry Shook, Pete Wade, Ray Edenton (g); Hargus Robbins (p); Buddy Harman (dm); string and horn arr Cam Mullins -1.

2-51523  **SONG OF SOLOMON**  (Lew DeWitt)
        American Cowboy Music Co., Inc.; BMI
        OD -- <u>9/10/75</u>, 10:00-12:30, Jerry Kennedy (g/db), Pete Drake (st g).
        Final mix -- 9/10/75
        SRM1-1051 -- *The Holy Bible, Old Testament*
        SRM2-101 -- *The Holy Bible, Old & New Testaments* (double)

2-51524  **SONG OF DAVID**  (Don Reid, Harold Reid) -1
        American Cowboy Music Co., Inc.; BMI
        Final mix -- 9/15/75
        SRM1-1051 -- *The Holy Bible, Old Testament*
        SRM2-101 -- *The Holy Bible, Old & New Testaments* (double)

2-51525  **HOW GREAT THOU ART**  (Carl Boberg, 1886. Translated from the
        original Swedish by Stuart K. Hine, 1949.) -2
        Manna Music, Inc.; BMI
        OD -- <u>8/22/75</u>, 10:00-12:00, Sheldon Kurland, Brenton Banks, Marvin Chantry, Gary Vanosdale, Roy Christensen, Byron Bach, Carl Gorodetzky, Chris Teal, Virginia Christensen, Steve Smith, Stephanie Woolf, George Binkley, Jerry Kennedy (g/db).

Final mix -- 9/15/75
73732 -- backed w/NOAH FOUND GRACE IN THE EYES OF THE LORD
SRM1-1052 -- *The Holy Bible, New Testament*
SRM2-101 -- *The Holy Bible, Old & New Testaments* (double)
PTV1003 -- *Memories . . . Now and Forever* (Canadian Rel)
SRM1-5024 -- *Best of the Statler Bros. Rides Again, Vol. II*
TLCW-14 -- *C&W Classics: The Statler Brothers* (TL)
RD7A-235 --*Best of SB, Their Greatest Hits & Finest Performances* (RD)

===========================================================

Mercury Custom Recording Studio                    November 21, 1974
                                                       (10:00-13:00)
Jerry Kennedy (g,db); Bob Moore (b); Buddy Harman (dm); Jerry Shook, Harold
Bradley, Ray Edenton (g); Richard Morris (timpani-1); Hargus Robbins (p); string
and horn arr Cam Mullins -2.

2-51526  **THE KINGDOM OF HEAVEN IS AT HAND**  (Lew DeWitt)
         American Cowboy Music Co., Inc.; BMI
         OD -- 9/10/75, 11:00-12:30, Jerry Kennedy (g/db), Pete Drake (st g).
         Final mix -- 9/15/75
         SRM1-1052 -- *The Holy Bible, New Testament*
         SRM2-101 -- *The Holy Bible, Old & New Testaments* (double)

2-51527  **THE KING IS COMING**  -1,-2
              (William Gaither, Gloria Gaither, Charles Milhoff)
         Gaither Music Co.; ASCAP
         OD -- 8/22/75, Strings, see 51525.
         OD -- 9/23/75, 10:00-11:15, Don Sheffield (trumpet), Eberhard Ramm
              (Fr hn), George Cunningham (trumpet), Roger E. Bissell
              (trombone).
         Final mix -- 9/23/75
         SRM1-1051 -- *The Holy Bible, Old Testament*
         SRM2-101 -- *The Holy Bible, Old & New Testaments* (double)

2-51528  Timpani Roll   -2
              *Note from the Mercury files* -- This has nothing to do with the
              actual recorded sides.  It is a timpani roll to be used behind a
              recitation, and we assigned a master number so we could keep up
              with it!   30 secs.          [Used on #51527]

2-51529  **THERE'S A MAN IN HERE**  (Harold Reid)
         American Cowboy Music Co., Inc.; BMI
         Final mix -- 9/15/75
         SRM1-1052 -- *The Holy Bible, New Testament*
         SRM2-101 -- *The Holy Bible, Old & New Testaments* (double)

**Note:** For information on #51527, see #52306, 9/23/75.

================================================================

Mercury Custom Recording Studio                                    April 8, 1975
                                                                 (14:00-17:00)
Jerry Kennedy (g,db); Bob Moore (b); Hargus Robbins (p); Chip Young, Pete
Wade, Ray Edenton, Harold Bradley (g); Buddy Harman (dm); Charlie McCoy
(vb); string and horn arr Cam Mullins -1.

2-51580   **WHO DO YOU THINK**   (Don Reid, Harold Reid) -1
          American Cowboy Music Co., Inc.; BMI
          OD -- 8/22/75, Strings, see 51525.
          Final mix -- 9/16/75
          55046 -- backed w/I BELIEVE IN SANTA'S CAUSE
          SRM1-1052 -- *The Holy Bible, New Testament*
          SRM2-101 -- *The Holy Bible, Old & New Testaments* (double)
          SRM1-5012 -- *Statler Brothers Christmas Card*

2-51581   **LORD, IS IT I?**   (Don Reid, Harold Reid)
          House of Cash, Inc./American Cowboy Music Co., Inc.; BMI
          OD -- Pete Drake (st g), date unknown.
          Final mix -- 9/16/75
          SRM1-1052 -- *The Holy Bible, New Testament*
          SRM2-101 -- *The Holy Bible, Old & New Testaments* (double)

2-51582   **THE BRAVE APOSTLES TWELVE**   (Don Reid)
          American Cowboy Music Co., Inc.; BMI
          Final mix -- 9/16/75
          SRM1-1052 -- *The Holy Bible, New Testament*
          SRM2-101 -- *The Holy Bible, Old & New Testaments* (double)

================================================================

Mercury Custom Recording Studio                                    April 9, 1975
                                                                 (14:00-17:00)
Jerry Kennedy (g,db); Bob Moore (b); Hargus Robbins (p); Chip Young, Pete
Wade, Ray Edenton, Harold Bradley (g); Buddy Harman (dm); Charlie McCoy
(hm-1,vb); Bobby Thompson (bjo-2).

2-51583   **THE TEACHER**   (Lew DeWitt) -1,-2
          American Cowboy Music Co., Inc.; BMI
          Final mix -- 9/17/75
          SRM1-1052 -- *The Holy Bible, New Testament*
          SRM2-101 -- *The Holy Bible, Old & New Testaments* (double)

2-51584   **FLOWERS ON THE WALL**   (Lew DeWitt) -2
          Southwind Music/Rightsong Music (Chappell); BMI
          Final mix -- 5/22/75

SRM1-1037 -- *Best of the Statler Brothers*
PTV1003 -- *Memories . . . Now and Forever* (Canadian Rel)
RB6-112 -- *Statler Brothers' Greatest Hits* (RD)
RD7A-235 --*Best of SB, Their Greatest Hits & Finest Performances* (RD)
NC 568 -- *The Statler Brothers Country* (K)
8077-V1 -- *The Very Best of the Statler Brothers* (Realm)

2-51585   **BEAT THE DEVIL**   (Don Reid) -1,-2
American Cowboy Music Co., Inc.; BMI
Final mix -- 9/17/75
SRM1-1052 -- *The Holy Bible, New Testament*
SRM2-101 -- *The Holy Bible, Old & New Testaments* (double)

2-51586   **THE KING OF LOVE**   (Harold Reid)
House of Cash, Inc.;BMI/American Cowboy Music Co., Inc.; BMI
Final mix -- 9/17/75
SRM1-1052 -- *The Holy Bible, New Testament*
SRM2-101 -- *The Holy Bible, Old & New Testaments* (double)

=========================================================

Mercury Custom Recording Studio                          April 10, 1975
                                                          (14:00-17:00)
Jerry Kennedy (db); Bob Moore (b); Charlie McCoy (hm-1,vb-2); Buddy Harman
(dm); Hargus Robbins (p); Ray Edenton, Chip Young, Pete Wade, Harold Bradley
(g); string and horn arr Cam Mullins -3.

2-51587   **THE LORD'S PRAYER**   -2,-3
(Biblical Text; Music composed by Albert Hay Malotte)
arr - Phil Balsley, Lew DeWitt, Don Reid, Harold Reid
G.Schirmer, Inc.; ASCAP
OD -- 8/22/75, Strings, see 51525.
Final mix -- 9/11/75
SRM1-1052 -- *The Holy Bible, New Testament*
SRM2-101 -- *The Holy Bible, Old & New Testaments* (double)

2-51588   **WOULD YOU RECOGNIZE JESUS?**   (Don Reid, Harold Reid) -1
American Cowboy Music Co., Inc.; BMI
Final mix -- 2/2/76
SRM1-1077 -- *Harold, Lew, Phil & Don*

=========================================================

EDIT:                                                September 23, 1975

2-52306   **THE KING IS COMING** (William Gaither, Gloria Gaither, Charles Milhoff)
Gaither Music Co.; ASCAP
OD -- 8/22/75, Strings, see 51525.
OD -- 9/23/75, 10:00-11:15, Don Sheffield (trumpet), Eberhard Ramm

(Fr hn), George Cunningham (trumpet), Roger E. Bissell (trombone).

Final mix -- 9/23/75

SRM1-1052 -- *The Holy Bible, New Testament*

SRM2-101 -- *The Holy Bible, Old & New Testaments* (double)

**Note from Mercury files:**     This is an edited version of master #51527. The timing on the original version is 3:44, and it will be used in its entirety on the Statler Brothers album THE HOLY BIBLE - THE OLD TESTAMENT. Timing on the edited version is 2:04, and this version is for use only on the Statler Brothers album THE HOLY BIBLE - THE NEW TESTAMENT, #SRM1-1052.

US Recording Studio                                                 January 27, 1976
                                                                        (14:00-17:00)

Bob Moore (b); Bobby Wood (p); Chip Young, Jerry Shook, Pete Wade, Harold Bradley (g); Buddy Harman (dm); Jerry Kennedy (db).

2-52354   **THE TIMES WE HAD**   (Don Reid)
          American Cowboy Music Co., Inc.; BMI
          OD -- Weldon Myrick (st g), date unknown.
          Final mix -- 2/27/76
          SRM1-1077 -- *Harold, Lew, Phil & Don*

2-52355   **MAGGIE**   (Don Reid)
          American Cowboy Music Co., Inc.; BMI
          Final mix -- 2/19/76
          SRD-50 -- DJ stereo release
          SRM1-1077 -- *Harold, Lew, Phil & Don*

2-52356   **AMANDA**   (Bob McDill)
          Gold Dust Music, Inc.; BMI
          Final mix -- 2/12/76
          SRM1-1077 -- *Harold, Lew, Phil & Don*
          RD7A-235 --*Best of SB, Their Greatest Hits & Finest Performances* (RD)

2-52357   **I'VE BEEN EVERYWHERE**   (Geoff Mack)
          Belinda Music, Inc.; BMI
          Final mix -- 2/12/76
          SRM1-1077 -- *Harold, Lew, Phil & Don*
          RD7A-235 --*Best of SB, Their Greatest Hits & Finest Performances* (RD)

US Recording Studio                                                 January 28, 1976
                                                                        (14:00-17:00)

Jerry Kennedy (db); Bob Moore (b); Ray Edenton, Harold Bradley, Chip Young, Pete Wade (g); Bobby Wood (p); Buddy Harman (dm); string arr Cam Mullins -1.

2-52358  **The Statler Brothers Quiz**  (Harold Reid, Don Reid)
American Cowboy Music Co., Inc.; BMI
Final mix -- 2/12/76
SRM1-1077 -- *Harold, Lew, Phil & Don*

2-52359  **Your Picture in the Paper**  (Don Reid) -1
American Cowboy Music Co., Inc.; BMI
OD -- Strings, date and musicians unknown.
OD -- Weldon Myrick (st g), date unknown.
Final mix -- 2/12/76
73785 -- backed w/ALL THE TIMES
CC-35038 -- backed w/I'LL GO TO MY GRAVE LOVING YOU
SRM1-1077 -- *Harold, Lew, Phil & Don*
RD7A-235 --*Best of SB, Their Greatest Hits & Finest Performances* (RD)
518-945 -- *30th Anniversary Celebration*
8077-V2 -- *The Very Best of the Statler Brothers* (Realm)

2-52360  **A FRIEND'S RADIO**  (Don Reid)
American Cowboy Music Co., Inc.; BMI
OD -- Weldon Myrick (st g); Charlie McCoy (hm), date unknown.
Final mix -- 2/19/76
SRM1-1077 -- *Harold, Lew, Phil & Don*

US Recording Studio                                            January 29, 1976
(14:00-17:00)
Hargus Robbins (p); Charlie McCoy (hm-1,vb); Harold Bradley, Ray Edenton, Pete
Wade, Chip Young (g); Jerry Kennedy (db); Bob Moore (b); Buddy Harman (dm).

2-52361  **VIRGINIA**  (Harold Reid, Don Reid)
American Cowboy Music Co., Inc.; BMI
OD -- Weldon Myrick (st g), date unknown.
Final mix -- 2/27/76
SRM1-1077 -- *Harold, Lew, Phil & Don*

2-52362  **ALL THE TIMES**  (Harold Reid, Don Reid)
American Cowboy Music Co., Inc.; BMI
Final mix -- 2/12/76
73785 -- backed w/YOUR PICTURE IN THE PAPER
SRM1-1077 -- *Harold, Lew, Phil & Don*

2-52363  **SOMETHING I HAVEN'T DONE YET**  (Don Reid) -1
American Cowboy Music Co., Inc.; BMI
Final mix -- 2/27/76
SRM1-1077 -- *Harold, Lew, Phil & Don*

US Recording Studio                                    <u>January 30, 1976</u>
                                                          (14:00-17:00)
Hargus Robbins (p); Charlie McCoy (hm-1,vb-2); Harold Bradley, Ray Edenton,
Pete Wade, Chip Young (g); Jerry Kennedy (g,db-3); Bob Moore (b); Buddy
Harman (dm).

2-52364  **THANK GOD I'VE GOT YOU**  (Don Reid) -2
         American Cowboy Music Co., Inc.; BMI
         Final mix -- 8/24/76
         73846 -- backed w/HAT AND BOOTS
         SRM1-1125 -- *The Country America Loves*
         PTV1003 -- *Memories . . . Now and Forever* (Canadian Rel)
         RD7A-235 --*Best of SB, Their Greatest Hits & Finest Performances* (RD)
         NC 568 -- *The Statler Brothers Country* (K)
         8077-V1 -- *The Very Best of the Statler Brothers* (Realm)

2-52365  **HAT AND BOOTS**  (Don Reid) -1,-3
         American Cowboy Music Co., Inc.; BMI
         Final mix -- 2/12/76
         SRM1-1125 -- *The Country America Loves*

2-52366  **YOURS LOVE**  (Harlan Howard) -2
         Wilderness Music Publishing Co., Inc.; BMI
         Final mix -- 2/12/76
         SRM1-5001 -- *Entertainers . . . On & Off the Record*

===============================================================

US Recording Studio                                    <u>October 19, 1976</u>
                                                          (15:00-17:00)
Jerry Kennedy (g,db-1); Bob Moore (b); Hargus Robbins (p); Buddy Harman (dm);
Charlie McCoy (hm,vb-2); Ray Edenton, Chip Young, Pete Wade, Harold Bradley
(g); string and horn arr Cam Mullins -3.

2-52479  **THE MOVIES**  (Lew DeWitt) -3
         American Cowboy Music Co., Inc.; BMI
         OD -- <u>12/3/76</u>, 10:00-13:00, Sheldon Kurland, Brenton Banks, Virginia
             Christensen, Stephanie Woolf, Martin Katahn, Carl Gorodetzky,
             Gary Vanosdale, Martin Chantry, Byron Bach, Lennie Haight,
             George Tidwell (trumpet), Roy Christensen, George Binkley, Don
             Sheffield (trumpet), Steven Sefsik (clarinet), Jerry Kennedy
             (g/db).
         Final mix -- 12/6/76
         73877 -- backed w/YOU COULD BE COMING TO ME
         SRM1-1125 -- *The Country America Loves*
         SRM1-5024 -- *Best of the Statler Bros. Rides Again, Vol. II*
         RD7A-235 --*Best of SB, Their Greatest Hits & Finest Performances* (RD)

NC 568 -- *The Statler Brothers Country* (K)
518-945 -- *30th Anniversary Celebration*
8077-V1 -- *The Very Best of the Statler Brothers* (Realm)

2-52480   **YOU COULD BE COMING TO ME**   (Don Reid, Harold Reid) -1,-2
American Cowboy Music Co., Inc.; BMI
OD -- Pete Drake (st g), date unknown.
Final mix -- 12/6/76
73877 -- backed w/THE MOVIES
SRM1-1125 -- *The Country America Loves*

2-52481   **YOU COMB HER HAIR EVERY MORNING**   -2
                    (Harlan Howard, Hank Cochran)
Tree Publishing Co., Inc.; BMI
OD -- Pete Drake (st g), date unknown.
Final mix -- 12/7/76
SRM1-1125 -- *The Country America Loves*

=================================================================

US Recording Studio                                    October 20, 1976
                                                          (14:00-17:00)
Jerry Kennedy (g,db-1); Bob Moore (b); Buddy Harman (dm); Ray Edenton, Chip
Young, Pete Wade, Harold Bradley (g); Charlie McCoy (hm-2,vb-3); Hargus
Robbins (p); string and horn arr Cam Mullins -4; arr D. Bergen White -5.

2-52482   **I WAS THERE**   (Don Reid) -1,-4
American Cowboy Music Co., Inc.; BMI
OD -- 12/3/76, Strings and horns, see 52479.
Final mix -- 12/7/76
73906 -- backed w/SOMEBODY NEW WILL BE COMING ALONG
SRM1-1125 -- *The Country America Loves*
PTV1003 -- *Memories . . . Now and Forever* (Canadian Rel)
TLCW-14 -- *C&W Classics: The Statler Brothers* (TL)
RD7A-235 --*Best of SB, Their Greatest Hits & Finest Performances* (RD)
NC 568 -- *The Statler Brothers Country* (K)
8077-V2 -- *The Very Best of the Statler Brothers* (Realm)

2-52483   **THE STAR**   (Don Reid) -2,-4
American Cowboy Music Co., Inc.; BMI
OD -- 12/3/76, Strings and horns, see 52479.
Final mix -- 12/6/76
SRM1-1173/SRM1-5001 -- *Short Stories*

2-52484   **A COUPLE MORE YEARS**   (Shel Silverstein, Dennis Locorriere) -3,-5
Evil Eye Music, Inc./Horse Hairs Music, Inc.; BMI
OD -- 12/9/76, 10:00-13:00, Sheldon Kurland, Brenton Banks, Carl

Gorodetzky, Marvin Chantry, Gary Vanosdale, Martha McCrory, Stephanie Woolf, Lennie Haight, Sam Terranova, Roy Christensen, Steve Smith, George Binkley.
OD -- Pete Drake (st g), date unknown.
Final mix -- 12/9/76
SRM1-1125 -- *The Country America Loves*

US Recording Studio                                   October 21, 1976
                                                          (14:00-17:00)
Jerry Kennedy (g,db); Bob Moore (b); Chip Young, Pete Wade, Harold Bradley, Ray Edenton (g); Hargus Robbins (p); Charlie McCoy (hm-1,vb-2); Buddy Harman (dm); string and horn arr D. Bergen White -3.

2-52485  **LET IT SHOW**  (Don Reid) -2
American Cowboy Music Co., Inc.; BMI
Final mix -- 12/9/76
SRM1-1125 -- *The Country America Loves*

2-52486  **ALL I CAN DO**  (Dolly Parton) -1
Owepar Publishing Co.; BMI
Final mix -- 12/9/76
SRM1-1125 -- *The Country America Loves*

2-52487  **(I'LL EVEN LOVE YOU) BETTER THAN I DID THEN**  -2,-3
(Don Reid, Harold Reid)
American Cowboy Music Co., Inc.; BMI
OD -- 12/9/76, Strings, see 52484.
OD -- 11/16/79, 9:00-10:00, Sound Stage Studios, Chip Young (g).
57012 -- backed w/ALMOST IN LOVE
SRM1-5024 -- *Best of the Statler Bros. Rides Again, Vol. II*
RB6-112 -- *Statler Brothers' Greatest Hits* (RD)
RD7A-235 --*Best of SB, Their Greatest Hits & Finest Performances* (RD)
NC 568 -- *The Statler Brothers Country* (K)
518-945 -- *30th Anniversary Celebration*

US Recording Studio                                   October 29, 1976
                                                          (14L00-17:00)
Jerry Kennedy (g,db); Bob Moore (b); Buddy Harman (dm); Ray Edenton, Pete Wade, Harold Bradley (g); Hargus Robbins (p); Charlie McCoy (hm-1,vb-2); string arr D. Bergen White -3.

2-52489  **SOMEBODY NEW WILL BE COMING ALONG**  (Don Reid) -2
American Cowboy Music Co., Inc.; BMI
Final mix -- 12/7/76
73906 -- backed w/I WAS THERE
SRM1-1125 -- *The Country America Loves*

2-52490   **QUITE A LONG, LONG TIME**   (Lew DeWitt) -2,-3
Southwind Music, Inc.; BMI
OD -- <u>6/3/77</u>, 10:00-13:00,  Sheldon Kurland, Roy Christensen, Steve
   Smith, Carl Gorodetzky, Virginia Christensen, Lennie Haight,
   Wilfred Lehmann, Katherine Ransom, Gary Vanosdale, Marvin
   Chantry, John Catchings, George Binkley, Jerry Kennedy (g/db);
   Grover "Shorty" Lavender (f).
OD -- <u>6/6/77</u>, 18:00-20:30, Weldon Myrick (st g).
Final mix -- 6/9/77
SRM1-1173/SRM1-5001 -- *Short Stories*

2-52491   **SILVER MEDALS & SWEET MEMORIES**   (Don Reid) -1,-3
American Cowboy Music Co., Inc.; BMI
OD -- <u>12/9/76</u>, Strings, see 52484.
Final mix -- 6/9/77
55000 -- backed w/REGULAR SATURDAY NIGHT SETBACK CARD GAME
SRM1-1173/SRM1-5001 -- *Short Stories*
SRM1-5024 -- *Best of the Statler Bros. Rides Again, Vol. II*
PTV1003 -- *Memories . . . Now and Forever* (Canadian Rel)
RD7A-235 --*Best of SB, Their Greatest Hits & Finest Performances* (RD)
518-945 -- *30th Anniversary Celebration*

2-52492   **THAT SUMMER**   (Don Reid) -1,-3
American Cowboy Music Co., Inc.; BMI
OD -- <u>6/3/77</u>, Strings, see 53090.
OD -- <u>6/7/77</u>, 18:00-20:30, Weldon Myrick (st g).
Final mix -- 6/9/77
SRM1-1173/SRM1-5001 -- *Short Stories*
518-945 -- *30th Anniversary Celebration*

**Note:**   #52492 is a recitation by Harold Reid.  The music tracks were recorded
first, with Harold laying down the vocal track immediately after the musicians left
the studio.  This was done to structure it and adjust the timing to make it come out
as they wanted it to sound.

==================================================================

US Recording Studio                                                      May 24, 1977
                                                                         (14:00-17:00)
Jerry Kennedy (g, fretted db-1); Bob Moore (b); Hargus Robbins (p); Chip Young,
Ray Edenton, Harold Bradley, Pete Wade (g); Buddy Harman (dm); Charlie McCoy
(hm,vb-2); string arr D. Bergen White -3.

2-53191   **CARRIED AWAY**   (Lew DeWitt) -1,-2
American Cowboy Music Co., Inc.; BMI/House of Cash, Inc.; BMI
Final mix -- 6/8/77
55013 -- backed w/SOME I WROTE
SRM1-1173/SRM1-5001 -- *Short Stories*

2-53192 **THE REGULAR SATURDAY NIGHT SETBACK CARD GAME**   -1,-2
(Don Reid, Harold Reid)
American Cowboy Music Co., Inc.; BMI
OD -- <u>6/6/77</u>, 18:00-20:30, Weldon Myrick (sl db).
Final mix -- 6/8/77.
55000 -- backed w/SILVER MEDALS & SWEET MEMORIES
SRM1-1173/SRM1-5001 -- *Short Stories*

2-53193 **DIFFERENT THINGS TO DIFFERENT PEOPLE** (Don Reid) -2,-3
American Cowboy Music Co., Inc.; BMI
OD -- <u>6/3/77</u>, Strings, see 53090.
OD -- <u>6/6/77</u>, 18:00-20:30, Weldon Myrick (st g).
Final mix -- 6/8/77.
SRM1-1173/SRM1-5001 -- *Short Stories*

2-3194 **GIVE MY LOVE TO ROSE**  (Johnny Cash) -1
Knox Music Co., Inc.; BMI
OD -- Weldon Myrick (st g), Shorty Lavender (f), date unknown.
Final mix -- 6/8/77.
SRM1-1173/SRM1-5001 -- *Short Stories*

=================================================================

US Recording Studio                                          May 25, 1977
                                                             (14:00-16:50)
Jerry Kennedy (g, fretted db-1); Bob Moore (b); Charlie McCoy (hm, vb-2); Pete
Drake (st g); Buddy Harman (dm); Hargus Robbins (p); Johnny Christopher, Chip
Young, Tommy Alsup (g); string arr D. Bergen White -3.

2-53195 **SOME I WROTE**  (Don Reid, Harold Reid) -1,-2,-3
American Cowboy Music Co., Inc.; BMI
OD -- <u>6/3/77</u>, Strings, see 53090.
OD -- <u>6/6/77</u>, 18:00-20:30, Weldon Myrick (sl db).
Final mix -- 6/9/77.
55013 -- backed w/CARRIED AWAY
SRM1-1173/SRM1-5001 -- *Short Stories*
PTV1003 -- *Memories . . . Now and Forever* (Canadian Rel)
SRM1-5024 -- *Best of the Statler Bros. Rides Again, Vol. II*
TLCW-14 -- *C&W Classics: The Statler Brothers* (TL)
RD7A-235 --*Best of SB, Their Greatest Hits & Finest Performances* (RD)
518-945 -- *30th Anniversary Celebration*

2-53196 **GRANDMA**  (Don Reid) -3
American Cowboy Music Co., Inc.; BMI
OD -- <u>6/6/77</u>, 18:00-20:30, Weldon Myrick (st g).
Final mix -- 6/9/77.
SRM1-1173/SRM1-5001 -- *Short Stories*

2-53197  **DON'T FORGET YOURSELF**  (Don Reid) -2
American Cowboy Music Co., Inc.; BMI
OD -- 5/15/80, Sound Stage Studios, 10:00-13:00, Sheldon Kurland, George Binkley, Dennis Molchan, Sam Terranova, Virginia Christensen, Lennie Haight, Stephanie Woolf, Wilfred Lehmann, Marvin Chantry, Gary Vanosdale, Roy Christensen, John Catchings.
Final mix -- 5/16/80
57037 -- backed w/WE GOT PAID BY CASH
SRM1-5027 -- *Tenth Anniversary*

US Recording Studio                                              May 26, 1977
                                                               (14:00-16:00)
Jerry Kennedy (g,db); Bob Moore (b); Buddy Harman (dm); Pete Wade, Chip Young, Harold Bradley, Ray Edenton (g); Hargus Robbins (p); Charlie McCoy (hm,vb).

2-53198  **IN THE GARDEN**  Traditional [C. Austin Miles, 1912]
                (Adapted -- Phil Balsley, Lew DeWitt, Don Reid, Harold Reid)
American Cowboy Music Co., Inc.; BMI
Final mix -- 1/26/81
SRM1-6002 -- *Years Ago*

2-53199  **IF IT MAKES ANY DIFFERENCE**  (Don Reid, Harold Reid)
American Cowboy Music Co., Inc.; BMI
-- unissued --

**Note:** #53199 was remade with Jimmy Fortune on 1/16/84, #57274.

US Recording Studio                                           January 13, 1978
                                                               (14:00-17:00)
Jerry Kennedy (g,db); Bob Moore (b); Buddy Harman (dm); Hargus Robbins (p); Weldon Myrick (st g); Harold Bradley, Pete Wade, Jerry Shook, Ray Edenton (g); string arr D. Bergen White -1.

2-54303  **I FORGOT MORE THAN YOU'LL EVER KNOW**   (Cecil A. Null)
Travis Music Co., Inc., BMI
Final mix -- 1/30/78
SRM1-5001 -- *Entertainers . . . On & Off the Record*
RD7A-235 --*Best of SB, Their Greatest Hits & Finest Performances* (RD)

2-54304  **WHO AM I TO SAY**  (Kim Reid) -1
American Cowboy Music Co., Inc.; BMI
OD -- 1/31/78, 10:00-12:00, Sheldon Kurland, George Binkley, Lennie Haight, Stephanie Woolf, Steve Smith, Pamela Sixfin Vanosdale,

Sam Terranova, Carl Gorodetzky, Marvin Chantry, Gary Vanosdale, Roy Christensen, John Catchings, Jerry Kennedy (g/db).
Final mix -- 1/31/78
55037 -- backed w/I DREAMED ABOUT YOU
CC-35042 -- backed w/DO YOU KNOW YOU ARE MY SUNSHINE
SRM1-5001 -- *Entertainers . . . On & Off the Record*
SRM1-5024 -- *Best of the Statler Bros. Rides Again, Vol. II*
RD7A-235 --*Best of SB, Their Greatest Hits & Finest Performances* (RD)
NC 568 -- *The Statler Brothers Country* (K)

2-54305 **I DREAMED ABOUT YOU**  (Don Reid)
American Cowboy Music Co., Inc.; BMI
Final mix -- 1/30/78
55037 -- backed w/Who Am I To Say
SRM1-5001 -- *Entertainers . . . On & Off the Record*

===========================================================

US Recording Studio                                     January 16, 1978
                                                         (14:00-17:00)
Jerry Kennedy (g,db); Pete Wade, Harold Bradley, Ray Edenton (g); Hargus Robbins (p); Bob Moore (b); Weldon Myrick (st g); Buddy Harman (dm); string arr D. Bergen White -1.

2-54306 **YOU'RE THE FIRST**  (Lew DeWitt)
American Cowboy Music Co., Inc.; BMI
Final mix -- 1/30/78
55022 -- backed w/DO YOU KNOW YOU ARE MY SUNSHINE
SRM1-5001 -- *Entertainers . . . On & Off the Record*

2-54307 **THE BEST THAT I CAN DO**  (Don Reid) -1
American Cowboy Music Co., Inc.; BMI
OD -- 1/31/78, Strings, see 54304.
55048 -- backed w/THE OFFICIAL HISTORIAN ON SHIRLEY JEAN BERRELL
SRM1-5001 -- *Entertainers . . . On & Off the Record*

2-54308 **THE OFFICIAL HISTORIAN ON SHIRLEY JEAN BERRELL**
(Don Reid, Harold Reid)
American Cowboy Music Co., Inc.; BMI
Final mix -- 2/7/78
55048 -- backed w/THE BEST THAT I CAN DO
SRM1-5001 -- *Entertainers . . . On & Off the Record*
SRM1-5024 -- *Best of the Statler Bros. Rides Again, Vol. II*
RB6-112 -- *Statler Brothers' Greatest Hits* (RD)
TLCW-14 -- *C&W Classics: The Statler Brothers* (TL)
RD7A-235 --*Best of SB, Their Greatest Hits & Finest Performances* (RD)

NC 568 -- *The Statler Brothers Country* (K)
518-945 -- *30th Anniversary Celebration*

---

US Recording Studio                                                   January 17, 1978
                                                                        (14:00-17:15)
Bob Moore (b); Weldon Myrick (st g); Buddy Harman (dm); Jerry Kennedy (g,db);
Pete Wade, Harold Bradley, Ray Edenton (g); Hargus Robbins (p); Charlie McCoy
(vb); Dale Sellers (rhythms); string and flute arr D. Bergen White -1.

2-54309   **BEFORE THE MAGIC TURNS TO MEMORY**   (Don Reid)
          American Cowboy Music Co., Inc.; BMI
          Final mix -- 1/30/78
          SRM1-5001 -- *Entertainers . . . On & Off the Record*

2-54310   **A CHRISTMAS MEDLEY**:  Traditional -1
                      (arr - Phil Balsley, Lew DeWitt, Don Reid, Harold Reid)
                      *Silent Night/O Holy Night/The First Noel/It Came Upon the*
                      *Midnight Clear/Silent Night*
          American Cowboy Music Co., Inc.; BMI
          OD -- Strings and flute, date unknown.  Musicians (*from the album*
                *cover*) -- Byron Bach, Brenton Banks, George Binkley, Marvin
                Chantry, Roy Christensen, Virginia Christensen, Carl Gorodetzky,
                Lennie Haight, Shelly Kurland, Wilfred Lehmann, Steve Smith,
                Chris Teal, Sam Terranova, Gary Vanosdale, Pamela Vanosdale,
                Stephanie Woolf.  Billy Puett (flute).
          Final mix -- 6/28/78
          SRM1-5012 -- *Statler Brothers Christmas Card*

---

US Recording Studio                                                   January 18, 1978
                                                                        (14:00-17:30)
Jerry Kennedy (g,db); Bob Moore (b); Buddy Harman (dm); Weldon Myrick (st g);
Hargus Robbins (p); Pete Wade, Harold Bradley, Jerry Shook, Ray Edenton (g);
string and flute arr D. Bergen White -1.

2-54311   **DO YOU KNOW YOU ARE MY SUNSHINE**   (Don Reid, Harold Reid) -1
          American Cowboy Music Co., Inc.; BMI
          OD -- 1/31/78, Strings, see 54304.
          Final mix -- 1/31/78
          76162 -- backed w/WHATEVER
          55022 -- backed w/YOU'RE THE FIRST
          CC-35042 -- backed w/WHO AM I TO SAY
          SRM1-5001 -- *Entertainers . . . On & Off the Record*
          SRM1-5024 -- *Best of the Statler Bros. Rides Again, Vol. II*
          RB6-112 -- *Statler Brothers' Greatest Hits* (RD)
          TLCW-14 -- *C&W Classics:  The Statler Brothers* (TL)

RD7A-235 --*Best of SB, Their Greatest Hits & Finest Performances* (RD)
NC 568 -- *The Statler Brothers Country* (K)
518-945 -- *30th Anniversary Celebration*

2-54312   **I BELIEVE IN SANTA'S CAUSE**   (Lew DeWitt, Buddy Church)
American Cowboy Music Co., Inc.; BMI
OD -- 6/29/78, Sound Stage Studios, 14:00-16:00, Jerry Kennedy (g/db),
        Buddy Spicher (f), Charlie McCoy (vb), Weldon Myrick (st g).
Final mix -- 6/30/78
55046 -- backed w/WHO DO YOU THINK
SRM1-5012 -- *Statler Brothers Christmas Card*
22660-4 -- *Christmas With the Statler Brothers*

2-54313   **WHITE CHRISTMAS**   (Irving Berlin) -1
Irving Berlin Music Corp.; ASCAP
OD -- 3/2/78, 15:30-17:00, Sheldon Kurland, Carl Gorodetzky, George
        Binkley, Gary Vanosdale, Lennie Haight, Steve Smith, John
        Catchings, Marvin Chantry, Stephanie Woolf, Pamela Sixfin,
        Wilfred Lehmann, Roy Christensen, Jerry Kennedy (g/db), Billy
        Puett (clarinet).
Final mix -- 5/31/78
SRM1-5012 -- *Statler Brothers Christmas Card*
22660-4 -- *Christmas With the Statler Brothers*

====================================================================

US Recording Studio                                      February 6, 1978
                                                         (14:00-17:00)
Bob Moore (b); Jerry Kennedy (g,db); Pete Wade, Chip Young, Ray Edenton,
Harold Bradley (g); Buddy Harman (dm); Hargus Robbins (p); Charlie McCoy
(vb); string and flute arr D. Bergen White -1.

2-54314   **AWAY IN A MANGER**   Traditional
                    [ascribed to Martin Luther, 1530; and Carl Müller]
                    (arr - Phil Balsley, Lew DeWitt, Don Reid, Harold Reid)
American Cowboy Music Co., Inc.; BMI
Final mix -- 5/31/78
DJ-577 -- included I NEVER SPEND A CHRISTMAS THAT I DON'T THINK
        OF YOU, JINGLE BELLS, and THE CAROLS THOSE KIDS USED TO
        SING
76130 -- backed w/I NEVER SPEND A CHRISTMAS THAT I DON'T THINK OF
        YOU
SRM1-5012 -- *Statler Brothers Christmas Card*

2-54315   **I NEVER SPEND A CHRISTMAS THAT I DON'T THINK OF YOU**   -1
                    (Don Reid)
American Cowboy Music Co., Inc.; BMI

OD -- 3/2/78, Strings and flute, see 54313.
Final mix -- 6/8/78
DJ-577 -- included AWAY IN A MANGER, JINGLE BELLS, and THE CAROLS
THOSE KIDS USED TO SING
76130 -- backed w/AWAY IN A MANGER
SRM1-5012 -- *Statler Brothers Christmas Card*

US Recording Studio                                                April 5, 1978
(14:00-17:00)
Bob Moore (b); Hargus Robbins (p); Buddy Harman (dm); Jerry Kennedy (g,db);
Chip Young, Ray Edenton, Harold Bradley (g); Pete Drake (st g); Bobby Thompson
(bjo-1); Charlie McCoy (org-2,hm-3,vb-4); string arr D. Bergen White -5.

2-54332  JINGLE BELLS  Traditional [J. Pierpoint]  -1-4
(arr - Phil Balsley, Lew DeWitt, Don Reid, Harold Reid)
American Cowboy Music Co., Inc.; BMI
Final mix -- 6/8/78
DJ-577 -- included I NEVER SPEND A CHRISTMAS THAT I DON'T THINK
OF YOU, AWAY IN A MANGER, and THE CAROLS THOSE KIDS USED
TO SING
SRM1-5012 -- *Statler Brothers Christmas Card*
22660-4 -- *Christmas With the Statler Brothers*

2-54334  CHRISTMAS TO ME  (Don Reid, Harold Reid)  -2,-3,-5
American Cowboy Music Co., Inc.; BMI
OD -- 6/29/78, Sound Stage Studios, 17:00-20:00, Sheldon Kurland,
Stephanie Woolf, George Binkley, Gary Vanosdale, Carl
Gorodetzky, Roy Christensen, Pamela Sixfin Vanosdale, Virginia
Christensen, Marvin Chantry, Lennie Haight, Steve Smith, John
Catchings.
Final mix -- 6/30/78
SRM1-5012 -- *Statler Brothers Christmas Card*

Sound Stage Studios                                               June 27, 1978
(14:00-17:00)
Bob Moore (b); Jerry Kennedy (g,db); Chip Young, Pete Wade, Harold Bradley,
Ray Edenton (g); Hargus Robbins (p); Buddy Harman (dm); Charlie McCoy
(hm,vb); string arr D. Bergen White -1.

2-54358  I'LL BE HOME FOR CHRISTMAS  -1
(Walter Kent, Kim Gannon, Buck Ram)
Gannon & Kent Music; ASCAP
OD -- 6/29/78, 14:00-16:00, Jerry Kennedy (g/db), Buddy Spicher (f),
Charlie McCoy (hm,vb), Weldon Myrick (st g).
OD -- 7/6/78, 17:00-19:00, Sheldon Kurland, Steve Smith, Lennie

Haight, Carl Gorodetzky, Stephanie Woolf, Pamela Sixfin Vanosdale, George Binkley, Wilfred Lehmann, Gary Vanosdale, Marvin Chantry, Roy Christensen, John Catchings.
Final mix -- 7/7/78
SRM1-5012 -- *Statler Brothers Christmas Card*
22660-4 -- *Christmas with the Statler Brothers*

2-54359  THE CAROLS THOSE KIDS USED TO SING  (Harold Reid, Don Reid)
American Cowboy Music Co., Inc.; BMI
OD -- 6/29/78, 14:00-16:00, Jerry Kennedy (g/db), Buddy Spicher (f), Charlie McCoy (hm,vb), Weldon Myrick (st g).
Final mix -- 6/30/78
DJ-577 -- included I NEVER SPEND A CHRISTMAS THAT I DON'T THINK OF YOU, JINGLE BELLS, and AWAY IN A MANGER
SRM1-5012 -- *Statler Brothers Christmas Card*

2-54360  SOMETHING YOU CAN'T BUY  (Don Reid, Harold Reid) -1
American Cowboy Music Co., Inc.; BMI
OD -- 6/29/78, 14:00-16:00, Jerry Kennedy (g/db), Buddy Spicher (f), Charlie McCoy (hm,vb), Weldon Myrick (st g).
OD -- 7/6/78, Strings, see 54358.
Final mix -- 7/7/78
SRM1-5012 -- *Statler Brothers Christmas Card*

====================================================================

Sound Stage Studios                                          September 28, 1978
(14:00-17:00)
Bob Moore (b); Harold Bradley, Chip Young, Pete Wade, Ray Edenton (g); Jerry Kennedy (g,db); Hargus Robbins (p); Buddy Harman (dm); string, flute and horn arr D. Bergen White -1.

2-54405  WHERE HE ALWAYS WANTED TO BE  (Harold Reid, Don Reid)
American Cowboy Music Co., Inc.; BMI
OD -- 1/31/79, 14:00-17:00, Ray Edenton (original *Jimmie Rodgers* guitar lick), Bob Wootton (original *Johnny Cash* guitar lick [in memory of the original *Luther Perkins*]), Billy Byrd (original *Ernest Tubb* guitar lick), Pete Kirby "Bashful Brother Oswald" (original *Roy Acuff* dobro lick), Grover "Shorty" Lavender (original *Grady Martin* chord [g]), Odell Martin (original *Merle Travis* guitar break), H.L. "Curly" Chalker (original *Hank Thompson* steel guitar lick), Don Helms (original *Hank Williams* steel guitar lick), Scotty Moore (original *Elvis Presley* guitar lick), Carl Perkins (original *Carl Perkins* guitar lick), Mac Wiseman (original Bluegrass guitar lick), Gordon Kennedy (g).
[Original notes from original album copy.  AH]

OD -- Ernest Tubb (g), and Johnny Gimble "emulating the original *Bob Wills* yell" (*from the album cover*), date unknown.

Final mix -- 2/16/79

SRM1-5016 -- *The Originals*

2-54406  **HOW TO BE A COUNTRY STAR**  (Harold Reid, Don Reid) -1

American Cowboy Music Co., Inc.; BMI

OD -- 1/23/79, 10:00-13:00, Sheldon Kurland, Stephanie Woolf, Carl Gorodetzky, Steve Smith, Wilfred Lehmann, George Binkley, Marvin Chantry, Pam Vanosdale, Lennie Haight, Gary Vanosdale, Roy Christensen, John Catchings. Billy Puett (flute), Don Sheffield (trumpet), Dennis Good (trombone), George Tidwell (trumpet).

Final mix -- 1/31/79

55057 -- backed w/A LITTLE FARTHER DOWN THE ROAD

SRM1-5016 -- *The Originals*

SRM1-5024 -- *Best of the Statler Bros. Rides Again, Vol. II*

PTV1003 -- *Memories . . . Now and Forever* (Canadian Rel)

RB6-112 -- *Statler Brothers' Greatest Hits* (RD)

TLCW-14 -- *C&W Classics: The Statler Brothers* (TL)

RD7A-235 --*Best of SB, Their Greatest Hits & Finest Performances* (RD)

NC 568 -- *The Statler Brothers Country* (K)

518-945 -- *30th Anniversary Celebration*

---

Sound Stage Studios                                                    January 15, 1979
                                                                      (14:00-17:00)

Jerry Kennedy (g,db); Bob Moore (b); Harold Bradley, Chip Young, Pete Wade, Ray Edenton (g); Hargus Robbins (p); Buddy Harman (dm); string, flute, and horn arr D. Bergen White -1.

2-54448  **A LITTLE FARTHER DOWN THE ROAD**  (Lew DeWitt)

American Cowboy Music Co., Inc.; BMI

Final mix -- 1/25/79

55057 -- backed w/HOW TO BE A COUNTRY STAR

SRM1-5016 -- *The Originals*

SRM1-5024 -- *Best of the Statler Bros. Rides Again, Vol. II*

2-54449  **MR. AUTRY**  (Harold Reid, Don Reid) -1

American Cowboy Music Co., Inc.; BMI

OD -- 1/23/79, Strings and horns, see 54406.

OD -- 1/23/79, 14:00-17:00, Weldon Myrick (st g).

Final mix -- 1/30/79

55066 -- backed w/HERE WE ARE AGAIN

SRM1-5016 -- *The Originals*

SRM1-5024 -- *Best of the Statler Bros. Rides Again, Vol. II*

RD7A-235 --*Best of SB, Their Greatest Hits & Finest Performances* (RD)

2-54450 **HERE WE ARE AGAIN** (Don Reid)
American Cowboy Music Co., Inc.; BMI
OD -- 1/23/79, 14:00-17:00, Weldon Myrick (st g).
55066 -- backed w/MR. AUTRY
SRM1-5016 -- *The Originals*
SRM1-5024 -- *Best of the Statler Bros. Rides Again, Vol. II*
RD7A-235 --*Best of SB, Their Greatest Hits & Finest Performances* (RD)
NC 568 -- *The Statler Brothers Country* (K)

================================================================

US Recording Studio                              January 16, 1979

2-55406 **THE STAR-SPANGLED BANNER**
DJ-557

**Note from Mercury files:** "Above selection is a special version. We have taken the original version (master #54452) and added a special spoken introduction. This new version will not be used for any commercial copies -- singles or LPs. It will be used only for a special promotional release -- DJ-557. For any and all commercial purposes, we will use the original master."

According to Jerry Kennedy, the spoken introduction was done by Sky Parker, a student at Belmont College in Nashville from Oklahoma. This is the same intro used by the Statlers at their concerts. It is recorded with each one on a different track. When Lew retired, his track was removed and Jimmy's added. The other three tracks remained unchanged. Jimmy's track was recorded at Sound Stage Studios in 1982.

================================================================

Sound Stage Studios                              January 16, 1979
                                                   (14:00-17:00)
Jerry Kennedy (g,db); Bob Moore (b); Chip Young, Pete Wade, Harold Bradley, Ray Edenton (g); Hargus Robbins (p); Buddy Harman (dm); string, flute, and horn arr D. Bergen White -1.

2-54451 **WHEN THE YANKEES CAME HOME** (Don Reid)
American Cowboy Music Co., Inc.; BMI
Final mix -- 1/25/79
SRM1-5016 -- *The Originals*

2-54452 **THE STAR-SPANGLED BANNER** (Francis Scott Key) -1
(arr & adapted -- Harold Reid, Lew DeWitt, Phil Balsley, Don Reid)
American Cowboy Music Co., Inc.; BMI
OD -- 1/23/79, Strings and horns, see 54406.
Final mix -- 1/30/79
SRM1-5016 -- *The Originals*

2-54453 **COUNTING MY MEMORIES** (Kim Reid)
American Cowboy Music Co., Inc.; BMI

OD -- 1/23/79, 14:00-17:00, Weldon Myrick (st g).
Final mix -- 1/31/79
SRM1-5016 -- *The Originals*

=======================================================

Sound Stage Studios                                          January 17, 1979
                                                               (14:00-17:00)
Joe McDorman (vo-1); Bob Moore (b); Jerry Kennedy (g,db); Chip Young, Pete
Wade, Harold Bradley (g); Ray Edenton (g, man-2); Hargus Robbins (p); Buddy
Harman (dm); Charlie McCoy (hm,vb-3), string, flute and horn arr D. Bergen
White -4.

2-54454   ALMOST IN LOVE   (Harold Reid, Don Reid) -2,-4
          American Cowboy Music Co., Inc.; BMI
          OD -- 1/23/79, 14:00-17:00, Weldon Myrick (st g).
          Final mix -- 1/30/79
          57012 -- backed w/BETTER THAN I DID THEN
          SRM1-5016 -- *The Originals*

2-54455   NOTHING AS ORIGINAL AS YOU   (Don Reid) -3,-4
          American Cowboy Music Co., Inc.; BMI
          OD -- 1/23/79, Strings and horns, see 54406.
          Final mix -- 1/30/79
          57007 -- backed w/COUNTING MY MEMORIES
          SRM1-5016 -- *The Originals*
          TLCW-14 -- *C&W Classics: The Statler Brothers* (TL)
          RD7A-235 --*Best of SB, Their Greatest Hits & Finest Performances* (RD)
          NC 568 -- *The Statler Brothers Country* (K)

2-54456   JUST A LITTLE TALK WITH JESUS   (Cleavant Derricks) -1,-4
          Stamps-Baxter Music Co.; BMI
          OD -- 1/23/79, Strings and horns, see 54406.
          Final mix -- 1/31/79
          SRM1-5016 -- *The Originals*
          TLCW-14 -- *C&W Classics: The Statler Brothers* (TL)
          RD7A-235 --*Best of SB, Their Greatest Hits & Finest Performances* (RD)

Note:     Joe McDorman was the man who originally organized the group when
          they were all kids. (Liner notes, *The Originals* album.)

=======================================================

                                                             January 22, 1980
                                                          (                    )

*(From the album cover)*  Harold Bradley, Ray Edenton, Jerry Kennedy, Pete Wade,
Chip Young [g]; Buddy Harman [dm]; Charlie McCoy [hm]; Bob Moore [b];
Weldon Myrick [st g]; Hargus Robbins [p]; Buddy Spicher [f]; Wynn Osborne
[bjo]; Marty Stuart [man]; Bill Wiggins [percussion]; string arr D. Bergen White.

2-55528   **CHARLOTTE'S WEB**   (Snuff Garrett, Cliff Croford, John Durrill)
Peso Music/Duchess Music; BMI
OD -- <u>1/22/80</u> (*immediately following initial recording session*) --
George Binkley, John Catchings, Marvin Chantry, Roy Christensen, Virginia Christensen, Carl Gorodetzky, Lennie Haight, Shelly Kurland, Wilfred Lehmann, Rebecca Lynch, Dennis Molchan, Sam Terranova, Gary Vanosdale, Carol Walker, Stephanie Woolf, Cindy Reynolds (harp).
57031 -- backed w/ONE LESS DAY TO GO
SRM1-5027/812-282 -- *Tenth Anniversary*
TLCW-14 -- *C&W Classics: The Statler Brothers* (TL)
RB6-112 -- *Statler Brothers' Greatest Hits* (RD)
RD7A-235 --*Best of SB, Their Greatest Hits & Finest Performances* (RD)
NC 568 -- *The Statler Brothers Country* (K)
518-945 -- *30th Anniversary Celebration*

**Note from Mercury files:**   Recorded by Universal Studios for the movie "Smokey & the Bandit II," and written by agreement between Universal Studios & Phonogram/Mercury. Phonogram may release as single and LP cut.
*(Instrumentation in brackets is my assumption, in lieu of documentation. AH)*

════════════════════════════════════════════════════════════

Sound Stage Studios                                          <u>April 29, 1980</u>
                                                             (14:00-17:00)
Jerry Kennedy (g,db); Bob Moore (b); Buddy Harman (dm); Chip Young, Ray Edenton, Pete Wade, Harold Bradley (g); Hargus Robbins (p,kb).

2-55509   **HOW ARE THINGS IN CLAY, KENTUCKY?**   (Harold Reid, Don Reid)
American Cowboy Music Co., Inc.; BMI
OD -- <u>5/12/80</u>, 10:00-12:00, Jerry Kennedy (g/db), Charlie McCoy (hm,org), Weldon Myrick (st g, sl db).
Final mix -- 5/12/80
57048 -- backed w/IN THE GARDEN
SRM1-5027 -- *Tenth Anniversary*

2-55510   **ONE LESS DAY TO GO**   (Harold Reid, Don Reid)
American Cowboy Music Co., Inc.; BMI
Final mix -- 5/16/80
57031 -- backed w/CHARLOTTE'S WEB
SRM1-5027 -- *Tenth Anniversary*

2-55511   **OLD CHEERLEADERS CRY**   (Kim Reid, Harold Reid)
American Cowboy Music Co., Inc.; BMI
OD -- <u>5/12/80</u>, 10:00-12:00, Jerry Kennedy (g/db), Charlie McCoy (hm,org), Weldon Myrick (st g).
Final mix -- 5/12/80
SRM1-5027 -- *Tenth Anniversary*

════════════════════════════════════════════════════════════

Sound Stage Studios <u>April 30, 1980</u>
(14:00-17:00)
Ray Edenton, Chip Young, Pete Wade, Harold Bradley (g); Jerry Kennedy (g,db);
Bob Moore (b); Hargus Robbins (p,kb); Buddy Spicher (f-1); Marty Stuart (man-2);
Weldon Myrick (st g-3); Wynn Osborne (bjo-4); Buddy Harman (dm); string arr D.
Bergen White -5.

2-55512 **NOBODY WANTS TO BE COUNTRY** (Harold Reid, Don Reid) -1,-2,-3,-4
American Cowboy Music Co., Inc.; BMI
OD -- <u>5/15/80</u>, 10:00-13:00,
Billy Puett (clarinet), Vic Willis (accordion).
Final mix -- 5/15/80
SRM1-5027 -- *Tenth Anniversary*

2-55513 **YEARS AGO** (Don Reid) -2,-4
American Cowboy Music Co., Inc.; BMI
Final mix -- 2/12/80
57059 -- backed w/DAD
SRM1-6002 -- *Years Ago*
518-945 -- *30th Anniversary Celebration*

2-55514 **WE GOT PAID BY CASH** (Harold Reid, Don Reid) -1
American Cowboy Music Co., Inc.; BMI
OD -- <u>5/12/80</u>, 10:00-12:00,
Jerry Kennedy (g/db), George Tidwell (trumpet).
OD -- <u>5/15/80</u>, Strings, see 53197.
Final mix -- 5/15/80
57037 -- backed w/DON'T FORGET YOURSELF
SRM1-5027 -- *Tenth Anniversary*
TLCW-14 -- *C&W Classics: The Statler Brothers* (TL)

Sound Stage Studios <u>May 1, 1980</u>
(14:00-17:00)
Jerry Kennedy (g,db-1); Chip Young, Pete Wade, Harold Bradley, Ray Edenton (g);
Bob Moore (b); Buddy Harman (dm); Hargus Robbins (p,kb).

2-55515 **NOBODY'S DARLIN' BUT MINE** (Jimmie Davis)
Duchess Music Corp., (MCA), BMI
OD -- <u>5/12/80</u>, 10:00-12:00), Jerry Kennedy (g/db),
Charlie McCoy (hm,vb), Weldon Myrick (st g, sl db).
Final mix -- 5/15/80
SRM1-5027 -- *Tenth Anniversary*

2-55516 **'TIL THE END** (Don Reid) -1
American Cowboy Music Co., Inc.; BMI

Final mix -- 5/12/80
SRM1-5027 -- *Tenth Anniversary*

2-55517  **THE KID'S LAST FIGHT**  (Bob Merrill)
Intersong Music, ASCAP
OD -- 5/15/80, 10:00-13:00, Ralph Childs (tuba).
Final mix -- 5/16/80
SRM1-5027 -- *Tenth Anniversary*

=========================================================

Sound Stage Studios                              March 12, 1981
                                                  (14:00-17:00)
Bob Moore (b); Jerry Kennedy (g,db); Pete Wade, Chip Young, Harold Bradley, Ray Edenton (g); Buddy Harman (dm); Hargus Robbins (p); Charlie McCoy (hm-1,vb-2); string arr D. Bergen White -3.

2-56605  **DON'T WAIT ON ME**  (Harold Reid, Don Reid) -2
American Cowboy Music Co., Inc.; BMI
OD -- 4/7/81, 10:00-13:30, Sheldon Kurland, David Boyle, George Binkley, Marvin Chantry, Roy Christensen, Connie Ellisor, Carl Gorodetzky, Martin Katahn, Dennis Molchan, Sam Terranova, Gary Vanosdale, Stephanie Woolf.
Final mix -- 4/21/81
57051 -- backed w/CHET ATKINS' HAND
SRM1-6002 -- *Years Ago*
TLCW-14 -- *C&W Classics: The Statler Brothers* (TL)

2-56606  **I DON'T KNOW WHY**  (Harold Reid, Don Reid)
American Cowboy Music Co., Inc.; BMI
OD -- 4/7/81, Strings, see 56605.
Final mix -- 4/6/82
SRM-4048 -- *The Legend goes on . . .*

2-56607  **A CHILD OF THE FIFTIES**  (Don Reid) -1
American Cowboy Music Co., Inc.; BMI
OD -- 4/7/81, Strings, see 56605.
Final mix -- 4/6/82
76184 -- backed w/ALL OVER AGAIN
SRM-4048 -- *The Legend goes on . . .*

=========================================================

Sound Stage Studios                              March 30, 1981
                                                  (14:00-17:00)
Jerry Kennedy (g,db); Bob Moore (b); Buddy Harman (dm); Chip Young, Pete Wade, Harold Bradley, Ray Edenton (g); Charlie McCoy (hm-1,vb-2); Hargus Robbins (p,kb).

2-56614 **THAT'S WHEN IT COMES HOME TO YOU** (Lew DeWitt) -2
American Cowboy Music Co., Inc.; BMI
Final mix -- 4/6/82
SRM-4048 -- *The Legend goes on . . .*

2-56615 **TODAY I WENT BACK** (Don Reid) -1
American Cowboy Music Co., Inc.; BMI
Final mix -- 4/23/81
SRM1-6002 -- *Years Ago*

2-56616 **MEMORIES ARE MADE OF THIS**
(Terry Gilkyson, Richard Dehr, Frank Miller)
Blackwood Music, Inc.; BMI
Final mix -- 4/23/81
SRM1-6002 -- *Years Ago*

=======================================================================

Sound Stage Studios                                          March 31, 1981
                                                             (14:00-17:00)
Jerry Kennedy (g,db); Bob Moore (b); Chip Young, Pete Wade, Harold Bradley,
Ray Edenton (g); Hargus Robbins (p,kb); Jerry Carrigan (dm); Weldon Myrick
(st g, sl db-1); string arr D. Bergen White -2.

2-56617 **CHET ATKINS' HAND** (Lew DeWitt)
American Cowboy Music Co., Inc.; BMI
Final mix -- 4/29/81
57051 -- backed w/DON'T WAIT ON ME
SRM1-6002 -- *Years Ago*

2-56618 **(I'LL LOVE YOU) ALL OVER AGAIN** (Don Reid) -1,-2
American Cowboy Music Co., Inc.; BMI
OD -- 4/7/81, Strings, see 56605.
Final mix -- 4/6/82
76184 -- backed w/A CHILD OF THE FIFTIES
SRM-4048 -- *The Legend goes on . . .*

2-56619 **WE AIN'T EVEN STARTED YET** (Harold Reid, Don Reid)
American Cowboy Music Co., Inc.; BMI
Final mix -- 4/29/81
76142 -- backed w/YOU'LL BE BACK
SRM1-6002 -- *Years Ago*

=======================================================================

Sound Stage Studios                                          April 27, 1981
                                                             (18:00-21:00)
Bob Moore (b); Charlie McCoy (hm,vb-1), Chip Young, Pete Wade, Ray Edenton,
Harold Bradley (g); Jerry Kennedy (g,db); Jerry Carrigan (dm); Hargus Robbins
(p,kb); string arr D. Bergen White -2.

2-56627  **YOU"LL BE BACK (EVERY NIGHT IN MY DREAMS)** -1,-2
      (Waylon Holyfield, Johnny Russell)
      Bibo Music Pub., ASCAP/Sunflower County Songs, Inc.; BMI
      OD -- 5/7/81, 10:00-11:30, Jerry Kennedy (g/db); Weldon Myrick (st g).
      OD -- 5/14/81, 14:00-17:00, Sheldon Kurland, George Binkley, Marvin
          Chantry, Roy Christensen, Conni Ellisor, Carl Gorodetzky,
          Dennis Molchan, Julia Tanner, Chris Teal, Sam Terranova, Gary
          Vanosdale, Stephanie Woolf.
      Final mix -- 5/14/81
      72142 -- backed w/WE AIN'T EVEN STARTED YET
      SRM1-6002 -- *Years Ago*
      RB6-112 -- *Statler Brothers' Greatest Hits* (RD)

2-56628  **WHATEVER** (Harold Reid, Don Reid)
      American Cowboy Music, Inc.; BMI
      -- rejected -- Remade 4/28/81, master #56630.

2-56629  **LOVE WAS ALL WE HAD** (Don Reid) -2
      American Cowboy Music Co., Inc.; BMI
      OD -- 5/7/81, 10:00-11:30, Jerry Kennedy (g/db); Weldon Myrick (st g).
      OD -- 5/14/81, Strings, see 56627.
      Final mix -- 5/15/81
      SRM1-6002 -- *Years Ago*
      TLCW-14 -- *C&W Classics: The Statler Brothers* (TL)

=============================================================

Sound Stage Studios                                        April 28, 1981
                                                   (14:00-17:00)
Harold Bradley, Ray Edenton, Chip Young (g); Jerry Kennedy (g,db); Hargus
Robbins (p,kb); Charlie McCoy (hm,vb), Bob Moore (b); Jerry Carrigan (dm);
string arr D. Bergen White -1.

2-56630  **WHATEVER** (Harold Reid, Don Reid)  ▶
      American Cowboy Music, Inc.; BMI
      OD -- 4/8/82, 10:00-12:00, Jerry Kennedy (g), Dennis Solee (sax),
                    Charlie McCoy (hm).
      Final mix -- 4/13/82
      76162 -- backed w/DO YOU KNOW YOU ARE MY SUNSHINE
      SRM-4048 -- *The Legend goes on . . .*
      433-962 060-8 -- *Brothers in Song* (video)
      800-633 289-3 -- *What We Love to Do* (video)

▶  Video ©1982, produced and directed by Scene Three Productions, Nashville,
Tennessee.
    This video is unique in two aspects. (1) The song was recorded with Lew, but
the video was made with Jimmy.  Jimmy is lipsinking Lew on the video.  It was

made during that quick transitional period between the two tenors, and there wasn't time to remake the recording. (2) It was the first video done to a record in Nashville at a time when there were few television programs on which videos were aired -- especially country music videos.

2-56631   **I HAD TOO MUCH TO DREAM** (Kim Reid) -1
American Cowboy Music Co., Inc.; BMI
Final mix -- 4/13/82
SRM-4048 -- *The Legend goes on . . .*

2-56632   **HOW DO YOU LIKE YOUR DREAM SO FAR** (Harold Reid, Don Reid) -1
American Cowboy Music Co., Inc.; BMI
OD -- 5/15/81, Strings, see 56627.
Final mix -- 4/2/82
SRM-4048 -- *The Legend goes on . . .*

2-56633   **DAD** (Harold Reid, Don Reid)
American Cowboy Music Co., Inc.; BMI
OD -- 5/7/81, 10:00-11:30, Jerry Kennedy (g/db), Weldon Myrick (st g).
Final mix -- 5/7/81
57059 -- backed w/YEARS AGO
SRM1-6002 -- *Years Ago*

====================================================================

Remixed from 56627:

2-56679   **YOU'LL BE BACK (EVERY NIGHT IN MY DREAMS)**
-- not used --

====================================================================

*"An Interview With Ex-Statler Lew DeWitt,"* by Donna LeLaney, **Country Music Roundup**, January, 1983 --

All but three songs were already recorded before the onset of Lew's illness in November, 1981. After recuperating a while, Lew returned to the studio to complete the last three cuts.

He proudly explained, "Toward the end of the first recuperation period, I got to feelin' better and we came down and finished that. I wasn't as strong as I thought I was when I got to the studio. It was with some difficulty that we got through the session, but we did get through it. It sounded good! I was pleased with the final result of it. Like I say, it was tougher than I really thought it was gonna be."

====================================================================

Sound Stage Studios                                    March 15, 1982
                                                       (14:00-17:00)
Jerry Kennedy (g, fretted db-1); Bob Moore (b); Hargus Robbins (p,kb); Buddy Harman (dm); Harold Bradley, Chip Young, Pete Wade, Ray Edenton (g); Weldon Myrick (st g, sl db-2); string arr D. Bergen White -3.

2-56681   **WHAT YOU ARE TO ME**   (Don Reid)  -3
          American Cowboy Music Co., Inc.; BMI
          OD -- 3/30/82, 10:13:00, George Binkley, John Catchings, Marvin
             Chantry, Roy Christensen, Virginia Christensen, Carl Gorodetzky,
             Lennie Haight, Dennis Molchan, Chris Teal, Gary Vanosdale,
             Pamela Vanosdale, Stephanie Woolf.
          OD -- 3/31/82, 14:00-17:00, Gordon Kennedy (g), Buddy Spicher (f),
             Jerry Kennedy (g/db), Ray Edenton (g), Charlie McCoy (hm,vb).
          Final mix -- 4/2/82
          SRM-4048 -- *The Legend goes on . . .*

2-56682   **I DON'T DANCE NO MORE**   (Don Reid)
          American Cowboy Music Co., Inc.; BMI
          OD -- 4/8/82, 10:00-12:00, Jerry Kennedy (g/db), Charlie McCoy
             (hm,vb), Hargus Robbins (p).
          Final mix -- 4/13/82
          SRM-4048 -- *The Legend goes on . . .*

2-56683   **LIFE'S RAILWAY TO HEAVEN**   Traditional   -1,-2
          (arr - Don Reid, Harold Reid, Lew DeWitt, Phil Balsley)
          American Cowboy Music Co., Inc.; BMI
          Final mix -- 4/27/82
          SRM-4048 -- *The Legend goes on . . .*

===========================================================

Lew had been extremely ill at this time, and had been hospitalized for surgery. He was finally able to return to the studio to finish the last session for what was to be his last album with the group, **The Legend goes on . . . .** I bought this album when it was first released, and I have listened to it over and over for years. I have always believed that LIFE'S RAILWAY TO HEAVEN was one of the best recordings he ever made. I had no idea it was the very last one with the group, nor how ill he had been.

Lew suggested his successor, Jimmy Fortune. Lew knew he would be unable to continue with the group, and felt it was in the group's best interest for him to retire. Jimmy was auditioned by Harold, Don and Phil, just like others who desired to be a part of the Statlers. As Don Reid put it, Jimmy was chosen because he was the best man for the job.

Strictly a personal opinion, I feel there is another factor at play.

The Blue Ridge Mountains of Virginia were settled by the Scotch-Irish many years ago. The descendants of those immigrants who live in that area today carry a rich legacy from those pioneers -- the sound of their language.

The Scotch-Irish is rich in the music of the Statler Brothers. It may not stand out as something you can pinpoint, but there is enough of it there to prick your ears -- to make you listen. You can tell there is something different. If you know what it is, you can find it.

The Statlers have never moved to Nashville, or any other large metropolitan area, continuing to live in the mountains where their roots run deep; raising their own families there, among the friends of their youth. That constant return to their beginnings has helped to maintain that legacy in their music.

I don't know how many others auditioned for Lew's place. Or how many of them may have been from Virginia -- and the Blue Ridge in particular. Someone without this legacy of history in his voice might not have blended in as well with the other three. And Jimmy is a marvelous tenor!

This Scotch-Irish heritage can be found in the very beginnings of Country Music from the Carter Family and Pop Stoneman up to Loretta Lynn. It is part of what makes them who they are -- and always will be.

The recording sessions with Jimmy Fortune are listed in the next chapter, rightfully entitled **"The Legend Goes On**."

# THE STATLER BROTHERS

Lester Roadhog Moran and The Cadillac Cowboys

**Nashville**
a PolyGram company

Photo courtesy of The Statler Brothers.

# WHAT WE LOVE TO DO

Going from town to town, knocking door-to-door
Writing songs on napkins to keep from getting bored
Starving for some work and a little bite to eat
Counting last night's money, and a'wonderin' where we sleep.
Wonderin' what she's doin' since the last time that I called
'Cause she's alone in Virginia, and I'm in Arkansas
Lord knows I love my music, and she knows I love her, too
She's a better man than I am to let me do the things I do.

We like to pick and sing, and it's not a nine to five
It may not be a real job, but it keeps our dream alive
We've sung for more than many, and some times quite a few,
Either way it doesn't matter -- it's what we love to do.

Each night is something different, 'cause we're learning more each day
We know now how the cards are dealt and we know now how to play
After weeks the days seem longer, but at home not long at all
Sun shines warm at our house, but out here it feels like fall
Backstage we say a small prayer, then do what we do best
The band begins our music, and we'll do all the rest
The ride home will be the long one as soon as the show is through
I know she'll be up waiting -- it's what we love to do.

We like to pick and sing, and it's not a nine to five
It may not be a real job, but it keeps our dream alive
We've sung for more than money and at times it helps us, too
Either way, it doesn't matter -- it's what we love to do.

*Wil Reid/Langdon Reid*
April 19, 1993
Beverly Manor Music, Inc.
Used by permission.

# CHAPTER 4

# The Legend Goes On: New Faces

The retirement of Lew DeWitt remains the only personnel change in this group. Jimmy Fortune became a part of the quartet and began recording with them in late 1982. This marks another major change in the Statlers' recording history and is covered in this chapter, but it is not the only change. His was a new face in the group, but new faces began appearing in the support group that is a part of the success of the Statlers. These new faces were composers whose songs were aptly suited for them -- the new writers were their own children. (Refer to the Composer Index.) Jimmy also made his mark as a writer with the group.

KEY TO ABBREVIATIONS and SYMBOL
"DJ" - 45 rpm singles issued only to disc jockeys, usually with the same title on
     both sides.
"SR" & "SRM" - stereo LP albums.
(6 digit numbers) - later stereo LP releases, change of numbering system;
     i.e., 518-945.
xxxxxx-7 - 6-digit number followed by "-7" indicates a single release.
"SRD" - stereo promotional LP issued only to DJs.
"CC" - 45 rpm released in the "Celebrity Country" series.
"MEPL" - a DJ-only issue of a 7-inch LP (untitled).
"CDP" - compact disc promo, DJ release
(5 digits) - a 45-rpm release, 7000 & 5000 numbers, i.e., 73141.
"TL" - Time-Life Country & Western series.
"HM" - Heartland Music
"BMI" - Broadcast Music, Inc.
"ASCAP" - American Society of Composers, Authors & Publishers
"SESAC" - Selected Editions of Standard American Catalogues
"CAPAC" - Composers, Authors, & Pubishers Association of Canada
▶ (VCR "Play" button) - Available on Video

INSTRUMENT ABBREVIATIONS --

| | | |
|---|---|---|
| g - guitar | dm - drums | org - organ |
| st g - steel guitar | hm - harmonica | uke - ukulele |
| el g - electric guitar | vb - vibes | b - bass |
| db - dobro | el b - electric bass | f - fiddle |
| sl db - slide dobro | kb - keyboard | p - piano |
| bjo - banjo | man - mandolin | Fr hn - French horn |

** All Mercury releases produced by Jerry Kennedy.
All releases are Mercury Records, unless otherwise noted.

===============================================================

Sound Stage Studios                                      December 7, 1982
Nashville                                                   (14:00-17:00)
Jerry Kennedy (g,db); Bob Moore (b); Buddy Harman (dm); Pete Wade, Ray
Edenton, Chip Young, Harold Bradley (g); Hargus Robbins (p); Charlie McCoy
(hm,vb).

2-56735 **THERE IS YOU**   (Harold Reid, Don Reid)
          American Cowboy Music, Inc.; BMI
          Final mix -- 3/7/83
          812-184 -- *Today*

2-56736 **GUILTY**   (Harold Reid, Don Reid)
          American Cowboy Music, Inc.; BMI
          rejected -- see 56755, 2/16/83

2-56737 **IF THAT ISN'T LOVE**   (no cc)
          unissued

===============================================================

Sound Stage Studios                                      February 15, 1983
Nashville                                                   (14:00-17:00)
Jerry Kennedy (g); Chip Young, Pete Wade, Ray Edenton (g); Michael Leech (b);
Hargus Robbins (p); Jerry Carrigan (dm); Charlie McCoy (hm-1,vb-2); string arr
D.Bergen White -3.

2-56751 **I NEVER WANT TO KISS YOU GOODBYE**   (Kim Reid) -2,-3
          American Cowboy Music, Inc.; BMI
          OD -- 3/16/83, 10:00-13:00, Carl Gorodetzky, George Binkley, Dennis
                Molchan, Walter Schwede, Pam Vanosdale, Marvin Chantry, Gary
                Vanosdale, Roy Christensen.
          Final mix -- 3/17/83
          812-988-7 -- backed w/GUILTY
          812-184 -- *Today*

2-56752 **ELIZABETH** (Jimmy Fortune) -1,-3 ▶
    American Cowboy Music, Inc.; BMI
    OD -- 3/2/83, 10:00-13:00, Carl Gorodetzky, George Binkley, Dennis
        Molchan, Walter Schwede, Pam Vanosdale, Stephanie Woolf,
        Lennie Haight, Chris Teal, Marvin Chantry, Gary Vanosdale, Roy
        Christensen, J. David Boyle.
    Final mix -- 3/7/83
    814-881-7 -- backed w/THE CLASS OF '57, Master #49794
    868-892-7 -- backed w/THERE'S STILL TIMES
    812-184 -- *Today*
    433-962 060-8 -- *Brothers in Song* (video)
    800-633 289-3 -- *What We Love to Do* (video)

2-56753 **OH BABY MINE (I GET SO LONELY)** (Pat Ballard) -2
    Edwin H. Morris & Co. (a division of MPL); ASCAP
    OD -- 2/23/83, 14:00-16:00, Jerry Kennedy (g/db); Weldon Myrick (st g);
        Samuel Levine (sax).
    Final mix -- 2/28/83
    811-488-7 -- backed w/I'M DYIN' A LITTLE EACH DAY
    812-184 -- *Today*
    3404-2 -- *Statler Bros. Sing the Classics*

**Note:** #56752 is the first song issued written by Jimmy Fortune, and went to
    Number One on the Billboard Charts..
▶ Video produced and directed by Jim Owens Productions, Nashville, Tenn.
====================================================

Sound Stage Studios                    February 16, 1983
Nashville                            (14:00-17:00)
Jerry Kennedy (g,db); Chip Young, Ray Edenton, Pete Wade (g); Hargus Robbins
(p); Jerry Carrigan (dm); Michael Leech (b); Charlie McCoy (vb).

2-56754 **SWEET BY AND BY** -- Traditional
        [Sanford E. Bennett, Joseph P. Webster, 1867]
        (arr -- Phil Balsley, Jimmy Fortune, Don Reid, Harold Reid)
    Statler Brothers Music, Inc.; BMI
    Final mix -- 3/14/83
    812-184 -- *Today*
    826-710 -- *Radio Gospel Favorites*

2-56755 **GUILTY** (Harold Reid, Don Reid) -Remake-
    American Cowboy Music, Inc.; BMI
    OD -- 3/3/83, 10:00-12:00, Jerry Kennedy (g/db); Don "Mousey" Morton
        (dm); Tommy Williams (f).
    -- reject -- see 56770, 3/9/83

2-56756 **RIGHT ON THE MONEY** (John Rimel)
      American Cowboy Music, Inc.; BMI
      OD -- Weldon Myrick (st g), date unknown.
      Final mix -- 3/15/83
      812-184 -- *Today*

================================================================

Sound Stage Studios                                    <u>February 17, 1983</u>
Nashville                                                  (14:00-17:00)
Jerry Kennedy (g,db); Chip Young, Pete Wade, Ray Edenton (g); Hargus Robbins (p); Jerry Carrigan (dm); Charlie McCoy (hm-1,vb-2); Michael Leech (b); string arr D.Bergen White-3.

2-56757 **I'M DYIN' A LITTLE EACH DAY** (Harold Reid) -2
      American Cowboy Music, Inc.; BMI
      OD -- <u>2/23/83</u>, 14:00-16:00 --
                  Jerry Kennedy (g/db); Weldon Myrick (st g).
      811-488-7 -- backed w/OH BABY MINE
      812-184 -- *Today*

2-56758 **PROMISE** (Jimmy Fortune) -1
      American Cowboy Music, Inc.; BMI
      Final mix -- 3/3/83
      812-184 -- *Today*

2-56759 **SOME MEMORIES LAST FOREVER** (Don Reid) -2,-3
      American Cowboy Music, Inc.; BMI
      OD -- <u>3/2/83</u>, Strings, see 56752.
      812-184 -- *Today*

================================================================

Sound Stage Studios                                    <u>March 9, 1983</u>
Nashville                                                  (18:30-21:00)
Jerry Kennedy (g,db); Chip Young, Ray Edenton, Pete Wade (g); Gene Chrisman (d); David Briggs (kb); Michael Leech (b); string arr D.Bergen White.

2-56770 **GUILTY** (Harold Reid, Don Reid) ▶
      American Cowboy Music, Inc.; BMI
      OD -- <u>3/16/83</u>, Strings, see 56751.
      Final mix -- 3/16/83
      812-988-7 -- backed w/I NEVER WANT TO KISS YOU GOODBYE
      870-681-7 -- backed w/LET'S GET STARTED IF WE'RE GONNA BREAK MY
           HEART
      812-184 -- *Today*
      433-962 060-8 -- *Brothers in Song* (video)
      800-633 289-3 -- *What We Love to Do* (video)

**Note:** Remake of master #56755, 2/16/83; and master #56736, 12/7/82. Story related to the author by Harold & Don Reid on 6/22/96 -- Harold: "We had a hard time with the ending to that song. Conway Twitty was working in another studio down the hall." Don -- "Conway said, 'Would you mind a suggestion from someone who really cares?' and he helped us work it out. He was a real friend."

▶ Video produced and directed by Scene Three Productions, Nashville, Tenn. Features the Cowboy Symphony Orchestra.

Sound Stage Studios                                                    June 27, 1983
Nashville                                                              (18:00-21:30)
Jerry Kennedy (g,db); Ray Edenton, Pete Wade (g); Jerry Carrigan (d); David Briggs (kb); Mike Leech (b).

2-57228 **ATLANTA BLUE** (Don Reid)  ▶
      Statler Brothers Music, Inc.; BMI
      818-700-7 -- backed w/IF IT MAKES ANY DIFFERENCE
      874-196-7 -- backed w/MORE THAN A NAME ON A WALL
      818-652 -- *Atlanta Blue*
      433-962 060-8 -- *Brothers in Song* (video)
      800-633 289-3 -- *What We Love to Do* (video)

2-57229 **NO LOVE LOST** (John Rimel, Jimmy Fortune)
      Statler Brothers Music, Inc.; BMI
      OD -- 2/13/84, 10:00-13:00, Woodland Sound Studios --
          Jerry Kennedy (g/db); Weldon Myrick (st g); David Innis (kb).
      818-652 -- *Atlanta Blue*

2-57230 **ANGEL IN HER FACE** (Don Reid)
      Statler Brothers Music, Inc.; BMI
      OD -- 2/13/84, 10:00-13:00, Woodland Sound Studios --
          Jerry Kennedy (g/db); Weldon Myrick (st g); David Innis (kb).
      818-652 -- *Atlanta Blue*

**Note:** An overdub session was recorded for master #57228, but **was not used** in the final mix, according to Jerry Kennedy. See master #57277 for personnel listing, string arr. D. Bergen White.

▶ Video ©1984, produced and directed by Scene Three Productions, Nashville, Tenn. Filmed on location in Atlanta, Georgia.

Sound Stage Studios                                                  January 16, 1984
Nashville                                                            (14:00-17:00)
Jerry Kennedy (g,db-1); Chip Young, Ray Edenton, Pete Wade (g); David Briggs (kb); Jerry Carrigan (dm); Mike Leech (b).

2-57274  **IF IT MAKES ANY DIFFERENCE**  (Don Reid, Harold Reid) -1
American Cowboy Music, Inc.; BMI
OD -- 2/13/84, 10:00-13:00, Woodland Sound Studios --
    Jerry Kennedy (g/db); Weldon Myrick (st g); David Innis (kb).
818-700-7 -- backed w/ATLANTA BLUE
818-652 -- *Atlanta Blue*

2-57275  **(LET'S JUST) TAKE ONE NIGHT AT A TIME**  (Kim Reid)
Statler Brothers Music, Inc.; BMI
OD -- 2/13/84, 10:00-13:00, Woodland Sound Studios --
    Jerry Kennedy (g/db); Weldon Myrick (st g); David Innis (kb).
OD -- banjo, date & musician unknown.
880-411-7 -- backed w/MY ONLY LOVE
818-652 -- *Atlanta Blue*

2-57276  **ONE SIZE FITS ALL**  (John Rimel)
Statler Brothers Music, Inc.; BMI
818-652 -- *Atlanta Blue*
826-710 -- *Radio Gospel Favorites*

Note:  #57276 is a remake of #53199, 5/26/77, which was never issued.
================================================================

Sound Stage Studios                                January 17, 1984
Nashville                                          (14:00-17:00)
Jerry Kennedy (g,db); Chip Young, Ray Edenton, Pete Wade (g); David Briggs
(kb); Mike Leech (b); Jerry Carrigan (dm); string and horn arr D.Bergen White.

2-57277  **ONE TAKES THE BLAME** (Don Reid)
Statler Brothers Music, Inc.; BMI
OD --   2/14/84, 10:00-13:00, Woodland Sound Studios -- Carl
    Gorodetzky, George Binkley, Dennis Molchan, Pam Vanosdale,
    Stephanie Woolf, Chris Teal, Lee Larrison, Larry Harvin, Gary
    Vanosdale, Virginia Christensen, Lennie Haight, Dan Furth, Roy
    Christensen, Martha McCrory.
OD -- Weldon Myrick (st g), date unknown.
880-130-7 -- backed w/GIVE IT YOUR BEST
818-652 -- *Atlanta Blue*

2-57278  ★ **HOLLY**★ **WOOD**★   (Don Reid)
Statler Brothers Music, Inc.; BMI
OD -- 2/14/84, 10:00-13:00, Woodland Sound Studios -- Roger Bissell
    (trombone), James "Buddy" Skipper (clarinet), George Tidwell
    (trumpet).
818-652 -- *Atlanta Blue*

2-57279  **MY ONLY LOVE** (Jimmy Fortune)  ▶
     Statler Brothers Music, Inc.; BMI
     OD -- 2/14/84, Strings, see 57277.
     880-411-7 -- backed w/TAKE ONE NIGHT AT A TIME
     818-652 -- *Atlanta Blue*
     433-962 060-8 -- *Brothers in Song* (video)
     800-633 289-3 -- *What We Love to Do* (video)

**Note from Mercury files:**  #57278 should always appear with the use of 5-pointed
     stars in the title, not asterisks.
▶  Video produced and directed by Jim Owens Productions, Nashville, Tenn.

=========================================================

Sound Stage Studios                                    January 18, 1984
Nashville                                                 (14:00-17:00)
Chip Young, Pete Wade, Ray Edenton (g); Jerry Kennedy (db); Mike Leech (b);
David Briggs (kb); Jerry Carrigan (dm).

2-57280  **GIVE IT YOUR BEST**  (Don Reid)
     Statler Brothers Music, Inc.; BMI
     880-130-7 -- backed w/ONE TAKES THE BLAME
     818-652 -- *Atlanta Blue*

=========================================================

Sound Stage Studios                                       April 17, 1984
Nashville                                                 (10:00-13:00)
Jerry Kennedy (g,db); Pete Wade, Ray Edenton (g); David Briggs (kb); Mike Leech
(b); Kenneth Malone (dm); string and horn arr D.Bergen White -1.

2-57316  **HELLO MARY LOU**  (Gene Pitney, Cayet Mangiaracina)
     Unichappel Music/Six Continents Music Pub. Co., Inc./Champion Music
        Corp.; BMI
     880-685-7 -- backed w/REMEMBERING YOU
     824-420 -- *Pardners in Rhyme*

2-57317  **AMAZING GRACE** -- Traditional    -1
        [John Newton, 1779; arr Edwin O. Excell, 1910]
        (arr -- Harold Reid, Phil Balsley, Jimmy Fortune, Don Reid)
     Statler Brothers Music, Inc.; BMI
     OD -- 1/31/85, 18:00-21:00, Young'Un Sound -- Carl Gorodetzky,
        George Binkley, Pam Sixfin, Dennis Molchan, Lee Larrison,
        Lennie Haight, Chris Teal, Stephanie Woolf, Gary Vanosdale,
        John Borg.
     OD -- 2/4/85, 11:00-13:00, Young'Un Sound -- Jerry Kennedy (db);
        Buddy Spicher (f); Chip Young (g).
     OD -- horns (musicians & instrumentation unknown), date unknown.

884-317-7 -- backed w/SWEETER AND SWEETER
824-420 -- *Pardners in Rhyme*
826-710 -- *Radio Gospel Favorites*

================================================================

Young'Un Sound                                    January 14, 1985
Nashville                                           (14:00-17:00)
Jerry Kennedy (g,db-1); Chip Young, Ray Edenton, Pete Wade (g); Jerry Carrigan (dm); Buddy Spicher (f); David Briggs (kb); Weldon Myrick (st g); Mike Leech (b).

2-58206   SWEETER AND SWEETER   (Don Reid, Harold Reid)   ▶
          Statler Brothers Music, Inc.; BMI
          884-317-7 -- backed w/AMAZING GRACE
          824-420 -- *Pardners in Rhyme*
          433-962 060-8 -- *Brothers in Song* (video)
          800-633 289-3 -- *What We Love to Do* (video)

2-58207   REMEMBERING YOU   (Harold Reid, Don Reid)  -1
          Statler Brothers Music, Inc.; BMI
          880-685-7 -- backed w/HELLO MARY LOU
          824-420 -- *Pardners in Rhyme*

2-58208   MEMORY LANE   (Jimmy Fortune)
          Statler Brothers Music, Inc.; BMI
          824-420 -- *Pardners in Rhyme*

▶  Video produced and directed by Jim Owens Productions, Nashville, Tenn.

================================================================

Young'Un Sound                                    January 15, 1985
Nashville                                           (14:00-17:30)
Jerry Kennedy (g,db); Chip Young (el g), Ray Edenton, Pete Wade (g); David Briggs (kb); Weldon Myrick (st g, sl db-1); Jerry Carrigan (dm); Mike Leech (b); string arr D.Bergen White -2.

2-58209   AUTUMN LEAVES (Jimmy Fortune, John Rimel)
          Statler Brothers Music, Inc.; BMI
          OD -- 2/4/85, 11:00-13:00 -- Jerry Kennedy (db);  Buddy Spicher (f);
                Chip Young (g).
          824-420 -- *Pardners in Rhyme*

2-58210   TOO MUCH ON MY HEART   (Jimmy Fortune)  -2
          Statler Brothers Music, Inc.; BMI
          OD -- 1/31/85, Strings, see 57317.
          OD -- Weldon Myrick (st g), date unknown.
          884-016-7 -- backed w/HER HEART OR MINE
          824-420 -- *Pardners in Rhyme*

2-58211  **HER HEART OR MINE**  (Harold Reid, Don Reid) -1
Statler Brothers Music, Inc.; BMI
884-016-7 -- backed w/TOO MUCH ON MY HEART
824-420 -- *Pardners in Rhyme*

═══════════════════════════════════════════════════════════

Young'Un Sound                                          January 16, 1985
Nashville                                               (14:00-17:00)
Chip Young, Pete Wade, Ray Edenton (g); Jerry Kennedy (g,db); Mike Leech (b);
Weldon Myrick (st g, sl db-1); Jerry Carrigan (dm); David Briggs (kb); string arr
D.Bergen White -2.

2-58212  **YOU DON'T WEAR BLUE SO WELL**
(Kim Reid, Karmen Reid, Kodi Reid)
Statler Brothers Music, Inc.; BMI
OD -- 2/4/85, 11:00-13:00, -- Jerry Kennedy (dbr);
Buddy Spicher (f); Chip Young (el g).
824-420 -- *Pardners in Rhyme*

2-58213  **I'M SORRY YOU HAD TO BE THE ONE** -1,-2
(Don Reid, Harold Reid, Jimmy Fortune)
Statler Brothers Music, Inc.; BMI
OD -- 1/31/85, Strings, see 57317.
824-420 -- *Pardners in Rhyme*

═══════════════════════════════════════════════════════════

Young'Un Sound                                          April 23, 1985
Nashville                                               (14:00-17:00)
Jerry Kennedy (g,db); Chip Young, Ray Edenton (g); Weldon Myrick (st g); Henry
Strzetecki (b); David Briggs (kb); Bela Fleck (bjo-1); Milton Sledge (dm).

2-58230  **OLD TOY TRAINS**  (Roger Miller)
Tree Publishing Co., Inc.; BMI
two takes made (which one used unknown)
OD -- 5/17/85, 10:00-13:00, Farrell Morris (percussion).
824-785 -- *Christmas Present*
22660-4 -- *Christmas with the Statler Bros.*

2-58231  **NO RESERVATION AT THE INN**  (Harold Reid, Don Reid) -1
Statler Brothers Music, Inc.; BMI
824-785 -- *Christmas Present*
22660-4 -- *Christmas with the Statler Bros.*

2-58232  **CHRISTMAS COUNTRY STYLE**  (Jimmy Fortune) -1
Statler Brothers Music, Inc.; BMI
two takes made (which one used unknown)

824-785 -- *Christmas Present*
22660-4 -- *Christmas with the Statler Bros.*

==================================================================

Young'Un Sound                                              <u>April 24, 1985</u>
Nashville                                                   (14:00-17:00)
Chip Young, Pete Wade, Ray Edenton (g); Jerry Kennedy (g,db); Jerry Carrigan (dm); Mike Leech (b); Bobby Ogdin (kb); string arr by D.Bergen White.

2-58233  BRAHMS' BETHLEHEM LULLABY -- Traditional
         [Johannes Brahms, Opus 49, No. 6]
         (arr -- Don Reid, Phil Balsley, Jimmy Fortune, Harold Reid)
         Statler Brothers Music, Inc.; BMI
         OD -- <u>5/17/85</u>, 10:00-13:00, 14:00-19:00; Carl Gorodetzky, George
         Binkley, Dennis Molchan, Pam Sixfin, Lee Larrison, Charles
         Everett, Stephanie Woolf, Phyllis Mazza, Gary Vanosdale, John
         Borg, Virginia Christensen, Connie Collopy, Roy Christensen,
         Mark Tanner.
         824-785 -- *Christmas Present*

2-58234  MARY'S SWEET SMILE
         (Harold Reid, Don Reid, Jimmy Fortune, Phil Balsley)
         Statler Brothers Music, Inc.; BMI
         OD -- <u>5/17/85</u>, Strings, see 58233.
         884-320-7 -- backed w/CHRISTMAS EVE (KODIA'S THEME)
         824-785 -- *Christmas Present*

2-58235  SOMEWHERE IN THE NIGHT   (Debo Reid, Don Reid)
         Statler Brothers Music, Inc.; BMI
         two takes -- used #2
         OD -- <u>5/17/85</u>, Strings, see 58233.
         824-785 -- *Christmas Present*

==================================================================

Young'Un Sound                                                <u>May 7, 1985</u>
Nashville                                                    (10:00-13:00)
Chip Young, Pete Wade, Ray Edenton (g); Jerry Kennedy (g,db); David Briggs (kb); Gene Chrisman (dm); Mike Leech (b); string arr D. Bergen White.

2-58236  CHRISTMAS EVE (KODIA'S THEME)  ▶
         (Debo Reid, Don Reid, Harold Reid)
         Statler Brothers Music, Inc.; BMI
         OD -- <u>5/17/85</u>, Strings, see 58233.
         884-320-7 -- backed w/MARY'S SWEET SMILE
         824-785 -- *Christmas Present*

2-58237  WHOSE BIRTHDAY IS CHRISTMAS  (Harold Reid)
         Statler Brothers Music, Inc.; BMI

OD -- <u>5/17/85</u>, Strings, see 58233.
824-785 -- *Christmas Present*

2-58238  **AN OLD-FASHIONED CHRISTMAS**  (John Rimel)
Statler Brothers Music, Inc.; BMI
OD -- <u>5/17/85</u>, Strings, see 58233.
OD -- <u>5/17/85</u>, Weldon Myrick (st g).
824-785 -- *Christmas Present*
22660-4 -- *Christmas with the Statler Bros.*

▶ The video was lifted from the TV special *"Statler Brothers Christmas Present."* It was directed by Steven A. Womack, and produced by Jim Owens Productions and Statler-Grant Productions for Multi-Media Entertainment. It was used on TNN's video programs, but was not issued for public release.

═══════════════════════════════════════════════════════

Young'Un Sound                                                     May 8, 1985
Nashville                                                          (10:00-13:00)
Chip Young, Pete Wade, Ray Edenton (g); Jerry Kennedy (g,db); David Briggs (kb); Gene Chrisman (dm); Mike Leech (b).

2-58239  **FOR MOMMA** (Don Reid, Harold Reid)
Statler Brothers Music, Inc.; BMI
824-785 -- *Christmas Present*

═══════════════════════════════════════════════════════

Young'Un Sound                                                    June 18, 1985
Nashville                                                         (14:00-17:00)
Chip Young, Pete Wade, Ray Edenton (g); Jerry Kennedy (g,db); David Briggs (kb); Gene Chrisman (dm); Mike Leech (b).

2-58262  **A BEAUTIFUL LIFE** -- Traditional  [William M. Golden, 1918]
                  Arr -- Statler Brothers
Statler Brothers Music, Inc.; BMI
826-710 -- *Radio Gospel Favorites*
HC2012 -- *Statler Bros. Gospel Favorites* [HM]

2-58263  **A DIFFERENT SONG**  (Don Reid) -- remake --
House of Cash, Inc.; BMI
826-710 -- *Radio Gospel Favorites*
HC2012 -- *Statler Bros. Gospel Favorites* [HM]

Note: #58263 is a remake of #2-48579, 11/16/71.

═══════════════════════════════════════════════════════

Master numbers 58264 through 58268 are out of date sequence. This set of numbers was set aside for the Heartland Music gospel favorites album. They were recorded January 27 through February 18, 1986.

═══════════════════════════════════════════════════════

Young'Un Sound                                                    June 19, 1985
Nashville                                                       (14:00-17:00)
Chip Young, Pete Wade, Ray Edenton (g); Jerry Kennedy (g,db); David Briggs (kb); Mike Leech (b); Jerry Carrigan (dm).

2-58272  **MORE LIKE DADDY THAN ME**  (Don Reid)
         Statler Brothers Music, Inc.; BMI
         888-219-7 -- backed w/FOREVER
         826-782 -- *Four for the Show*

2-58273  **COUNT ON ME**  (Don Reid)
         Statler Brothers Music, Inc.; BMI
         884-721-7 -- backed w/WILL YOU BE THERE
         826-782 -- *Four for the Show*
         834-626 -- *Greatest Hits, Vol. 3*

Young'Un Sound                                                  January 14, 1986
Nashville                                                       (14:00-17:00)
Chip Young, Ray Edenton, Pete Wade (g); Jerry Kennedy (g,db); Gene Chrisman (dm); David Briggs (kb); Mike Leech (b); string arr D. Bergen White.-1

2-58274  **WILL YOU BE THERE**  (Don Reid, Debo Reid) -1
         Statler Brothers Music, Inc.; BMI
         OD -- 2/7/86, Jerry Kennedy (g/db); Weldon Myrick (st g).
         OD -- 2/19/86, 10:00-13:00, Carl Gorodetzky, George Binkley, Pamela
               Sixfin, Dennis Molchan, Lee Larrison, Charles Everett, Chris
               Teal, Stephanie Woolf, Gary Vanosdale, John Borg.
         884-721-7 -- backed w/COUNT ON ME
         826-782 -- *Four for the Show*

2-58275  **FOR CRYIN' OUT LOUD**  (John Rimel, Jimmy Fortune)
         Statler Brothers Music, Inc.; BMI
         OD -- 2/7/86, Jerry Kennedy (g/db); Weldon Myrick (st g).
         826-782 -- *Four for the Show*

Young'Un Sound                                                  January 15, 1986
Nashville                                                       (14:00-17:00)
Chip Young, Pete Wade, Ray Edenton (g); Jerry Kennedy (g,db); Hoot Hester (f); Weldon Myrick (st g, sl db-1); David Briggs (kb); Mike Leech (b); Gene Chrisman (dm).

2-58276  **YOU OUGHTA BE HERE WITH ME**  (Roger Miller)
         Tree Publishing Co., Inc. & Roger Miller Music; BMI
         [From the Broadway play *Big River*]
         826-782 -- *Four for the Show*

2-58277  **WE GOT THE MEM'RIES**  (Harold Reid, Don Reid) -1
Statler Brothers Music, Inc.; BMI
888-042-7 -- backed w/ONLY YOU
826-782 -- *Four for the Show*

2-58278  **I DON'T DREAM ANYMORE**  (Don Reid, Debo Reid)
Statler Brothers Music, Inc.; BMI
826-782 -- *Four for the Show*

=================================================================

Young'Un Sound                                    January 16, 1986
Nashville                                          (10:00-13:00)
Chip Young, Ray Edenton, Pete Wade (g); Jerry Kennedy (g,db); David Briggs
(kb); Gene Chrisman (dm); Mike Leech (b); string arr D. Bergen White.

2-58279  **FOREVER**  (Jimmy Fortune)
Statler Brothers Music, Inc.; BMI
OD -- 2/19/86, Strings, see WILL YOU BE THERE, 1/14/86.
888-219-7 -- backed w/MORE LIKE DADDY THAN ME
826-782 -- *Four for the Show*

=================================================================

Young'Un Sound                                    January 27, 1986
Nashville                                          (14:00-17:00)
Jerry Kennedy (g,db); Chip Young, Pete Wade, Ray Edenton (g); Mike Leech (b);
Gene Chrisman (dm); Larry Butler (kb-1); string arr D. Bergen White -2.

2-58264  **BLESSED BE**  (Kim Reid) -2
Statler Brothers Music, Inc.; BMI
OD -- 2/19/86, Strings, see WILL YOU BE THERE, 1/14/86.
Final mix -- 2/21/86
826-710 -- *Radio Gospel Favorites*
HC2012 -- *TheStatler Brothers Gospel Favorites* (HM)

2-58265  **I BELIEVE I'LL LIVE FOR HIM**  (Harold Reid, Don Reid)
Statler Brothers Music, Inc.; BMI
Final mix -- 2/21/86
826-782 -- *Four for the Show*
826-710 -- *Radio Gospel Favorites*

2-58266  **OVER THE SUNSET MOUNTAINS**  (John W. Peterson) -1
John W. Peterson Music Co.; ASCAP
826-710 -- *Radio Gospel Favorites*

**Note:** As related by Jimmy Fortune, "I mentioned one day in conversation that
OVER THE SUNSET MOUNTAINS was my mother's favorite hymn. Harold, Phil, and
Don weren't familiar with the song, but we learned it and put it on our next album."

=================================================================

Young'Un Sound                                                    January 28, 1986
Nashville                                                         (14:00-17:00)
Chip Young, Ray Edenton, Pete Wade (g); Jerry Kennedy (g,db); Gene Chrisman
(dm); Mike Leech (b); Larry Butler (kb).

2-58267  **WE WON'T BE HOME UNTIL THEN**  (Don Reid)
         Statler Brothers Music, Inc.; BMI
         Final mix -- 2/21/86
         826-710 -- *Radio Gospel Favorites*

---

Young'Un Sound                                                    February 18, 1986
Nashville                                                         (14:00-17:00)
Chip Young, Ray Edenton, Pete Wade (g); Jerry Kennedy (g,db); Mike Leech (b);
Gene Chrisman (dm); David Briggs (kb).

2-58268  **THERE IS POWER IN THE BLOOD**  Traditional  [Lewis E. Jones, 1899]
                 (arr -- Phil Balsley, Jimmy Fortune, Don Reid, Harold Reid)
         Statler Brothers Music, Inc.; BMI
         Final mix -- 3/3/86
         826-710 -- *Radio Gospel Favorites*
         HC2012 -- *TheStatler Brothers Gospel Favorites* (HM)

2-58280  **ONLY YOU**  (Buck Ram, Ande Rand) -1  ▶
         Hollis Music, Inc; BMI
         OD -- 2/19/86, Strings, see WILL YOU BE THERE, 1/14/86.
         888-042-7 -- backed w/WE GOT THE MEM'RIES
         826-782 -- *Four for the Show*
         3404-2 -- *Statler Bros. Sing the Classics*
         800-633 289-3 -- *What We Love to Do* (video)

▶  Video produced and directed by Jim Owens Productions, Nashville, Tenn.

---

Young'Un Sound                                                    June 16, 1986
Nashville                                                         (14:00-17:00)
Chip Young, Pete Wade, Ray Edenton (g); Jerry Kennedy (g,db); Bobby Ogdin
(kb); Mike Leech (b); Gene Chrisman (dm); string arr D.Bergen White -1.

2-58370  **BEYOND ROMANCE**  (Jimmy Fortune, John Rimel) -1
         Statler Brothers Music, Inc.; BMI
         OD -- Strings, date unknown. Musicians -- (*from the album cover*) Carl
              Gorodetzky, George Binkley III, John Borg, John Catchings, Roy
              Christensen, Virginia Christensen, Jim Grosjean, Lee Larrison,
              Ted Madsen, Dennis Molchan, Laura Molyneaux, Pamela Sixfin,
              Gary Vanosdale, Stephanie Woolf.
         Final mix -- 3/25/87

870-442-7 -- backed w/AM I CRAZY
832-404 -- *Maple Street Memories*

2-58371  MAPLE STREET MEMORIES  (Don Reid)  ▶
Statler Brothers Music, Inc.; BMI
Final mix -- 3/27/87
PRO562-7 -- DJ issue
888-920-7 -- backed w/JESUS SHOWED ME SO
832-404 -- *Maple Street Memories*
800-633 289-3 -- *What We Love to Do* (video)

▶  Video produced and directed by Jim Owens Productions, Nashville, Tenn.
═══════════════════════════════════════════════════════
Custom Mastering, Inc.                          July 16, 1986

Interview with Statler Brothers and Jerry Kennedy.
PRO 736 -- DJ issue
═══════════════════════════════════════════════════════
Young'Un Sound                              November 17, 1986
Nashville                                      (14:00-17:00)
Mike Leech (b); Gene Chrisman (dm); David Briggs (kb); Ray Edenton, Chip
Young, Pete Wade (g); Billy Puett (flute, clarinet, sax); Farrell Morris (timpani);
Eberhard Ramm (Fr hn); Marianne Osiel (oboe). *Strings* -- Carl Gorodetzky,
George Binkley, Dennis Molchan, Pamela Sixfin, Lee Larrison, David Davidson,
Laura Molyneaux, Ted Madsen, John Borg, Gary Vanosdale, Virginia Christensen,
Kathryn Plummer, Roy Christensen, Mark Lammer.  String arr D. Bergen White.

2-59109  DÉJÀ VU  (Harold Reid, Don Reid, Debo Reid)
Statler Brothers Music, Inc.; BMI
Final mix -- 3/26/87
888 650-7 -- backed w/I'LL BE THE ONE
832 404 -- *Maple Street Memories*

**Note:**  As related to the author by Jerry Kennedy on 7/26/96, they did not want to
do a string overdub on this song.  They wanted all the musicians in the studio at
once to get the feeling of presence that would give.  However, there was not room
for the singers (the Statlers) in the studio at the same time!  The vocals were
actually done as an overdub to this first recording, immediately after the musicians
left the studio.  This is the second time the Statlers ever intentionally recorded to
a sound track.  (See #52492, Oct. 29, 1976.)
═══════════════════════════════════════════════════════
Young'Un Sound                        Tuesday, November 18, 1986
Nashville                                      (15:00-17:00)
Jerry Kennedy (g,db); Chip Young, Ray Edenton, Pete Wade (g); David Briggs
(kb); Gene Chrisman (dm); Mike Leech (b).

2-59123  **AM I CRAZY**  (Jimmy Fortune)
           Statler Brothers Music, Inc.; BMI
           OD -- Strings, date unknown.  See 58370, 6/16/86.
           Final mix -- 3/26/87
           870-442-7 -- backed w/BEYOND ROMANCE
           832-404 -- *Maple Street Memories*

Young'Un Sound                                    December 8, 1986
Nashville                                          (10:00-12:00)
Chip Young, Pete Wade (g); Jerry Kennedy (g,db); David Briggs (kb); Buddy
Spicher (f); string arr D.Bergen White.  Jean McCracken and Diana Rae (vocals).

2-59122  **OUR STREET/TELL ME WHY**
2-58450           (Harold Reid, Don Reid) /
                  (Mitchell Parish, Michael Edwards, Sigmund Spaeth)
                  Statler Brothers Music, Inc.; BMI/Mills Music, Inc.; ASCAP
                  Final mix -- 3/24/87
                  832-404 -- *Maple Street Memories*

Young'Un Sound                                    January 13, 1987
Nashville                                          (          )
*(From the album cover.)*  Ray Edenton, Chip Young (g); David Briggs, Bobby
Ogdin (kb); Gene Chrisman (dm); Mike Leech (b); Weldon Myrick (st g-1); Pete
Wade, Jerry Kennedy (g,db); Bela Fleck (bjo-2); Buddy Spicher (f); string arr
D.Bergen White -3.

2-59108  **I'LL BE THE ONE**  (Don Reid, Debo Reid) -2,-3
           Statler Brothers Music, Inc.; BMI
           OD -- Strings, date unknown.  See 58370, 6/16/86.
           Final Mix -- 1/13/87
           872-604-7 -- backed w/MOON PRETTY MOON
           888-650-7 -- backed w/DÉJÀ VU
           832-404 -- *Maple Street Memories*

2-59110  **THE BEST I KNOW HOW**  (Kim Reid) -1
           Statler Brothers Music, Inc.; BMI
           Final mix -- 3/26/87
           870-164-7 -- backed w/I LOST MY HEART TO YOU
           832-404 -- *Maple Street Memories*

Young'Un Sound                                    January 14, 1987
Nashville                                          (      )
*(From the album cover.)*  Ray Edenton, Chip Young (g); David Briggs, Bobby
Ogdin (kb); Gene Chrisman (dm); Mike Leech (b); Weldon Myrick (st g-1); Pete
Wade, Jerry Kennedy (g,db-2); Bela Fleck (bjo-3); Buddy Spicher (f); string arr D.
Bergen White -4.

2-59125   **I LOST MY HEART TO YOU**   (Jimmy Fortune, John Rimel) -2,-3,-4
Statler Brothers Music, Inc.; BMI
OD -- Strings, date unknown. See 58370, 6/16/86.
Final mix -- 3/25/87
870-164-7 -- backed w/THE BEST I KNOW HOW
832-404 -- *Maple Street Memories*

2-59126   **JESUS SHOWED ME SO**   (Harold Reid, Don Reid)   -1
Statler Brothers Music, Inc.; BMI
Final mix -- 3/25/87
888-920-7 -- backed w/MAPLE STREET MEMORIES
832-404 -- *Maple Street Memories*

---

At this point, Mercury Records ceased the use of "master numbers." The system
now is a File ID number. See Introduction for explanations of both master numbers
and File ID numbers. Overdubs are referred back to session dates.

---

Young'Un Sound                                           January 12, 1988
Nashville                                                    (14:00-17:00)
Jimmy Fortune (g-1); Jerry Kennedy (g,db); Larry Paxton (el g); Ray Edenton (g);
David Briggs (kb); Chip Young (g); Gene Chrisman (dm); Pete Wade (g); string
arr D. Bergen White -2.

98928     **HOLDING ON**   (Jimmy Fortune, John Rimel) -1,-2
Statler Brothers Music; BMI
OD -- 6/8/88, 10:00-13:00 -- Carl Gorodetzky, Dennis Molchan, Pamela
    Sixfin, George Binkley, Laura Molyneaux, Ted Madsen, Conni
    Ellisor, Lee Larrison, John Borg, Richard Grosjean, Kristin
    Wilkinson, Robert Mason, Roy Christensen, Gary Vanosdale.
OD -- 3/5/90, Javelina Studios, 10:00-13:00,
    Brent Rowan (g), Roy Huskey, Jr. (acoustic b).
842-518 -- *Music, Memories & You*

96126     **MOON PRETTY MOON**   (Kim Reid)
69070     Statler Brothers Music, Inc.; BMI
98928     872-604-7 -- backed w/I'LL BE THE ONE
834-626 -- *Greatest Hits, Vol. 3*

---

Young'Un Sound                                           January 13, 1988
Nashville                                                    (14:00-17:00)
Jerry Kennedy (g,db-1); Chip Young (g); Hargus Robbins (p); Pete Wade (g); Ray
Edenton (g); Larry Paxton (el b); Gene Chrisman (dm).

98928    **NOBODY ELSE**  (Don Reid)  -1   ▶
104960   Statler Brothers Music, Inc.; BMI
         OD -- 6/9/88, 10:00-13:00 -- Jerry Kennedy (g/db); Hoot Hester (f);
              Weldon Myrick (st g); Chip Young (g).
         878-386-7 -- backed w/HE IS THERE
         CDP 325 -- DJ release CD
         842-518 -- *Music, Memories & You*
         800-633 289-3 -- *What We Love to Do* (video)

98928    **OLD HABITS OF HEART**
98929         -Unissued-

▶ Video produced and directed by Scene Three Productions, Nashville, Tenn.

====================================================================
Young'Un Sound                                        May 23, 1988
Nashville                                            (14:00-17:00)
Jerry Kennedy (g,db); Gene Chrisman (dm); Hargus Robbins (p); Mike Leech (el
b); Ray Edenton (g); Pete Wade (g, fretted db-1).

98928    **WHAT'S ON MY MIND**  (Don Reid)
98929    Statler Brothers Music, Inc.; BMI -- two takes, used #2
         OD -- 6/8/88, Strings, see HOLDING ON, 1/12/88.
         842-518 -- *Music, Memories & You*

68277    **LET'S GET STARTED IF WE'RE GONNA BREAK MY HEART** -1   ▶
96126         (Harold Reid, Don Reid, Debo Reid)
98928    Statler Brothers Music, Inc.; BMI
         870-681-7 -- backed w/GUILTY
         834-626 -- *Greatest Hits, Vol. 3*
         800-633 289-3 -- *What We Love to Do* (video)

▶ Video produced and directed by Jim Owens Productions, Nashville, Tenn.

====================================================================
Young'Un Sound                                        May 24, 1988
Nashville                                            (14:00-17:00)
Jerry Kennedy (g,db); Chip Young, Pete Wade, Ray Edenton (g); Gene Chrisman
(dm); Mike Leech (b);  David Briggs (p,kb).

96126    **MORE THAN A NAME ON A WALL**  (Jimmy Fortune, John Rimel)
69145    Statler Brothers Music, Inc.; BMI
98928    OD -- 6/8/88, Strings, see HOLDING ON, 1/12/88.
         874-196-7 -- backed w/ATLANTA BLUE
         834-626 -- *Greatest Hits, Vol. 3*

98928     **JEALOUS EYES** (Debo Reid, Don Reid)
98929     Statler Brothers Music, Inc.; BMI
         two takes made (which one used unknown)
         OD -- 3/5/90, Javelina Studios, 10:00-13:00 --
             Brent Rowan (g), Roy Huskey, Jr. (acoustic b).
         842-518 -- *Music, Memories & You*

===========================================================

Young'Un Sound                         May 25, 1988
Nashville                                 14:00-17:00
Jerry Kennedy (db); Chip Young, Pete Wade, Ray Edenton (g); David Briggs (p,kb); Mike Leech (b); Weldon Myrick (st g, sl db-1); Buddy Spicher (f); Gene Chrisman (dm).

98928     **MY MUSIC, MY MEMORIES, AND YOU** (Don Reid, Harold Reid) -1
105077   Statler Brothers Music, Inc.; BMI
106089   875-498-7 -- backed w/SMALL, SMALL WORLD
         842-518 -- *Music, Memories & You*

98924     **WHEN THE ROLL IS CALLED UP YONDER** Traditional
         [James M. Black, 1893]
         (arr -- Statler Brothers) -- no instrumental accompaniment
         Statler Brothers Music, Inc.; BMI
         HC2012 -- *TheStatler Brothers Gospel Favorites* (HM)

===========================================================

Stargem Studio                       November 16, 1988
                                      14:00-17:00
Chip Young, Ray Edenton, Pete Wade, Jerry Kennedy (g); Buddy Spicher (f); Mike Leech (b); Gene Chrisman (dm); Weldon Myrick (st g); David Briggs (p,kb).

98929     **I NEVER ONCE GOT TIRED OF YOU**
105077          (Harold Reid, Don Reid, Debo Reid)
         Statler Brothers Music, Inc.; BMI -- two takes, used #2
         842-518 -- *Music, Memories & You*

98929     **YOU GAVE YOURSELF AWAY** (Jimmy Fortune, John Rimel)
         Statler Brothers Music, Inc.; BMI -- two takes, used #1
         OD -- 3/5/90, Javelina Studios, 10:00-13:00 --
             Brent Rowan (g), Roy Huskey, Jr. (acoustic b).
         842-518 -- *Music, Memories & You*

===========================================================

Stargem Studio                       November 17, 1988
                                      14:00-17:00
Jerry Kennedy (g,db); Chip Young, Pete Wade, Ray Edenton (g); Mike Leech (b); Gene Chrisman (dm); David Briggs (p,kb).

98929      **THINK OF ME**   (Don Reid, Harold Reid)
105077     Statler Brothers Music, Inc.; BMI -- two takes, used #2
           OD -- 3/5/90, Javelina Studios, 10:00-13:00 --
                Brent Rowan (g), Roy Huskey, Jr. (acoustic b).
           842-518 -- *Music, Memories & You*

===============================================================

Capitol Music Hall                                            June 23, 1989
Wheeling, West Virginia -- LIVE  CONCERT
 **The Cowboy Symphony Orchestra** -- Billy "Boopie" James (b); Carroll "Bull"
Durham (p); Don "Mousey" Morton (dm); Jerry Hensley, Charlie Hamm (g).

98265      **THE OFFICIAL HISTORIAN ON SHIRLEY JEAN BERRELL**
                (Don Reid, Harold Reid)
           American Cowboy Music, Inc.; BMI
           OD --8/8/89, Scruggs Sound Studio, 10:00-13:00 -- James, Hensley,
                Morton, Durham, Hamm.
           876-876-7 -- backed w/WALKING HEARTACHE IN DISGUISE -- LIVE

98265      **A HURT I CAN'T HANDLE**   (Jimmy Fortune)
           Statler Brothers Music, Inc.; BMI
           OD --8/8/89, Scruggs Sound Studio, 10:00-13:00 -- James, Hensley,
                Morton, Durham, Hamm.
           875-112-7 -- backed w/DON'T WAIT ON ME -- LIVE

98265      **BED OF ROSE'S**   (Harold Reid)
           House of Cash, Inc.; BMI
           OD --8/8/89, Scruggs Sound Studio, 10:00-13:00 -- James, Hensley,
                Morton, Durham, Hamm.

98265      **FOGGY MOUNTAIN BREAKDOWN** -- Instrumental

98265      **WHEN THE ROLL IS CALLED UP YONDER**   Traditional
                [James M. Black, 1893]--No instrumental accompaniment.
                (Arr - Phil Balsley, Jimmy Fortune, Don Reid, Harold Reid)
           Statler Brothers Music, Inc.; BMI

98265      **I'LL FLY AWAY**   (Albert E. Brumley)  Arr by the Statler Brothers
           Albert E. Brumley & Sons, SESAC

98265      **WALKING HEARTACHE IN DISGUISE**
                (Harold Reid, Don Reid, Debo Reid)
           Statler Brothers Music, Inc.; BMI
           OD -- see above, 8/8/89.
           876-876-7 -- backed w/THE OFFICIAL HISTORIAN ON SHIRLEY JEAN
                BERRELL -- LIVE

98265    **TOMORROW NEVER COMES**   (Ernest Tubb, Johnny Bond)
         Noma Music Inc./Unichappell Music, Inc.; BMI

98265    **DON'T WAIT ON ME**   (Harold Reid, Don Reid)
         American Cowboy Music Co., Inc.; BMI
         875-112-7 -- backed w/A HURT I CAN'T HANDLE -- LIVE
         **Note:** This is where Harold explains why they had to change the words
         to this song!

98265    **I'LL GO TO MY GRAVE LOVING YOU**   (Don Reid, Harold Reid)
         American Cowboy Music Co., Inc.; BMI
         3404-2 -- *Statler Bros. Sing the Classics*

98265    **THIS OLE HOUSE**   (Stuart Hamblen)
         Hamblen Music Co., Inc.; BMI

**Note:** All are released on 875-112 -- *Live and Sold Out*
========================================================

Eleven Eleven Sound                                    March 26, 1990
Nashville                                                  18:00-21:00
Chip Young, Ray Edenton, Pete Wade (g); Jerry Kennedy (g,db); Mike Leech (b);
Gene Chrisman (dm); David Briggs (p,kb).

104960   **HE IS THERE**   (Kim Reid)
         Statler Brothers Music, Inc.; BMI
         OD -- Strings, date unknown.  Musicians -- (*from the album cover*) Carl
             Gorodetzky, George Binkley, John Borg, Roy Christensen, Conni
             Ellisor, Jim Grosjean, Lee Larrison, Ted Madsen, Bob Mason,
             Dennis Molchan, Laura Molyneaux, Pam Sixfin, Gary Vanosdale,
             Kris Wilkinson.
         878-386-7 -- backed w/NOBODY ELSE
         842-518 -- *Music, Memories & You*

104960   **SMALL, SMALL WORLD**   (Gary Scruggs, Thom Schuler)   ▶
105891   Statler Brothers Music, Inc.; BMI
         875-498-7 -- backed w/MY MUSIC, MY MEMORIES AND YOU
         842-518 -- *Music, Memories & You*
         800-633 289-3 -- *What We Love to Do* (video)

▶  Video produced and directed by Jim Owens Productions, Nashville, Tenn.
========================================================

Soundshop Recording Studios                           November 14, 1990
Nashville                                                  14:00-17:00
Jerry Kennedy (g); Chip Young, Mark Casstevens (acoustic g); David Briggs,
Bobby Ogdin (p,kb); Brent Mason (el g); David Hungate (b); Jerry Kroon (dm).

106415    **DYNAMITE**  (Wil Reid)
          Statler Brothers Music, Inc.; BMI -- two takes, used #2
          848-370 -- *All-American Country*

106415    **FALLING IN LOVE**  (Don Reid, Debo Reid)
          Statler Brothers Music, Inc.; BMI -- two takes, used #2
          848-370 -- *All-American Country*

===============================================================

Soundshop Recording Studios                         December 4, 1990
Nashville                                                10:00-13:00
Jerry Kennedy (g); Chip Young, Mark Casstevens (acoustic g); David Briggs,
Bobby Ogdin (p,kb); Weldon Myrick (st g, sl db); Brent Rowan (el g); Larry Paxton
(b); Jerry Kroon (dm).

106415    **IF I'D PAID MORE ATTENTION TO YOU**  (Jimmy Fortune)
          Statler Brothers Music, Inc.; BMI -- three takes, used #3
          848-370 -- *All-American Country*

106415    **THERE'S STILL TIMES**  (Don Reid)
          Statler Brothers Music, Inc.; BMI -- four takes, used #4
          868-892-7 -- backed w/ELIZABETH
          848-370 -- *All-American Country*

===============================================================

Soundshop Recording Studios                         February 6, 1991
Nashville                                                10:00-13:00
Jerry Kennedy (g); Chip Young, Kenneth Bell (acoustic g); Hargus Robbins, David
Briggs (p, kb); Larry Paxton (b); Steve Turner (dm); Brent Rowan (el g).

106415    **REMEMBER ME**  (John Northrup, Gordon Payne)
106089    _____; ASCAP -- three takes, used #3
106406    OD -- 2/7/91, 10:00-13:00 -- David Briggs (p,kb).
          868-140-7 -- backed w/MY MUSIC, MY MEMORIES AND YOU
          848-370 -- *All-American Country*

**Note:**  REMEMBER ME was released as a single on 2/22/91, on the album in June,
1991, before the beginning of Desert Shield.  The conflict became known as Desert
Storm in December, 1991.  It was not written for this current event, but it was
appropriate.

106415    **YOU'VE BEEN LIKE A MOTHER TO ME**  (Don Reid) -- remake -- ▶
          American Cowboy Music, Inc.; BMI
          OD -- 2/7/91, 10:00-13:00 -- David Briggs (p,kb).
          868-484-7 -- backed w/JESUS IS THE ANSWER EVERY TIME
          848-370 -- *All-American Country*
          800-633 289-3 -- *What We Love to Do* (video)

**Note:** YOU'VE BEEN LIKE A MOTHER TO ME is a remake of master #2-51473, 9/30/74.

▶ Video directed by Richard Jernigan for Marilyn Leaman Productions.

=========================================================

Eleven Eleven Recording Studios                          February 19, 1991
Nashville                                                         10:00-13:00
Jerry Kennedy (g); David Briggs, Bobby Ogdin (p,kb); Weldon Myrick (st g); Brent
Rowan (el g); Larry Paxton (b); Chip Young, Kenneth Bell (acoustic g); Steve
Turner (dm).

106415   PUT IT ON THE CARD   (Tony Haleldon, Stan Munsey, Jr.)
         _____; BMI  -- three takes, used #3
         848-370 -- *All-American Country*

106415   EVERYTHING YOU SEE IN YOUR DREAMS   (Don Reid, Harold Reid)
         Statler Brothers Music, Inc.; BMI -- two takes, used #2
         848-370 -- *All-American Country*

106415   JESUS IS THE ANSWER EVERY TIME   (Don Reid, Harold Reid)
         Statler Brothers Music, Inc.; BMI -- two takes, used #2
         868-484-7 -- backed w/YOU'VE BEEN LIKE A MOTHER TO ME
         848-370 -- *All-American Country*
         514-858 -- *Today's Gospel Favorites*

=========================================================

Eleven Eleven Sound                                      February 20, 1991
Nashville                                                        10:00-13:00
Jerry Kennedy (g); David Briggs, Bobby Ogdin (p,kb); Brent Rowan (el g); Larry
Paxton (b); Kenneth Bell, Chip Young (acoustic g); Steve Turner (dm).

98929    WHO DO YOU THINK YOU ARE   (Frank Dycus, Dean Dillon)
106415   _____; SESAC/BMI
         848-370 -- *All-American Country*

=========================================================

Soundshop Recording Studio                               February 24, 1992
Nashville                                                        14:00-17:00
Jerry Kennedy (g); Brent Rowan (el g); Gary Smith (p); Steve Turner (dm); Mark
Casstevens (g); Larry Paxton (el b); David Briggs (p,kb).

114653   THE REST OF MY LIFE   (Don Reid)
         Statler Brothers Music, Inc.; BMI
         OD -- 3/18/92, 14:00-17:00 -- Glen Duncan (f); James Vest (st g).
         512-275 -- *Words & Music*

114653    **A LIFETIME OF LOVING YOU IN VAIN**
          (Don Reid, Debo Reid, Langdon Reid)
          Statler Brothers Music, Inc.; BMI
          512-275 -- *Words & Music*

===============================================================

Soundshop Recording Studio                        February 25, 1992
Nashville                                              14:00-17:00
Jerry Kennedy (g,db); Brent Rowan (el g); Gary Smith (p); Steve Turner (dm);
Mark Casstevens (g); Larry Paxton (el b); David Briggs (p,kb).

114653    **IS IT YOUR PLACE OR MINE**   (Kim Reid)
          Statler Brothers Music, Inc.; BMI
          OD -- 3/18/92, 14:00-17:00 -- Glen Duncan (f), James Vest (st g).
          512-275 -- *Words & Music*

114653    **SAME WAY EVERY TIME**   (Don Reid)
          Statler Brothers Music, Inc.; BMI
          512-275 -- *Words & Music*

114653    **NOBODY LOVES HERE ANYMORE**   (LaDonna Brewer-Capps)
          C B C Music; ASCAP
          OD -- 3/18/92, 14:00-17:00 -- Glen Duncan (f), James Vest (st g).
          512-275 -- *Words & Music*

===============================================================

Soundshop Recording Studio                        February 26, 1992
Nashville                                              14:00-17:00
Jerry Kennedy, Mark Casstevens (acoustic g); Brent Rowan (el g); Pete Wade,
James Capps (acoustic g, el g); Gary Smith (p); Steve Turner (dm); Larry Paxton
(el b); David Briggs (kb).

114653    **TO MAKE A LONG STORY SHORT**   (Wayland Holyfield,
                  Ron Irving, Susan Holden, Larry Wayne Clark)
          April Music, Inc.; BMI / Ides of March Music; ASCAP / Minkey Music;
                  CAPAC / Brainchild Music; CAPAC
          512-275 -- *Words & Music*

114653    **THANK YOU FOR BREAKING MY HEART**   (Jim Martin)
          Sweet Tater Tunes, Inc.; ASCAP
          512-275 -- *Words & Music*

===============================================================

Soundshop Recording Studio                          February 27, 1992
Nashville                                                  14:00-17:00
Jerry Kennedy (acoustic g); Brent Rowan (el g); Gary Smith (p); Steve Turner
(dm); Larry Paxton (el b); James Capps (g).

114653   **HE'S ALWAYS THERE FOR YOU**   (Langdon Reid)
         Statler Brothers Music, Inc.; BMI
         512-275 -- *Words & Music*

════════════════════════════════════════════════════════════════════

Soundshop Recording Studio                             April 13, 1992
Nashville                                                  14:00-17:00
Jerry Kennedy (acoustic g); Mark Casstevens (acoustic g, man-1); Pete Wade (g);
Gary Smith (p); Steve Turner (dm); Larry Paxton (el b); James Capps (g).

114653   **SOME I WROTE**   (Harold Reid, Don Reid)
         American Cowboy Music Co., Inc.; BMI
         Remake of master #2-53195, 5/25/77.
         512-275 -- *Words & Music*

114653   **IT ONLY HURTS FOR A LITTLE WHILE**  -1
         (Mack David, Fred Spielman)
         _____; ASCAP
         512-275 -- *Words & Music*
         3404-2 -- *Statler Bros. Sing the Classics*

════════════════════════════════════════════════════════════════════

Soundshop Recording Studio -- Heartland Project           April 14, 1992
Nashville                                                  14:00-17:00
Jerry Kennedy (g,db); Pete Wade (g); Gary Smith (p); Steve Turner (dm); James
Capps (g); Mark Casstevens (g); Duncan Mullins (b).

120560   **THE OLD RUGGED CROSS** Traditional [George Bennard, 1913]
                  (arr Harold Reid, Don Reid, Jimmy Fortune, Phil Balsley)
         Statler Brothers Music, Inc.; BMI
         HC2012 -- *Statler Bros. Gospel Favorites* (HM)

120560   **PRECIOUS MEMORIES** Traditional [J.B.F. Wright, 1938]
                  (arr Harold Reid, Don Reid, Jimmy Fortune, Phil Balsley)
         Statler Brothers Music, Inc.; BMI
         HC2012 -- *Statler Bros. Gospel Favorites* (HM)

120560   **ROCK OF AGES** Traditional
         [Augustus M. Toplady, 1776; Thomas Hastings, 1830]
                  (arr Harold Reid, Don Reid, Jimmy Fortune, Phil Balsley)
         Statler Brothers Music, Inc.; BMI
         OD -- Strings, date and musicians unknown.
         HC2012 -- *Statler Bros. Gospel Favorites* (HM)

════════════════════════════════════════════════════════════════════

Soundshop Recording Studio -- Heartland Project                    April 15, 1992
Nashville                                                           14:00-17:00
Jerry Kennedy (g,db); Pete Wade (g); Hargus Robbins (p,kb); Steve Turner (dm);
James Capps (g); Mark Casstevens (g); Duncan Mullins (b).

120574    **TURN YOUR RADIO ON**   (Albert E. Brumley)
          Stamps-Baxter Music Co.; BMI
          HC2012 -- *Statler Bros. Gospel Favorites* (HM)

 120574   **LOVE LIFTED ME**   Traditional
          [James Rowe, Howard E. Smith, 1912]
          (Arr by Harold Reid, Don Reid, Jimmy Fortune, Phil Balsley)
          Statler Brothers Music, Inc.; BMI
          HC2012 -- *Statler Bros. Gospel Favorites* (HM)

120574    **NOAH FOUND GRACE IN THE EYES OF THE LORD**
          (Richard Schmertz)
          Ludlow Music, Inc.; BMI
          Remake of master #2-50326.
          HC2012 -- *Statler Bros. Gospel Favorites* (HM)

===============================================================

Soundshop Recording Studio -- Heartland Project                    April 16, 1992
Nashville                                                           14:00-17:00
Jerry Kennedy (g,db); Pete Wade (g); Hargus Robbins (p,kb); Steve Turner (dm);
James Capps (g); Mark Casstevens (g); Duncan Mullins (b); Larry Paxton (b).

120560    **IN THE GARDEN**   Traditional   [C. Austin Miles, 1912]
          (arr - Phil Balsley, Lew DeWitt, Don Reid, Harold Reid)
          Statler Brothers Music, Inc.; BMI
          OD -- Strings, date and musicians unknown.
          Remake of master #2-53198.
          HC2012 -- *Statler Bros. Gospel Favorites* (HM)

120560    **HOW GREAT THOU ART**   (Carl Boberg, 1886.  Translated from the
          original Swedish by Stuart K. Hine, 1949)
          Manna Music, Inc.; ASCAP
          OD -- Strings, date and musicians unknown.
          Remake of master #2-51525.
          HC2012 -- *Statler Bros. Gospel Favorites* (HM)

120560    **JUST A LITTLE TALK WITH JESUS**   (Cleavant Derricks)
          Stamps-Baxter Music, Inc.; BMI
          Remake of master #2-54456.
          HC2012 -- *Statler Bros. Gospel Favorites* (HM)

===============================================================

Eleven Eleven Sound                                April 19, 1993
                                                   14:00-17:00
Jerry Kennedy (g,db); Gary Smith (p); Buddy Spicher (f-1); Weldon Myrick (st g);
Bobby Wray (b); Mark Casstevens (g); Brent Rowan (g); Tommy Wells (dm);
string arr D. Bergen White -2.

522704    **WHAT WE LOVE TO DO**  (Wil Reid, Langdon Reid)  -1  ▶
          Beverly Manor Music; BMI
          OD -- 6/28/93 (Mon), 10:00-13:00 -- Jerry Kennedy (g/db), Hoot Hester
            (f), Hargus Robbins (p,kb), Sonny Garrish (st g, sl db), Roy
            Huskey, Jr. (acoustic b).
          514-744 -- *Home*
          800-633 289-3 -- *What We Love to Do* (video)

522704    **I'VE NEVER LIVED THIS LONG BEFORE**  (Don Reid, Harold Reid)  -2
          Beverly Manor Music; BMI
          OD -- 6/29/93 (Tues), 10:00-13:00 -- Carl Gorodetzky, Lee Larrison,
            Alan Umstead, Laura Molyneaux, David Davidson, David Angell,
            Catherine Umstead, Gary Vanosdale, James Grosjean, Robert
            Mason.
          514-744 -- *Home*

▶  Video produced and directed by Steven Miller and Brad Murano for Film Xero.
Features All-American Band.

===============================================================

Eleven Eleven Sound                                April 20, 1993
                                                   14:00-17:00
Jerry Kennedy (g,db); Gary Smith (p); Mark Casstevens (g); Brent Rowan (g);
Kenny Malone (dm); Larry Paxton (b); string arr by D. Bergen White -1.

522704    **HE'LL ALWAYS HAVE YOU AGAIN**  (Kim Reid)  -1
          Beverly Manor Music; BMI
          OD -- 6/29/93, Strings, see I'VE NEVER LIVED THIS LONG BEFORE,
            4/19/93.
          514-744 -- *Home*

522704    **CHATTANOOGA SHOESHINE BOY**  (Harry Stone, Jack Stapp)
          Acuff-Rose Music, Inc.; BMI
          OD -- 6/28/93 (Mon), 10:00-13:00 -- Jerry Kennedy (g/db); Hargus
            Robbins (p,kb); Sonny Garrish (sl db); Roy Huskey, Jr.
            (acoustic b).
          514-744 -- *Home*
          3404-2 -- *Statler Bros. Sing the Classics*

===============================================================

Eleven Eleven Sound                                    (Thursday) May 20, 1993
                                                                  14:00-17:00
"Girls Next Door" - Doris King, Cindy Nixon Psanos, Diane Williams Foust, and
Tammy Stephens Smith (vo-1); Jerry Kennedy (g,db); Gary Smith (p); Mark
Casstevens (g); Brent Rowan (g); Larry Paxton (b); Steve Turner (dm).

522704   THE ALL-GIRL-ALL-GOSPEL QUARTET   (Don Reid) -1
         Beverly Manor Music; BMI
         OD -- 6/28/93 (Mon), 10:00-13:00 -- Jerry Kennedy (g/db); Hoot Hester
              (f); Hargus Robbins (p,kb); Sonny Garrish (st g, sl db); Roy
              Huskey, Jr. (acoustic b).
         514-744 -- *Home*

522704   DREAM ON   (Don Reid)
         Beverly Manor Music; BMI
         OD -- 6/29/93, Strings, see I'VE NEVER LIVED THIS LONG BEFORE,
              4/19/93.
         514-744 -- *Home*

===============================================================

Eleven Eleven Sound                                      (Friday) May 21, 1993
                                                                  14:00-17:00
Jerry Kennedy (g); Gary Smith (p); Steve Turner (dm); Larry Paxton (b); Mark
Casstevens (g); Brent Rowan (g).

522704   MY PAST IS LOOKING BRIGHTER (ALL THE TIME)
         (Michael Huffman, Gene Dobbins, Bob Morrison)
         _____; ASCAP
         OD -- 6/28/93 (Mon), 10:00-13:00 -- Jerry Kennedy (g); Hargus Robbins
              (p,kb); Sonny Garrish (st g, sl db); Roy Huskey, Jr. (acoustic b).
         OD -- 7/23/93, 10:00-13:00 --
              Jerry Kennedy (g/db); Hargus Robbins (p,kb).
         514-744 -- *Home*

522704   FEELIN' MIGHTY FINE   (Mosie Lister)
         Lilenas Publishing Co.; SESAC
         514-744 -- *Home*

**Note:** The correct title for the song by Mosie Lister is I'M FEELING FINE.

===============================================================

Soundshop Recording Studios                            (Tuesday) June 8, 1993
                                                                  14:00-17:00
Jerry Kennedy, Pete Wade (g); Mark Casstevens (g); Hargus Robbins (p,kb);
Kenny Malone (dm); Sonny Garrish (st g, sl db-1); Bobby Wray (b).

522704   THAT HAUNTED OLD HOUSE   (Wil Reid, Harold Reid)
         Beverly Manor Music; BMI
         514-744 -- *Home*

522704   **CHET, YOU'RE THE REASON** (Don Reid, Debo Reid, Langdon Reid) -1
         Beverly Manor Music; BMI
         OD -- 7/1/93 -- Chet Atkins (g).
         514-744 -- *Home*

===============================================================

Soundshop A Recording Studios                          (Monday) May 1, 1995
Heartland Project                                            14:00-17:00
Jerry Kennedy (g,db); Mark Casstevens (g); Hargus Robbins (p,kb); Gene
Chrisman (dm); James Capps (g); Mike Leech (b).

_____   **HAVE I TOLD YOU LATELY** (Scott Wiseman)
         Duchess Music Corp.
         OD -- 6/5/95, 10:00-13:00 -- Jerry Kennedy (g/db);
              Sonny Garrish (sl db); Glen Duncan (f).
         HM3404 -- *Statler Bros. Sing the Classics*

_____   **LOVE LETTERS** (J. Fred Coots, Nick Kenny, Charles Kenny)
         Toy Town Tunes, Inc./Bourne Co.
         HM3404 -- *Statler Bros. Sing the Classics*

_____   **SHE THINKS I STILL CARE** (Dickey Lee)
         Songs of Polygram Int'l, Inc./ Glad Music Co.
         OD -- 6/5/95, 10:00-13:00 -- Jerry Kennedy (g/db); Sonny Garrish (st g,
              sl db); Glen Duncan (f).
         Remake of Master #2-48584, 11/17/71.
         HM3404 -- *Statler Bros. Sing the Classics*

===============================================================

Soundshop A Recording Studios                          (Tuesday) May 2, 1995
Heartland Project                                            14:00-17:00
Jerry Kennedy (g,db); Mark Casstevens (g); Hargus Robbins (p,kb); Gene
Chrisman (dm); James Capps (g); Mike Leech (b); string arr D. Bergen White -1.

_____   **THE NAUGHTY LADY OF SHADY LANE** -1
              (Sid Tepper, Roy C. Bennett)
         Chappell & Co.
         OD -- 6/6/95, 10:00-13:00; 14:00-17:00 -- Carl Gorodetzky, Pamela
              Sixfin, Lee Larrison, Mary K. Vanosdale, David Davidson, Conni
              Ellisor, Ted Madsen, Alan Umstead, Richard Grosjean, Kristin
              Wilkinson, Robert Mason, John Catchings.
         HM3404 -- *Statler Bros. Sing the Classics*

_____   **MEMORIES ARE MADE OF THIS**
              (Terry Gilkyson, Richard Dehr, Frank Miller)
         EMI Blackwood Music Inc.
         OD -- Wendy Suits and Jeanine Walker (vo), date unknown.

Remake of master #2-56616, 3/30/81.
HM3404 -- *Statler Bros. Sing the Classics*

_____    **UNCHAINED MELODY** (Hy Zaret, Alex North) -1
Frank Music Corp.
OD -- 6/6/95, Strings, see THE NAUGHTY LADY OF SHADY LANE, 5/2/95.
HM3404 -- *Statler Bros. Sing the Classics*

═══════════════════════════════════════════════════════════

Soundshop A Recording Studios                          (Wed.) May 3, 1995
Heartland Project                                        14:00-17:00
Jerry Kennedy (g,db); Mark Casstevens (g, bjo-1); Hargus Robbins (p,kb); Gene
Chrisman (dm); James Capps (g); Mike Leech (b); string arr D. Bergen White -2.

_____    **THE BALLAD OF TOM DOOLEY**    -1
              (Frank Warner, John A. Lomax, Alan Lomax)
TRO-Ludlow Music, Inc.
HM3404 -- *Statler Bros. Sing the Classics*

_____    **LOVE ME TENDER** (Vera Matson, Elvis Presley) -2
Elvis Presley Music, Admin. by R&H Music Co.
OD -- 6/6/95, Strings, see THE NAUGHTY LADY OF SHADY LANE, 5/2/95.
HM3404 -- *Statler Bros. Sing the Classics*

_____    **THE BATTLE OF NEW ORLEANS** (Jimmy Driftwood)
Warden Music, Inc.
-- Rejected --

═══════════════════════════════════════════════════════════

Soundshop A Recording Studios                          (Thurs.) May 4, 1995
Heartland Project                                        14:00-17:00
Jerry Kennedy (g,db); Mark Casstevens (g,bjo-1); Hargus Robbins (p,kb); Gene
Chrisman (dm); James Capps (g); Mike Leech (b); string arr D. Bergen White -2.

_____    **THE BATTLE OF NEW ORLEANS** (Jimmy Driftwood) -1
Warden Music, Inc.
HM3404 -- *Statler Bros. Sing the Classics*

_____    **HE'S GOT THE WHOLE WORLD IN HIS HANDS** (Trad.) -2
              Arr. by Harold Reid, Phil Balsley, Jimmy Fortune, Don Reid
Beverly Manor Music; Admin. by CMI
OD -- 6/6/95, Strings, see THE NAUGHTY LADY OF SHADY LANE, 5/2/95.
HM3404 -- *Statler Bros. Sing the Classics*

_____    **GOODNIGHT SWEETHEART** (Calvin Carter, James Hudson) -2
Arc Music Corp.
OD -- 6/6/95, Strings, see THE NAUGHTY LADY OF SHADY LANE, 5/2/95.
HM3404 -- *Statler Bros. Sing the Classics*

═══════════════════════════════════════════════════════════

Soundshop A Recording Studios                    (Monday) May 22, 1995
Heartland Project                                       14:00-17:00
Jerry Kennedy (g,db); Mark Casstevens (g,man-1); Hargus Robbins (p,kb); Gene
Chrisman (dm); James Capps (g); Mike Leech (b); string arr D. Bergen White -2.

_____     GONE   (Smokey Rogers) -2
            Unichappel Music, Inc./Dallas Music, Admin. by CMI
            OD -- 6/6/95, Strings, see THE NAUGHTY LADY OF SHADY LANE, 5/2/95.
            HM3404 -- *Statler Bros. Sing the Classics*

_____     MAKING BELIEVE   (Jimmy Work) -1
            Acuff-Rose Music, Inc.
            OD -- Glen Duncan (f); Sonny Garrish (st g); date unknown.
            HM3404 -- *Statler Bros. Sing the Classics*

Soundshop A Recording Studios                    (Tuesday) May 23, 1995
Heartland Project                                       14:00-17:00
Jerry Kennedy (g,db); Mark Casstevens (g); Hargus Robbins (p,kb); Gene
Chrisman (dm); James Capps (g); Mike Leech (b); string arr D. Bergen White -1.

_____     I CAN'T STOP LOVING YOU   (Don Gibson)
            Acuff-Rose Music, Inc.
            OD -- Glen Duncan (f); Sonny Garrish (st g); date unknown.
            HM3404 -- *Statler Bros. Sing the Classics*

_____     MOMENTS TO REMEMBER   (Robert Allen, Al Stillman) -1
            Charlie Deitcher Productions, Inc./Larry Spier, Inc.
            OD -- 6/6/95, Strings, see THE NAUGHTY LADY OF SHADY LANE, 5/2/95.
            OD -- Crystal Gayle (vo), date unknown.
            Remake of Master #2-48461, 4/14/71.
            HM3404 -- *Statler Bros. Sing the Classics*

Soundshop A Recording Studios                    (Wednesday) May 24, 1995
Heartland Project                                       14:00-17:00
Jerry Kennedy (g,db); Mark Casstevens (g); Hargus Robbins (p,kb); Gene
Chrisman (dm); James Capps (g); Mike Leech (b); string arr D. Bergen White -1.

_____     BYE BYE LOVE   (Boudleaux Bryant, Felice Bryant)
            House of Bryant Publications
            HM3404 -- *Statler Bros. Sing the Classics*

_____     THE GREAT PRETENDER   (Buck Ram) -1
            Panther Music Corp.
            OD -- 6/6/95, Strings, see THE NAUGHTY LADY OF SHADY LANE, 5/2/95.
            HM3404 -- *Statler Bros. Sing the Classics*

"Stay tuned, Folks,

cause we ain't even

started yet!"

-- Harold Reid

# CHAPTER 5

# Index of Releases

Italics designate a Johnny Cash release. Titles in brackets are flip sides that do not include the Statler Brothers. This is a numerical listing. A Song Title Index is included in this work for ease in locating sessions.

## SINGLES:  45 rpm records & compact discs

### COLUMBIA

4-43069 ........... June 23, 1964
Wreck of the Old '97
Hammer & Nails

4-43146 ......... October 6, 1964
Your Foolish Game
I Still Miss Someone

4-43313 .............. *June, 1965*
*Mister Garfield*
*The Streets of Laredo*

4-43315 ........... June 14, 1965
Billy Christian
Flowers on the Wall

4-43342 .............. *July, 1965*
*The Sons of Katie Elder*
*A Certain Kinda Hurtin'*

4-43420 ........... *October, 1965*
*Happy to Be with You*
*[Pickin' Time]*

4-43526 ......... January 31, 1966
The Doodlin' Song
My Darling Hildegarde

4-43624 ............ May 16, 1966
The Right One
Is That What You'd Have Me Do

4-43868 ......... October 17, 1966
That'll Be the Day
Makin' Rounds

4-44011 .......... *February, 1967*
[Jackson]
Pack Up Your Sorrows

4-44070 ............ April 3, 1967
Ruthless
Do You Love Me Tonight

4-44245 ............ July 25, 1967
You Can't Have Your Kate
        & Edith, Too
Walking in the Sunshine

4-44288 ......... *September, 1967*
[Red Velvet]
The Wind Changes

4-44480 .......... March 19, 1968
Jump for Joy
Take a Bow Rufus Humfry

4-44608 ........ September 3, 1968
I'm the Boy
Sissy

4-44689 ......... *November, 1968*
*Daddy Sang Bass*
*He Turned the Water Into Wine*

4-33134 ....... December 17, 1968
Flowers on the Wall
Ruthless

4-44899 ............ May 29, 1969
How Great Thou Art
Oh Happy Day

4-33153 .............. *May, 1969*
*Hall of Fame Series*
*[Folsom Prison Blues-Live]*
*Daddy Sang Bass*

4-45211 .............. *July, 1970*
*[Sunday Mornin Coming Down]*
*I'm Gonna Try to Be That Way*

4-45786 ............. *April, 1973*
[Children]
The Last Supper

+-------------------------------+
|           **MERCURY**         |
+-------------------------------+

73141 .......... September, 1970
Bed of Roses
The Last Goodbye

73194 .............. March, 1971
This Part of the World
New York City

73229 ................ July, 1971
Pictures
Making Memories

73253 .......... November, 1971
You Can't Go Home
Second Thoughts

73275 ............ February, 1972
Do You Remember These
Since Then

73315 ................ July, 1972
The Class of '57
Every Time I Trust a Gal

73360 ............. January, 1973
Monday Morning Secretary
A Special Song for Wanda

73392 ............... May, 1973
Woman without a Home
I'll Be Your Baby Tonight

73415 ............. August, 1973
Carry Me Back
I Wish I Could Be

55057 . . . . . . . . . . . . . . March, 1979
How to Be a Country Star
A Little Farther Down the Road

55066 . . . . . . . . . . . . . . June, 1979
Here We Are Again
Mr. Autry

57007 . . . . . . . . . . . . . October, 1979
Nothing As Original As You
Counting My Memories

57012 . . . . . . . . . . . . . January, 1980
Better Than I Did Then
Almost in Love

57031 . . . . . . . . . . . . . June, 1980
Charlotte's Web
One Less Day to Go

57037 . . . . . . . . . . . . October, 1980
Don't Forget Yourself
We Got Paid by Cash

57048 . . . . . . . . . . . . February, 1981
How Are Things in Clay,
    Kentucky?
In the Garden

57051 . . . . . . . . . . . . . . May, 1981
Chet Atkins' Hand
Don't Wait on Me

57059 . . . . . . . . . . September, 1981
Years Ago
Dad

811 488-7 . . . . . . . . March 29, 1983
Oh Baby Mine
I'm Dyin' a Little Each Day

812 988-7 . . . . . . . . . . July 26, 1983
Guilty
I Never Want to Kiss You
    Goodbye

814 881-7 . . . . . . . November, 1983
Elizabeth
The Class of '57 (master #49794)

818 700-7 . . . . . . . . . . March, 1984
Atlanta Blue
If It Makes Any Difference

868 140-7/4 . . . . . February 22, 1991
Remember Me
My Music, My Memories & You

868-484-7 . . . . . . . . . . May 28, 1991
You've Been Like a Mother to
    Me  (2/6/91)
Jesus Is the Answer

868 892-7 . . . . . . . . August 9, 1991
There's Still Times
Elizabeth

870 164-7 . . . . . . . . . January, 1988
The Best I Know How
I Lost My Heart to You

870 442-7 . . . . . . . . . . . May, 1988
Am I Crazy
Beyond Romance

870 681-7 . . . . . . . September, 1988
Let's Get Started If We're Gonna
    Break My Heart
Guilty

872 604-7 . . . . . . . . . January, 1989
Moon Pretty Moon
I'll Be the One

874 196-7 . . . . . . . . . . . April, 1989
More Than a Name on a Wall
Atlanta Blue

875 112-7/4 . . . . . . October 13, 1989
A Hurt I Can't Handle - LIVE
Don't Wait on Me - LIVE w/intro

## DJ Releases

DJ-577 . . . . . . . . . November, 1982
-- *Extended Play*
    I Never Spend a Christmas
    Jingle Bells
    Away in a Manger
    The Carols Those Kids Used to
        Sing

MEPL-11 . . . . . . . . . . . . . . . . . . . . . .
    Open End Interview
    Since Then
    I'll Take Care of You

MEPL-25 . . . . . . . . . . . . . . . . . . . . . .
    When My Blue Moon Turns to
        Gold
    The Saturday Morning Radio
        Show
    1953-Dear John-Honky Tonk
        Blues

PRO 448-7 . . . . . . . September, 1986
    There Is Power in the Blood

PRO 562-7 . . . . . . . . . October, 1987
    Maple Street Memories

PRO 736-7 . . . . . . . . . . . . . . . . . . . . .
    Interview w/Statler Brothers &
        Jerry Kennedy

PRO 750-7 . . . . . . . September, 1989
    Don't Wait on Me - Live w/intro
    Don't Wait on Me - Edited
        version.
*Note: Label reads "US★99 10-In-A-*
*Row Country, Commemorative*
*Edition"*

SRD-50 . . . . . . . . . . . . . . . . . . . . . . .
    Maggie

---

## MERCURY
## Celebrity Country Series

CC-34030 . . . . . . . . . . . . . . . . . . . . .
    Bed of Rose's
    Pictures

CC-35035 . . . . . . . . . . . . . . . . . . . . .
    Do You Remember These
    The Class of '57

CC-35038 . . . . . . . . . . January, 1977
    I'll Go to My Grave Loving You
    Your Picture in the Paper

CC-35042 . . . . . . . November, 1978
    Do You Know You Are My
        Sunshine
    Who Am I to Say

## Long-Play Albums

Italics --Johnny Cash Releases, titles shown here are the ones on which the Statlers appear.

Gold album - 500,000 units sold; Platinum album - 1,000,000 units sold. A unit is one LP, cassette tape, 8-track tape, or compact disc.

\* Anthology albums, compilation of several artists.

---

### COLUMBIA

CL-2231/CS-9031
**Kentucky Derby Day\***
Hammer & Nails

C30324/CA30324
**Country Hymns\***
Church in the Wildwood

AE2-1018
**Hall of Fame, Vol. III**
Flowers on the Wall

CL-2309/CS-9109
*Orange Blossom Special*
Amen

DL6420/DS6420
*Sons of Katie Elder*
Sons of Katie Elder

C2L38/C2S838
*Ballads of the True West*
A Letter from Home

CL-2446/CS-9246 *Mean As Hell*
A Letter from Home
Twenty-five Minutes to Go
Stampede

KCS9726 *The Holy Land*
Land of Israel
Nazarene
Town of Cana
He Turned the Water Into Wine
Beautiful Words
The Ten Commandments
Daddy Sang Bass
Come to the Wailing Wall
The Fourth Man

KC-30100 *The Johnny Cash Show*
There Ain't No Easy Run
These Hands
I'm Gonna Try to Be That Way
Detroit City

KC30887
*The Johnny Cash Collection*
Daddy Sang Bass

KC31754
*Johnny Cash Family Christmas*
King of Love
Merry Christmas Mary
Old Fashioned Tree (Lew DeWitt)

C-32240
*Sunday Morning Coming Down*
I'm Gonna Try to Be That Way

KG32253 *The Gospel Road*
I See Men as Trees Walking

Blessed Are
The Lord's Prayer/Amen Chorus
Feast of the Passover
Lord, Is It I?
The Last Supper
Ascension/Amen Chorus

C-10777 *Johnny Cash & Friends*
Daddy Sang Bass

CL-2449/CS-9249 . . January 3, 1966
**Flowers on the Wall**
Flowers on the Wall
My Darling Hildegarde
King of the Road
Memphis
I'm Not Quite Through Crying
My Reward
This Ole House
Billy Christian
The Doodlin' Song
Quite a Long, Long Time
The Whiffenpoof Song
I Still Miss Someone

CL-2537/CS-9337 *Happiness Is You*
Happiness Is You
Guess Things Happen That Way
She Came from the Mountains
Happy to Be With You

CL-2719/CS-9519; PCT9519
**SB Sing the Big Hits**
. . . . . . . . . . . . . . . . . . Aug. 28, 1967
Ruthless
You Can't Have Your
    Kate & Edith, Too
Release Me (And Let Me
    Love Again)
Walking in the Sunshine
Funny, Familiar, Forgotten
    Feelings
Ruby, Don't Take Your
    Love to Town

Green, Green Grass of Home
There Goes My Everything
Almost Persuaded
I Can't Help It (If I'm Still in
    Love With You)
Shenandoah

CL-2728/CS-9528
*Carryin' on With Cash & Carter*
Pack Up Your Sorrows
    (Phil Balsley, only.)

CS-9878 . . . . . . . . . . . June 25, 1969
**Oh Happy Day**
Oh Happy Day
How Great Thou Art
King of Love
Are You Washed in the Blood
Pass Me Not
Daddy Sang Bass
Less of Me
Things God Gave
Led Out
Just in Time
Fourth Man

CG31557 . . . . . . . . . . July 26, 1972
**The World of the Statler
    Brothers**
Flowers on the Wall
King of the Road
Memphis
I'm Not Quite Through Cryin'
My Reward
This Ole House
Billy Christian
Quite a Long, Long Time
The Whiffenpoof Song
I Still Miss Someone
Shenandoah
Ruthless
Green, Green Grass of Home
Release Me
Walking in the Sunshine
Ruby, Don't Take Your
    Love to Town

You Can't Have Your Kate
   & Edith, Too
There Goes My Everything
Almost Persuaded
I Can't Help It

BT 16554
**Always Here**
Funny, Familiar Forgotten
   Feelings
My Darling Hildegarde
Memphis
How Great Thou Art
Flowers on the Wall
The Doodlin' Song
Quite a Long, Long Time
Daddy Sang Bass

BT 16745
**Best of the Statler Brothers**
Flowers on the Wall
Ruby, Don't Take Your Love to
   Town
There Goes My Everything
I'm Not Quite Through Crying
Green, Green Grass of Home
King of the Road
Do You Love Me Tonight
This Ole House

BT24276
**How Great Thou Art**
This Ole House
King of Love
Daddy Sang Bass
Hammer & Nails
Oh Happy Day
Less of Me
Are You Washed
Pass Me Not
Things God Gave Me
How Great Thou Art

A18491 . . . . . . . . . . CD only, 1993
**Oh, Happy Day** --
Flowers on the Wall
King of the Road
Ruby, Don't Take Your Love to
   Town
Green, Green Grass of Home
I'm Not Quite Through Cryin'
There Goes My Everything
That'll Be the Day
Daddy Sang Bass
This Ole House
Oh, Happy Day

A24362 . . . . . . . . . . CD only, 1993
**The Statler Brothers/**
**The Oak Ridge Boys**
How Great Thou Art
This Ole House
Oh Happy Day
King of Love
Daddy Sang Bass

CWS2
**Welcome to Columbia Country***
Ruthless

CK-64764 . . . . . . . . . . March, 1996
**Flowers on the Wall:  The**
**Essential Statler Brothers**
**1964-1969**
        Columbia Legacy Series
Wreck of the Old '97  [sic]
Hammers & Nails
I Still Miss Someone
Flowers on the Wall
This Ole House
My Darling Hildegarde
Green Grass
The Right One
That'll Be the Day
Half a Man
Ruthless
Shenandoah

You Can't Have Your Kate &
    Edith, Too
Jump for Joy
Sissy
I'm the Boy
Less of Me
Oh Happy Day

STS 2004
Columbia Star Series
    *The Heart of Johnny Cash* --
The Sons of Katie Elder
A Certain Kinda Hurtin'
Happiness Is You

## HARMONY
### Columbia Budget Series

HL-7414 Kentucky Derby Day*
    Hammer & Nails

HS-11214
America's Greatest Country Stars
        Live & in Person*
    Same as: HL-7414

H-30610 . . . . . . . . . . April 19, 1971
        **Big Country Hits**
    Flowers on the Wall
    King of the Road
    Green, Green Grass of Home
    Ruby, Don't Take Your
        Love to Town
    Walking in the Sunshine
    Daddy Sang Bass
    Almost Persuaded
    I Can't Help It
    Oh Happy Day

KH-30916 *Understand Your Man*
    A Certain Kinda Hurtin'

KH-31256 *Give My Love to Rose*
    Pack Up Your Sorrows
    (Phil Balsley, only.)

K-31325 -- ROY ACUFF,
JOHNNY HORTON, STATLER
BROTHERS & LIL' JIMMY
DICKENS TOGETHER*
    Daddy Sang Bass
    Memphis
    Billy Christian

KH-31570 . . . . . . . August 30, 1972
    **How Great Thou Art**
    Oh Happy Day
    How Great Thou Art
    King of Love
    Are You Washed in the Blood
    Things God Gave Me
    Just in Time
    Led Out of Bondage
    The Fourth Man
    Pass Me Not
    Less of Me

KH-31602
    *The Johnny Cash Songbook*
    I'm Gonna Try to Be That Way

P2-13048  **Country Thunder***
    Class of '57

P2-13429
    **Gospel's Top 20--The All Time
        Favorites***
    Church in the Wildwood

DS-365
    **30 Great Hits by 30 Great
        Country Artists***
    Release Me

C 10779
    **Hymns of Gold**
        (Columbia Special Products)
    Are You Washed in the Blood

P 12620  **Hymns of Gold, Vol. II**
    (Columbia Special Products)
    Oh, Happy Day

KH-32256 . . . . . . . . . May 25, 1973
    **Do You Love Me Tonight**
    **& Other Favorites**
    That'll Be the Day
    Hammers & Nails
    Green Grass
    The Right One
    Do You Love Me Tonight
    Is That What You'd Have Me Do
    I'm the Boy
    Makin' Rounds
    Half a Man
    Staunton, VA

## European Releases

BFX-15030 *Johnny and June*
    Thunderball

BFX-15033 *Tall Man*
    Rodeo Hand

**Abbreviations Used**
LPR - LP album reissue
CS - cassette
CSR - cassette reissue
8T - stereo 8 track tape
CD - compact disc

## MERCURY

SRM-61317 . . . . . . . . Dec. 15, 1970
    **Bed of Rose's**
8T - MC-8-61317
LPR - ML-8005  (Apr. 1, 1981)
LPR - 826-247-1 (Feb. 13, 1986)
CSR - ML4-8005  (Apr. 1, 1981)
CSR - 826-247-4  (Feb. 13, 1986)
    Bed of Rose's
    New York City
    All I Have to Offer You Is Me
    Neighborhood Girl
    Fifteen Years Ago
    The Junkie's Prayer
    We
    This Part of the World
    Tomorrow Never Comes
    Me and Bobby McGee
    The Last Goodbye

SRM-61349 . . . . . . . . Aug. 20, 1971
    **Pictures of Moments**
    **to Remember**
CS - MCR-4-61349 (Aug. 20, 1971)
8T - MC-8-61349  (Aug. 20, 1971)
    Pictures
    Moments to Remember
    Second Thoughts
    Just Someone I Used to Know
    I Wonder How the Old Folks
      Are at Home
    Things
    You Can't Go Home
    Tender Years
    Making Memories
    Faded Love
    When You and I Were
      Young, Maggie

SRM-61358 . . . . . . . . . . April, 1972
**Innerview**
CS - MCR-4-61358
8T - MCR-8-61358
LPR - 826-259-1 (Feb. 13, 1986)
CSR - 826-259-4 (Feb. 13, 1986)
 Do You Remember These
 I'd Rather Be Sorry
 Everyday Will Be Sunday, Bye
  & Bye
 She Thinks I Still Care
 Got Leavin' on Her Mind
 I'll Take Care of You
 Take Me Home Country Roads
 Daddy
 Never Ending Song of Love
 A Different Song
 Since Then

SR-61367 . . . . . . . . . . . . . . . . 1972
**Country Music Then & Now**
CS - MCR-4-61367
8T - MC-8-61367
CSR - 810-461-4S (Mar. 14, 1983)
LPR - 826-260-1 (Feb. 13, 1986)
CSR - 826-260-4 (Feb. 13, 1986)
 When My Blue Moon Turns to
  Gold
 No One Will Ever Know
 Saturday Morning Radio Show
 Class of '57
 A Stranger in My Place
 Jesus, Take Another Look at Me
 1953-Dear John-Honky Tonk
  Blues
 Under It All
 Every Time I Trust a Gal

SR-61374 . . . . . . . . . . Dec. 15, 1972
**Statler Brothers Sing**
**Country Symphonies in E Major**
CS - MCR-4-61374
8T - MC-8-61374
CSR - 518-940-4 (March 22, 1994)
CD - 518-940-2 (March 22, 1994)

 Monday Morning Secretary
 Burning Bridges
 I Wanna Carry Your
  Sweet Memories
 I Believe in Music
 A Special Song for Wanda
 I'll Be Your Baby Tonight
 Woman Without a Home
 Delta Dawn
 Wedding Bells
 Too Many Rivers
 They Can't Take You Out of Me

SRM-1676 . . . . . . . . . Sept. 1, 1973
**Carry Me Back**
CS - MCR-4-1-676
8T - MC-8-1-676
LPR - 812-264-1 (Feb. 13, 1986)
 Carry Me Back
 The Woman I Still Love
 What Do I Care
 If We Never Had
 Take Good Care of Her
 The Streets of San Francisco
 Whatever Happened to
  Randolph Scott
 I Wish I Could Be
 We Owe It All to Yesterday
 When I Stop Dreaming
 The Strand

SRM-1692 . . . . . . . . . . May 13, 1974
 Jerry Kennedy & Friends
 Rollin' in My Sweet Baby's Arms

SRM-1-707 . . . . . . . . . . . . . . 1974
**Thank You, World**
CS - MCR-4-1-707 (8-21-81)
8T - MC-8-1-707
 Thank You, World
 City Lights
 Sweet Charlotte Ann
 Left-Handed Woman
 The Blackwood Brothers
  by the Statler Brothers

Cowboy Buckaroo
She's Too Good
Baptism of Jesse Taylor, The
Streets of Baltimore
Margie's at the Lincoln Park Inn
Boy Inside of Me

SRM-1-708 ............... 1974
**Alive at Johnny Mack**
**Brown High School**
CS - MCR-4-1-708
CSR - 518-944-4 [May 1994]*
8T - MC-8-1-708
CD - 518-944-2 [May 1994]*
Lester "Roadhog" Moran &
    the Cadillac Cowboys
*Alive at the Johnny Mack Brown*
    *High School*
    Little Liza Jane
    Hey Joe
    Filipino Baby
    Sixteen Tons
    Rubber Dolly
    Wildwood Flower/Keep on
        the Sunny Side/Waterloo
*The Saturday Morning Radio Show*
    *No. 2*
    Freight Train
    He'll Have to Go
    Hello Darlin'/Hello Walls/Funny
        How Time Slips Away
    Church in the Wildwood
*Rainbow Valley Confidential*
    *Audition Tape*
*Contains two additions, see 518-944.

SRM-1-1019 ....... Dec. 15, 1974
**Sons of the Motherland**
CS - MCR-4-1-1019
8T - MC-8-1-1019
    All American Girl
    A Letter from Shirley Miller
    A Few Old Memories
    You Can't Judge a Book by Its
        Cover

Together
Susan When She Tried
You've Been Like a Mother to
    Me
Eight More Miles to Louisville
One More Summer in Virginia
I'll Be Here
So Mary Could Make It Home

SRM-1-1037 ......... July 7, 1975
**Best of the Statler Brothers**
CS - MCR-4-1-1037
8T - MC-8-1-1037
LPR - 822-524-1 (May, 1987)
CSR - 822-524-4 (May, 1987)
CD - 822-524-2  (Oct., 1987)
    Bed of Rose's
    Whatever Happened to
        Randolph Scott
    Do You Remember These
    Carry Me Back
    Flowers on the Wall
    Class of '57, The
    I'll Go to My Grave Loving You
    Pictures
    Thank You, World
    New York City
    Susan When She Tried
**GOLD ALBUM -- 1977**
**PLATINUM -- 1978**
**DOUBLE PLATINUM -- 1980**
**TRIPLE PLATINUM -- 1995**

SRM-1-1051 ............... 1975
**The Holy Bible--Old Testament**
LPR - 826 267-1 - (Feb. 13, 1986)
CS - MCR-4-1-1051
8T - MC-8-1-1051
CD - 826-267-2 (Oct. 17, 1983)
    In the Beginning
    Eve
    Noah Found Grace in
        the Eyes of the Lord
    Have a Little Faith
    The Dreamer

The King Is Coming
Led Out of Bondage
The Ten Commandments
Samson
Song of David
Song of Solomon
The Fourth Man
**GOLD ALBUM -- 1995**

SRM-1-1052 . . . . . . . . . . . . . . 1975
**The Holy Bible --New Testament**
LPR - 826 268-1 (Feb. 13, 1986)
CS - MCR-4-1-1052
8T - MC-8-1-1052
CD - 826-268-2 (Sept. 6, 1988)
    Who Do You Think?
    The Kingdom of Heaven Is at
       Hand
    Beat the Devil
    The Brave Apostles Twelve
    The Teacher
    The Lord's Prayer
    There's a Man in Here
    How Great Thou Art
    Lord, Is It I?
    The King of Love
    The King Is Coming
**GOLD ALBUM -- 1993**

SRM-2-2101 . . . . . . . . . . . . . . 1975
**The Holy Bible**
**Old & New Testaments**
LPR - 826 264-1 (Feb. 14, 1986)
CS - MCR-4-2-2101
8T - MC-8-2-2101
CSR - 826-264-4 (Sept. 30, 1979)
    [SRM1-1051 and SRM1-1052
    combined.]

SRM-1-1077 . . . . . . March 19, 1976
**Harold, Lew, Phil & Don**
CS - MCR-4-1-1077  (Mar. 19, 1976)
8T - MC-8-1-1077  (Mar. 19, 1976)
LPR - 826-691-1  (July 18, 1988)
CSR - 826-269-4  (July 18, 1988)

Your Picture in the Paper
All the Times
Maggie
Virginia
I've Been Everywhere
Amanda
A Friend's Radio
Something I Haven't Done Yet
Times We Had, The
Would You Recognize Jesus?
The Statler Brothers Quiz

SRM-1-1125 . . . . . . January 7, 1977
**The Country America Loves**
CS - MCR-4-1-1125  (Jan. 7, 1977)
8T - MC-8-1-1175  (Jan. 7, 1977)
LPR - 826-275-1  (July 18, 1988)
CSR - 826-275-4  (July 18, 1988)
    Movies, The
    Let It Show
    All I Can Do
    You Could Be Coming to Me
    Hat and Boots
    I Was There
    Thank God I've Got You
    Blue Eyes Cryin' in the Rain
    Somebody New Will Be
       Coming Along
    You Comb Her Hair Every
       Morning
    Couple More Years, A

SRM-1-1173/SRM-1-5001
**Short Stories** -- 1977
LPR - 8260280-1 - (July 18, 1988)
CS - MCR-4-1-5001
CSR - 826-280-4 (July 18, 1988)
8T - MC-8-1-5001
    Silver Medals & Sweet
       Memories
    Regular Saturday Nite
       Setback Card Game
    That Summer
    He Went to the Cross Loving
       You

Quite a Long, Long Time
Carried Away
Star, The
Grandma
Different Things to
    Different People
Give My love to Rose
Some I Wrote

SRM-1-5007 . . . . . . March 13, 1978
**Entertainers . . . On**
**& Off the Record**
CS-MCR-4-1-5007 (March 13, 1978)
8T - MC-8-1-5007 (March 13, 1978)
LPR - 812-283-1 (May 12, 1983)
CSR - 812-283-4 (May 12, 1983)
CD - 812-283-2 (March 22, 1994)
    Yours Love
    The Best That I Can Do
    You're the First
    Tomorrow Is Your Friend
    The Official Historian on
        Shirley Jean Berrell
    Who Am I to Say?
    I Forgot More Than
        You'll Ever Know
    When You Are Sixty-Five
    I Dreamed About You
    Before the Magic Turns to
Memory
**GOLD ALBUM -- 1978**

SRM-1-5012 . . . . . . . . . Sept. 1978
**SB Christmas Card**
CS - MCR-4-1-5012 (Sept. 1978)
8T - MC-8-1-5012 (Sept. 1978)
LPR - 822-743-1
CSR - 822-743-4
CD - 822-743-2 (Sept. 1988)
    I Believe in Santa's Cause
    I'll Be Home for Christmas
    Jingle Bells
    I Never Spend a Christmas
        that I Don't Think of You
    White Christmas

Christmas to Me
Who Do You Think?
Away in a Manger
Something You Can't Buy
Carols Those Kids Used to Sing,
    The
Christmas Medley, A (Silent
    Night-O Holy Night-First
    Noel-It Came Upon a
    Midnight Clear)
**GOLD ALBUM -- 1982**
**PLATINUM ALBUM -- 1993**

SRM-1-5016 . . . . . . March 29, 1979
**The Originals**
CS - MCR-4-1-5016 (March, 1979)
8T - MC-8-1-5016 (March, 1979)
CSR - 826 281-4 (July 18, 1988)
    How to Be a Country Star
    When the Yankees Came Home
    Here We Are Again
    Where He Always Wanted to Be
    Mr. Autry
    Nothing As Original As You
    Counting My Memories
    A Little Farther Down the Road
    Just a Little Talk With Jesus
    Almost in Love
    Star-Spangled Banner, The
**GOLD ALBUM -- 1981**

SRM-1-5024 . . . . . . . Dec. 31, 1979
**The Best of the Statler Brothers**
**Rides Again, Vol. II**
LPR - 822 525-1 (May 4, 1987)
CS - MCR-4-1-5024 (Dec. 31, 1979)
CSR - 822 525-4 - (May 4, 1987)
8T - MC-8-1-5024 (Dec. 31, 1979)
CD - 822 525-2 (Nov. 21, 1989)
    Do You Know You Are My
        Sunshine
    Here We Are Again
    Movies, The
    Your Picture in the Paper
    Some I Wrote

How Great Thou Art
(I'll Even Love You) Better Than
     I Did Then
How to Be a Country Star
Silver Medals & Sweet
     Memories
Who Am I to Say
Official Historian on Shirley
     Jean Berrell, The
**GOLD ALBUM -- 1981**

SRM-1-5027 ........ July 24, 1980
     **Tenth Anniversary**
CS - MCR-4-1-5027  (July 24, 1980)
8T - MC-8-1-5027   (July 24, 1980)
LPR - 812-282-1  (Feb. 13, 1986)
CSR - 812-282-4  (May 12, 1983)
CD -  812-282-2  (March 22, 1994)
     Don't Forget Yourself
     The Kid's Last Fight
     How Are Things in Clay,
          Kentucky?
     One Less Day to Go
     Nobody Wants to Be Country
     We Got Paid by Cash
     Old Cheerleaders Cry
     'Til the End
     Nobody's Darlin' But Mine
     Charlotte's Web
**GOLD ALBUM -- 1995**

SRM-1-6002 ........ June 18, 1981
     **Years Ago**
CS - MCR-4-1-6002  (June 18, 1981)
8T - MC-8-1-6002   (June 18, 1981)
CSR - 826-282-4  (March 22, 1994)
CD - 826-282-2  (March 22, 1994)
     Don't Wait on Me
     Today I Went Back
     In the Garden
     Chet Atkins' Hand
     You'll Be Back (Every Night
          in My Dreams)
     Years Ago
     Love Was All We Had

We Ain't Even Started Yet
Dad
Memories Are Made of This

SRM-4048 ......... June 10, 1982
     **The Legend goes on ...**
CS - MCR-4-1-4048  (June 10, 1982)
8T - MC-8-1-4048   (June 10, 1982)
LPR - 826-278-1   (July 18, 1988)
CSR - 826-278-4   (July 18, 1988)
     Whatever
     I Had Too Much to Dream
     I Don't Know Why
     Life's Railway to Heaven
     How Do You Like Your
          Dream So Far
     A Child of the Fifties
     That's When It Comes Home to
          You
     I Don't Dance No More
     What You Are to Me
     (I'll Love You) All Over Again

*Here the Mercury numbering system
changes. The first six digits are the
release number, the last digits (-1,-2,-
4) designate LP (-1), compact disc
(-2), cassette (-4). Multiple forms are
shown as -1/4, or -2/4.*

812-184-1/4 ............... 1983
     **Today**
     Oh, Baby Mine (I Get So
          Lonely)
     Some Memories Last Forever
     Promise
     I'm Dyin' a Little Each Day
     There Is You
     Guilty
     Elizabeth
     Right on the Money
     I Never Want to Kiss You
          Goodbye

Sweet By and By
**GOLD ALBUM -- 1993**
_____

818-652-1/4 . . . . . . . . . . . . . . . 1984
**Atlanta Blue**
CD - 818-652-2 (Nov. 21, 1989)
Reissued - Oct, 5, 1987
    Atlanta Blue
    If It Makes Any Difference
    (Let's Just) Take One
        Night at a Time
    Angel in Her Face
    ★Holly★Wood★
    One Takes the Blame
    Give It Your Best
    No Love Lost
    One Size Fits All
    My Only Love
**GOLD ALBUM -- 1995**
_____

824-420-1/4 . . . . . . . . . . April,1985
**Pardners in Rhyme**
CD - 824-420-2 (Nov. 21, 1989)
Reissued - Oct. 5, 1987
    Hello, Mary Lou
    Sweeter and Sweeter
    Memory Lane
    Remembering You
    Too Much on My Heart
    I'm Sorry You Had to Be the One
    Her Heart or Mine
    You Don't Wear Blue So Well
    Autumn Leaves
    Amazing Grace
**GOLD ALBUM -- 1995**
_____

824-785-1/4 . . . . . . . Sept. 23, 1985
**Christmas Present**
824-785-2 (Nov. 25, 1985
    Christmas Eve (Kodia's Theme)
    Christmas Country Style
    Brahms' Bethlehem Lullaby
    Somewhere in the Night
    An Old Fashioned Christmas
    No Reservation at the Inn

    Mary's Sweet Smile
    Whose Birthday Is Christmas
    Old Toy Trains
    For Momma
_____

826-782-1/4 . . . . . . . . . . May, 1986
**Four for the Show**
Reissued - (-1, -4) July 18, 1988
CD - 826-782-2 (Nov. 21, 1989)
    Count on Me
    You Oughta Be Here with Me
    We Got the Mem'ries
    I Don't Dream Anymore
    Forever
    Only You
    For Cryin' Out Loud
    Will You Be There?
    I Believe I'll Live for Him
    More Like Daddy Than Me
_____

826-710-1 . . . . . . . . Sept. 15, 1986
**Radio Gospel Favorites**
CD - 826-710-2 (August 15, 1988)
CS - 826-710-4 (July 9, 1990)
    There Is Power in the Blood
    We Won't Be Home Until Then
    One Size Fits All
    Sweet By And By
    I Believe I'll Live for Him
    A Different Story
    Blessed Be
    A Beautiful Life
    Amazing Grace
    Over the Sunset Mountains
**GOLD ALBUM -- 1993**
_____

832-404-1 . . . . . . . . . July 20, 1987
**Maple Street Memories**
CS - 832-404-4 (Sept. 25, 1990)
CD - 832-404-2 (Sept. 25, 1990)
    Our Street/Tell Me Why
    Maple Street Mem'ries
    Deja Vu
    Am I Crazy
    The Best I Know How

I'll Be the One
Beyond Romance
I Lost My Heart to You
Jesus Showed Me So

834-626-1/2/4 . . . . . . . Oct. 3, 1988
**The Greatest Hits, Vol. III**
Let's Get Started If We're
    Gonna Break My Heart
Elizabeth
Count on Me
Best I Know How, The
Moon Pretty Moon
More Than a Name on a Wall
Guilty
My Only Love
I'll Be the One
Atlanta Blue

838-231-1/2/4 . . . . . . . Oct. 3, 1989
**Live and Sold Out**
Official Historian of Shirley
    Jean Berrell, The
A Hurt I Can't Handle
Bed of Rose's
Foggy Mountain Breakdown
    (Band)
When the Roll Is Called Up
    Yonder
I'll Fly Away
Walking Heartache in Disguise
Tomorrow Never Comes
Don't Wait on Me
I'll Go to My Grave Loving You
This Ole House

842-518-2/4 . . . . . . . . June 19, 1990
**Music, Memories and You**
Small, Small World
Nobody Else
Jealous Eyes
Holding On
Think of Me
You Gave Yourself Away
I Never Once Got Tired of You

What's on My Mind
He Is There
My Music, My Memories and
    You

848-370-2/4 . . . . . . . . . . . June, 1991
**All-American Country**
Remember Me
Dynamite
Everything You See in Your
    Dreams
Who Do You Think You Are
There's Still Times
Put It on the Card
If I'd Paid More Attention to You
Jesus Is the Answer Every Time
Fallin' in Love
You've Been Like a Mother to
    Me

512-275-2/4 . . . . . . . . . Aug.18, 1992
**Words and Music**
To Make a Long Story Short
It Only Hurts for a Little While
Lifetime of Loving You in Vain
Rest of My Life, The
Some I Wrote
Nobody Loves Here Anymore
Same Way Every Time
Is It Your Place or Mine
He's Always There for You
Thank You for Breaking My
    Heart

514-858-4 . . . . . . . . . June 22, 1993
**Today's Gospel Favorites**
Turn Your Radio On
A Different Song
Blessed Be
Love Lifted Me
Jesus Is the Answer Every Time
Just a Little Talk with Jesus
Precious Memories
Rock of Ages
I Believe I'll Live for Him

I'll Fly Away
**GOLD ALBUM -- 1995**

514-744-2/4 . . . . . . . . Oct. 25, 1993
**Home**
Dream On
The All-Girl-All-Gospel Quartet
Chattanooga Shoe Shine Boy
He'll Always Have You Again
Feeling Mighty Fine
My Past Is Looking Brighter
    (All the Time)
That Haunted Old House
Chet, You're the Reason
I've Never Lived This Long
    Before
What We Love to Do


518-944-4 . . . . . . . . . . . May, 1994
**The Complete Lester "Roadhog"**
**Moran & the Cadillac Cowboys**
The Saturday Morning Radio
    Show
Alive at the Johnny Mack Brown
    High School
Saturday Morning Radio Show #2
Rainbow Valley Confidential
    Audition Tape
Interview with Ralph Emery
    (4-1-74)**
Phone-in interview with Ralph
    Emery on WSM Radio (6-5-
    75)**
**Not included on original release,
SRM-1-1708.


518-945 Package -- . . . . May, 1994
 **The Statler Brothers'**
 **30ᵗʰ Anniversary Celebration** --
    includes 518-944-4; 518-946-4;
    518-947-4; and 518-948-4.
    -------------
518-946-4  Tape One
Flowers on the Wall
Ruthless

You Can't Have Your Kate
    & Edith Too
Bed of Roses [sic]
Do You Remember These
Class of '57
Woman Without a Home
Carry Me Back
Whatever Happened to
    Randolph Scott
Thank You World
Susan When She Tried
I'll Go to My Grave Loving You
Your Picture in the Paper
The Movies
Silver Medals
That Summer
Some I Wrote
Do You Know You Are My
    Sunshine
Who Am I to Say
The Official Historian on
    Shirley Jean Berrell
How to Be a Country Star
(I'll Even Love You) Better
    Than I Did Then
    --------------
518-947-4  Tape Two
Charlotte's Web
Don't Wait on Me
Years Ago
A Child of the Fifties
Oh Baby Mine
Guilty
Elizabeth
Atlanta Blue
Hollywood
One Takes the Blame
My Only Love
Hello Mary Lou
Amazing Grace
Sweeter and Sweeter
Too Much on My Heart
Count on Me
Forever
I'll Be the One

More Like Daddy Than Me
--------------
518-948-4  <u>Tape Three</u>
  Maple Street Memories
  The Best I Know How
  More Than a Name on a Wall
  Let's Get Started If We're
      Gonna Break My Heart
  Moon Pretty Moon
  Walking Heartache in Disguise
  Tomorrow Never Comes
  This Ole House
  Nobody Else
  Jealous Eyes
  Small, Small World
  You've Been Like a Mother to
      Me
  Fallin' in Love
  He's Always There for You
  Is It Your Place or Mine
  It Only Hurts for a Little While
  How Great Thou Art
  Chattanooga Shoeshine Boy
  Feeling Mighty Fine
  What We Love to Do

---

## MERCURY POLYGRAM
### Special Markets

22660-4
  **Christmas With the Statler Bros.**
  Christmas Country Style
  An Old Fashioned Christmas
  No Reservation at the Inn
  Old Toy Trains
  I Believe in Santa's Cause
  I'll Be Home for Christmas
  Jingle Bells
  White Christmas

---

## MERCURY
### Foreign Releases

[No effort was made to list all foreign releases. These surfaced and are listed.]

PTV 1003  - Canadian
  **Memories...Now and Forever**
  How to Be a Country Star
  How Great Thou Art
  Whatever Happened to
      Randolph Scott
  Bed of Roses [sic]
  Flowers on the Wall
  I Was There
  Some I Wrote
  Thank You World
  Susan When She Tried
  Silver Medals and Sweet
      Memories
  I'll Go to My Grave Loving You
  Do You Remember These
  The Class of '57
  Thank God I've Got You
  Pictures
  Carry Me Back
  **GOLD ALBUM -- 1979**

Note:   Does not correspond to any
        U.S. release.

6338 100 - Dutch
  **Country Music Then & Now**
  (Same as U.S. release.)

# READERS' DIGEST

*The Best of the Statler Brothers -
- Their Greatest Hits and Finest
Performances* -- released 1983 --
Reissued Oct., 1994
RD7A-235-1 -- BCD2-5681
  Flowers on the Wall
  Do You Know You Are My
    Sunshine?
  Class of '57
  Do You Remember These
  Bed of Rose's
  Charlotte's Web
  Better Than I Did Then
  Who Am I to Say?
  How to Be a Country Star
  Official Historian of Shirley
    Jean Berrell
  The Movies
  Some I Wrote
  Thank God I've Got You
  Silver Medals & Sweet
    Memories
  Mr. Autry
  Nothing As Original As You
  Here We Are Again
  I Was There
  I'll Go to My Grave Loving You
  Your Picture in the Paper
  Whatever Happened to
    Randolph Scott
  Susan When She Tried
  Thank You World
  New York City
  Carry Me Back
  Pictures
  You Can't Go Home
          --------------
RD7A-235-2 -- BCD2-568-2
  All-American Girl
  Woman Without a Home

Monday Morning Secretary
I've Been Everywhere
Amanda
Take Good Care of Her
Take Me Home Country Roads
How Great Thou Art
Just a Little Talk With Jesus
He Went to the Cross Loving
  You
The Lord's Prayer
Jesus Take Another Look at Me
Blue Eyes Cryin' in the Rain
Faded Love
When My Blue Moon Turns
  to Gold Again
Tender Years
Delta Dawn
Never Ending Song of Love
I Forgot More Than You'll
  Ever Know
All I Have to Offer You Is Me
She Thinks I Still Care
I Believe in Music
Me & Bobby McGee
_____

RB6-112-1/1 . . . . . . . . . . . . . . 1985
          **SB Greatest Hits**
Flowers on the Wall
Do You Know You Are
  My Sunshine?
Class of '57
(I'll Even Love You) Better
  Than I Did Then
Official Historian of Shirley
  Jean Berrell, The
Do You Remember These
Charlotte's Web
Bed of Rose's
How to Be a Country Star
Whatever Happened to
  Randolph Scott
You'll Be Back
_____

## SUNRISE MEDIA

SM-3008
**History of Country Music\***
Flowers on the Wall

## CBS REALM RECORDS

8077
**The Very Best of
the Statler Brothers**
Record One -- V1 8077
  Flowers on the Wall
  The Class of '57
  Monday Morning Secretary
  You Can't Go Home
  The Movies
  Do You Remember These
  I'll Go to My Grave Loving You
  Thank God I've Got You
  All American Girl
  Carry Me Back
Record Two -- V2 8077
  Bed of Rose's
  Pictures
  Your Picture in the Paper
  New York City
  How Great Thou Art
  Susan When She Tried
  Whatever Happened to
      Randolph Scott
  Thank You World
  Woman without a Home
  I Was There

## TIME-LIFE RECORDS
### Country & Western
### Classics

TLCW-14 . . . . . . . . . . . . . . . . . 1982
**The Statler Brothers**
Record One
  Wreck of the Old '97
  Flowers on the Wall
  Billy Christian
  The Right One
  That'll Be the Day
  Ruthless
  You Can't Have Your Kate
      and Edith Too
  Jump for Joy
  Staunton, VA
  Bed of Rose's
  Me and Bobby McGee
  New York City
  Pictures
  Do You Remember These
      --------------
Record Two
  1953-Dear John-Honky-Tonk
      Blues
  Class of '57
  Monday Morning Secretary
  What Do I Care
  Whatever Happened to
      Randolph Scott
  Carry Me Back
  We Owe It All to Yesterday
  Susan When She Tried
  Thank You World
  Baptism of Jesse Taylor
  Blackwood Bros. by the Statler
      Bros., The
  Samson
  I'll Go to My Grave Loving You
      --------------

Record Three
    All American Girl
    How Great Thou Art
    I Was There
    Some I Wrote
    Official Historian on Shirley
        Jean Berrell
    Do You Know You Are
        My Sunshine?
    How to Be a Country Star
    Just a Little Talk With Jesus
    Nothing As Original As You
    Charlotte's Web
    We Got Paid by Cash
    Don't Wait on Me
    Love Was All We Had

## K-TEL RECORDS

NC 568 . . . . . . . . . . . . . . . . . . . 1983
**The Statler Brothers Country**
    I'll Go to My Grave Loving You
    Do You Know You Are My
        Sunshine
    Better Than I Did Then
    The Official Historian on Shirley
        Jean Berrell
    Thank God I've Got You
    I Was There
    Who Am I to Say
    Nothing As Original As You
    Flowers on the Wall
    Bed of Rose's
    Charlotte's Web
    How to Be a Country Star
    The Movies
    Here We Are Again
    Do You Remember These
    The Class of '57

## HEARTLAND MUSIC

HL 1016 . . . . . . . . . . . . . . . . . . 1984
**The Very Best of
the Statler Brothers**
    Don't Wait on Me
    (I'll Even Love You) Better Than
        I Did Then
    Elizabeth
    Guilty
    Oh Baby Mine
    Atlanta Blue
    One Takes the Blame
    My Only Love
    Hollywood [sic]
    Flowers on the Wall
    Do You Remember These
    I'll Go to My Grave Loving You
    Class of '57
    Do You Know You Are My
        Sunshine
    Who Am I to Say
    Charlotte's Web
    The Official Historian on Shirley
        Jean Berrell
    You'll Be Back

HC 2012 (cassette) . . . . . . July, 1992
HL 2012 (LP) . . . . . . . . . . . July, 1992
**Statler Bros. Gospel Favorites**
HC 2012-1 Tape One
    When the Roll Is Called Up
        Yonder
    Rock of Ages
    Noah Found Grace in the Eyes
        of the Lord
    The Old Rugged Cross
    Blessed Be
    One Size Fits All
    Sweet By and By
    Turn Your Radio On

Amazing Grace
Love Lifted Me
There Is Power in the Blood
This Ole House

HC 2012-2 Tape Two
Precious Memories
How Great Thou Art
Jesus Is the Answer Everytime
Over the Sunset Mountains
I Believe I'll Live for Him
In the Garden
A Different Song
Just a Little Talk with Jesus
A Beautiful Life
I'll Fly Away

Double Set, CD and cassette
HL3404 . . . . . . . . . . October, 1995
**The Statler Brothers**
**Sing the Classics**
Volume One
Memories Are Made of This
The Great Pretender
Gone
Naughty Lady of Shady Lane
She Thinks I Still Care
I'll Go to My Grave Loving You
Moments to Remember
Chattanooga Shoe Shine Boy
Making Believe
Tom Dooley
Love Letters in the Sand
Hello Mary Lou

--------------

Volume Two
Unchained Melody
The Battle of New Orleans
I Can't Stop Loving You
Bye Bye Love
Only You
Have I Told You Lately That I
Love You
Oh, Baby Mine (I Get So
Lonely)

It Only Hurts for a Little While
He's Got the Whole World in His
Hands
Bed of Roses [sic]
Love Me Tender
Goodnight Sweetheart Goodnight

**PUBLISHER'S
CLEARING HOUSE**

#15069 . . . . . . . . . . . . . . . . . . . . 1993
**The Statler Brothers**
**36 All-Time Favorites**
Volume One --
Maple Street Mem'ries
Remember Me
Who Do You Think You Are
My Only Love
Elizabeth
Fallin' in Love
Am I Crazy
Let's Get Started if We're Gonna
Break My Heart
I'll Be the One
More Than a Name on a Wall
The Best I Know How
Jesus Showed Me So

-----------

Volume Two --
Do You Remember These
Deja Vu
The Class of '57
Count on Me
Beyond Romance
There's Still Times
Moon Pretty Moon
Put It on the Card
Oh Baby Mine

Too Much on My Heart
If I'd Paid More Attention to You
I Was There

--------------

Volume Three --
Bed of Rose's
I'll Go to My Grave Loving You
Everything You See in Your
Dreams

You've Been Like a Mother to
Me
I Lost My Heart to You
Dynamite
Guilty
Atlanta Blue
Do You Know You Are
My Sunshine
Jesus Is the Answer Every Time
Forever
In the Garden

# VIDEO RELEASES

RCA/Columbia Pictures Home
Video
43396 20608 . . . . . . . . . . . . 1985
**Brothers in Song**
Sweeter and Sweeter
My Only Love
Whatever
Elizabeth
Atlanta Blue
Guilty

Mercury 800-633 289-3 . . . . 1994
**What We Love to Do**
My Only Love
Sweeter & Sweeter
Atlanta Blue
Elizabeth
Whatever
Only You
Maple Street Memories
Let's Get Started
Guilty
Small Small World
Nobody Else
You've Been Like a Mother to
Me
What We Love to Do

# CHAPTER 6

# Album Notes

An inside album sleeve from Columbia Records printed in 1969 reads as follows:

> "Here's How Records Give You More of What You Want: . . . They're attractive, informative, and easy to store. Record albums are never out of place. Because of the aesthetic appeal of the jacket design, they're beautifully at home in any living room or library. They've also got important information on the backs -- about the artists, about the performances or about the program."

With the advent of eight-track and cassette tapes, we lost a lot of the information available to us on the LP album covers. The coming of the compact disc has brought a lot of that back, but it will never be the same.

That same sleeve bears the slogan,
> "And remember . . . it always happens first on records."

My purpose here is to provide information to collectors to determine the relative worth of searching for a particular LP album cover. This is limited to original issue Columbia, Harmony, Mercury, and Heartland Music (when originally issued there). This does not include other anthology or compiliation sets.

**FLOWERS ON THE WALL** -- Columbia CL2449/CS9249  (Jan. 3, 1965)
Produced by Don Law & Frank Jones. Liner notes by Ren Grevatt. Cover photo by Don Hunstein. Front cover -- picture of Statlers in a stairwell. No musicians named on cover.

**THE BIG HITS** -- Columbia CL2719/CS9519 (Aug. 28, 1967)
Produced by Bob Johnston. Cover photo: Columbia Records Photo Studio -- Sandy Speiser/Don Hunstein. Front cover -- Statlers next to wheels of large train locomotive. No musicians named.

**OH HAPPY DAY** -- Columbia CS9878  (June 25, 1969)
Produced by George Richey.  Liner notes by Johnny Cash.  Cover photo, Al Clayton.  Front cover -- Statlers dressed in suits, setting is green field, posed leaning against trees.  No musicians named.

**BIG COUNTRY HITS** -- H30610 (April 19, 1971) Columbia Harmony label.
Liner notes by William Ouver.  Cover photo, Al Clayton.  Front cover picture made at same session as cover of *Oh Happy Day* album -- different pose.  No musicians named.

**THE WORLD OF THE STATLER BROTHERS** -- Columbia CG31557
          2-record set  (July 26, 1972)
Cover design, Bill Barnes; Assemblage, Pat Strzelecki.  Cover photos, Don Hunstein, Slick Lawson, Pike Davis.  Inside photos, Sandy Speiser.  Front and back identical picture made to look like an unfinished framed tapestry:  Statlers walking up a hillside (earth tones), sky and rainbow stitched in colors, real flowers and butterfly added to picture.  Reissued Columbia masters.  Folded double album, inside has black & white concert pictures.

**DO YOU LOVE ME TONIGHT and OTHER FAVORITES** -- KH32256
          Columbia Harmony   (May 25, 1973)
Front cover a concert picture taken at an upward angle, entire cover in red overtones.  Reissued Columbia masters, including one previously unissued title, seven that had been issued only as singles, and the title that was pulled after three weeks.

**BED OF ROSE'S** -- Mercury SRM-61317 (Dec. 15, 1970), Mercury Studios
          Produced by Jerry Kennedy.  No album photo or design credits given.
          Front cover -- concert picture.  Liner notes are interviews with the wives of the Statler Brothers.
          Musicians -- Harold Bradley, Ray Edenton, Chip Young (g); Jerry Kennedy (g,db); Bob Moore (b); Buddy Harman (dm); Pig Robbins (p); Bobby Thompson (bjo); Pete Drake (st g); Charlie McCoy (hm,vb,org).

**PICTURES OF MOMENTS TO REMEMBER** -- SRM-61349  (Aug. 20, 1971)
          Produced by Jerry Kennedy.  Art director, Des Strobel.  Design, John Youssi.
          Front and back covers are pictures of Statlers of younger vintage.  Liner notes by Carl Perkins.
          Musicians -- Ray Edenton, Chip Young (g); Harold Bradley (g,uke); Buddy Harman (dm); Bob Moore (b); Floyd Cramer Produced by Jerry Kennedy for JK Productions, Inc., Pig Robbins (p); Pete Drake (steel g); Earl Scruggs (bjo); Jerry Kennedy (db); Charlie McCoy (org,vb,hm).
Arr. Cam Mullins --

| | |
|---|---|
| Just Someone I Used to Know | You Can't Go Home |
| Faded Love | Moments to Remember |

**INNERVIEW** -- SRM-61358 (April, 1972), Produced by Jerry Kennedy.
No album design credits given. Front cover -- candid pictures form frame around center group shot. Musicians not listed on the album cover. Liner notes are Ralph Emery's interview with the Statler Brothers.

**COUNTRY MUSIC THEN & NOW** -- SRM-61367 (1972)
Produced by Jerry Kennedy. Art director, Des Strobel. Design, John Youssi. Photography, Roger Allen Vincent.
Front cover pictures, Roadhog & the Cadillac Cowboys (black & white) - "THEN", and one of the Statlers, color, "NOW" (cover). Liner notes -- letter from Roadhog (in smudged pencil on lined paper).
Musicians -- Harold Bradley, Ray Edenton, Chip Young (g); Jerry Kennedy (g,db); Buddy Harman (dm); Bob Moore (b); Hargus "Pig" Robbins (keyb,p); Charlie McCoy (hrm,vb); Pete Drake (steel g); Buddy Spicher (f); George Tidwell (trumpet).
Arranged by Cam Mullins --

| | |
|---|---|
| When My Blue Moon Turns to Gold | The Class of '57 |
| No One Will Ever Know | A Stranger in My Place |

**THE STATLER BROTHERS SING**
**COUNTRY SYMPHONIES IN E MAJOR** -- SRM-61374 (Dec. 15, 1972)
Produced by Jerry Kennedy. Design, John Youssi, Photo, Joe Horton.
Recorded at Mercury Memorial Music Hall, Nashville
Front cover -- picture of Statlers in tuxedoes, white gloves, and black cowboy hats, seated in formal ballroom before music stand. Liner notes -- written as a concert program.
Musicians -- Ray Edenton, Chip Young, Harold Bradley (g); Jerry Kennedy (g,db, sitar); Pete Drake (steel g); Bob Moore (b); Hargus "Pig" Robbins (p,org); Charlie McCoy (vb,hm); Buddy Spicher (f); Bob Thompson (bjo); Buddy Harman (dm).

**CARRY ME BACK** -- SRM-1676 (Sept. 1, 1973), Produced by Jerry Kennedy.
Album design, Joe Kotleba. Photography, Roger Vincent, Tom Zamiar.
Pictures front & back with their wives; front is '50's style, back is contemporary 1973.
Musicians -- Harold Bradley, Ray Edenton, Jerry Shook, Chip Young (g); Jerry Kennedy (g,db); Buddy Harman (dm); Bob Moore (b); Pig Robbins (keyb); Pete Drake (steel g); Charlie McCoy (hm,vb).
String arr. Cam Mullins --

| | |
|---|---|
| Carry Me Back | We Owe It All to Yesterday |
| The Woman I Still Love | The Strand |
| The Streets of San Francisco | |

**THANK YOU WORLD** -- SRM-1707 (1974),  Produced by Jerry Kennedy.
Album design, Joe Kotleba.  Photography, Woody Robertson.
Liner notes -- open letter from the Statler Brothers (lyrics to title song).
Includes list of awards received 1965 through 1973.
Musicians -- Harold Bradley, Ray Edenton, Pete Wade, Chip Young (g); Jerry
Kennedy (g,db); Buddy Harman (dm); Bob Moore (b); Pig Robbins (p,org); Larry
Butler (p); Pete Drake (steel g); Charlie McCoy (hm,vb); Johnny Gimble (f).
String arr. Cam Mullins --

| | |
|---|---|
| City Lights | Streets of Baltimore |
| Sweet Charlotte Ann | Boy Inside of Me |

**ALIVE AT JOHNNY MACK BROWN HIGH SCHOOL** -- SRM-1708 (1974)
Produced by Jerry Kennedy.  Photo graffitti, Woody Robertson.
LESTER "ROADHOG" MORAN & His Cadillac Cowboys
Pictures of Roadhog & the gang -- handwritten liner notes, including Mercury
logos and catalog numbers, for that "hand-made" look.  Includes letter from the
Statler Brothers that reads more like a disclaimer than an endorsement!
Ray Edenton (g); Bob Moore (b); Buddy Spicher (f); Wichita (el g).
[Nowhere on this album is the name "Statler Brothers" used to refer to the
artists on this recording.]

**SONS OF THE MOTHERLAND** -- SRM1-1019 (Dec. 15, 1974)
Produced by Jerry Kennedy.  Design and photography, Woody Robertson.
Front cover -- Red, white and blue, w/stars.  Pen and ink drawings of Statlers
representative of faces on Mt. Rushmore.  Liner notes -- notes by the Statlers on
each song on the record, w/pictures.
Musicians -- Harold Bradley, Ray Edenton, Jerry Shook, Pete Wade, Chip
Young (g); Jerry Kennedy (db); Pete Drake (steel g); Buddy Harman (dm); Bob
Moore (b); Pig Robbins, Bobby Wood (p); Charlie McCoy (hm,vb); Buddy Spicher
(f); Mary Ann Mullins (tuba).
String arr. Cam Mullins --                    You've Been Like a Mother to Me
One More Summer in Virginia         All American Girl
Things of Note:
Eight More Miles to Louisville -- Grandpa Jones (bjo)
You Can't Judge a Book by Its Cover -- Bobby Thompson (bjo)

**THE BEST OF THE STATLER BROTHERS**  -- SRM1-1037 (July 7, 1975)
Produced by Jerry Kennedy.  Photography, Michael Mauney.
Art director, Jim Schubert, AGI.
Front cover, picture of their wives only.  Back cover, picture of all four
couples.  Liner notes by Harold, Don, Lew, and Phil.  No musicians listed.

**THE HOLY BIBLE - OLD TESTAMENT** -- SRM1-1051 (1975)
Produced by Jerry Kennedy.
Black leather-grain look cover. Liner notes by The Statlers. No musicians listed.

**THE HOLY BIBLE - NEW TESTAMENT** -- SRM1-1052 (1975)
Produced by Jerry Kennedy. Liner photograph, Dan Morrill.
Art direction, Jim Schubert, AGI. Design, Joe Kotleba.
White leather-grain look cover. Liner notes by The Statlers. No musicians listed.

**HOLY BIBLE (DOUBLE)** -- SRM-2-101, (1975); Produced by Jerry Kennedy.
Photograph, Dan Morrill. Art direction, Jim Schubert, AGI.
Design, Joe Kotleba.
Double folded cover, red leather-grain look, inside notes written by Statlers.
Musicians -- Byron Bach, Brenton Banks, Roger Bissell, George Binkley III, Harold Bradley, Marvin Chantry, Roy Christensen, Virginia Christensen, George Cunningham, Pete Drake, Ray Edenton, Carl Gorodetzky, Buddy Harman, Jerry Kennedy, Shelly Kurland, Charlie McCoy, Bob Moore, Farrell Morris, Eberhard Ramm, Hargus "Pig" Robbins, Don Sheffield, Jerry Shook, Steven M. Smith, Buddy Spicher, Chris Teal, Bobby Thompson, Gary Vanosdale, Pete Wade, Stephanie Woolf, Chip Young.

**HAROLD, LEW, PHIL & DON** -- SRM1-1077 (March 19, 1976)
Produced by Jerry Kennedy. Photo, Garvey & Dean Winegar.
Front cover -- solid blue w/oval picture of Statlers in center. Liner notes are the questions (and answers) to the Statler Brothers Quiz.
Musicians -- Harold Bradley, Ray Edenton, Jerry Shook, Pete Wade, Chip Young (g); Weldon Myrick (st g); Jerry Kennedy (db), Buddy Harmon (dm), Bob Moore (b), Pig Robbins, Bobby Wood (p), Charlie McCoy (hrm, vb).
String arr. Cam Mullins -- Your Picture In the Paper

**THE COUNTRY AMERICA LOVES** -- SRM1-1125 (January 7, 1977).
Produced by Jerry Kennedy. Photography, Deane & Garvey Winegar. Art direction, Jim Schubert (AGI). Suits designed by Vic Urrasio.
Liner notes by the Statlers. Front cover is the Red, White, & Blue suits, with flag belt buckles. Picture is framed by red, white and blue ribbon. On the original issue, the ribbon is embossed and the texture of the album is like the fabric of a flag. Later issues have smooth covers.
Musicians -- Byron Bach, Brenton Banks, George Binkley III, Harold Bradley, Marvin Chantry, Roy Christensen, Virginia Christensen, Pete Drake, Ray Edenton, Solie Fott, Carl Gorodetsky, Lennie Haight, Buddy Harman, Martin Katahn, Jerry Kennedy, Shelly Kurland, Charlie McCoy, Martha McCrory, Bob Moore, Pig Robbins, Steve Sefsik, Don Sheffield, Jerry Shook, Steven M. Smith, Christian

Teal, Samuel Terranova, George Tidwell, David Vanderkooi, Gary Vanosdale, Pete Wade, Stephanie Woolf, Chip Young.
String & horn arr. Cam Mullins

| The Movies | Thank God I've Got You |
| I Was There | Blue Eyes Cryin' in the Rain |

String arr. by D. Bergen White -- A Couple More Years


**SHORT STORIES** -- SRM1-1173/SRM1-5001 (1977).
Produced by Jerry Kennedy., U.S. Recording Studios, Inc.
Photography, Deane & Garvey Winegar. Front cover -- Statlers in library setting.
Musicians -- Tommy Allsup, Byron Bach, Brenton Banks, George Binkley III, Harold Bradley, John Catchings, Marvin Chantry, Roy Christensen, Virginia Christensen, Johnny Christopher, Pete Drake, Ray Edenton, Carl Gorodetzky, Lennie Haight, Buddy Harman, Martin Katahn, Jerry Kennedy, Shelly Kurland, Shorty Lavender, Wilfred Lehmann, Charlie McCoy, Martha McCrory, Bob Moore, Weldon Myrick, Katherine Ransom, Hargus "Pig" Robbins, Steve Sefsik, Don Sheffield, Steven M. Smith, Samuel Terranova, George Tidwell III, Gary Vanosdale, Pete Wade, Stephanie Woolf, Chip Young.
String & horn arr. Cam Mullins (No titles marked.)
String arr. D.Bergen White --

| Silver Medals and Sweet Memories | The Star |
| Quite a Long, Long Time | That Summer |
| Different Things to Different People | Some I Wrote |


**ENTERTAINERS . . . ON & OFF THE RECORD**
SRM-1-5007 (March 13, 1978)
Produced by Jerry Kennedy. Photography, Deane & Garvey Winegar.
Front cover -- Statlers in outside setting. Back cover -- concert picture, brown and white suits. Both pictures are offset by yellow border.
Musicians -- Byron Bach, Brenton Banks, George Binkley III, Harold Bradley, John Allan Catchings, Marvin Chantry, Roy Christensen, Stephen Clapp, Ray Edenton, Solie Fott, Carl Gorodetzky, Lennie Haight, Buddy Harman, Lillian Hunt, Martin Katahn, Jerry Kennedy, Shelly Kurland, Charlie McCoy, Martha McCrory, Bob Moore, Weldon Myrick, Hargus "Pig" Robbins, Dale Sellers, Jerry Shook, Steven M. Smith, Samuel Terranova, Gary Vanosdale, Pamela Vanosdale, Pete Wade, Stephanie Woolf, Chip Young.
String arr. D.Bergen White --

| | Who Am I to Say |
| Do You Know You Are My Sunshine | The Best That I Can Do |

String arr. Cam Mullins -- Tomorrow Is Your Friend


**CHRISTMAS CARD** -- SRM-1-5012 (Sept. 1978) Produced by Jerry Kennedy.
Photography, Dean & Garvey Winegar. Design, Steve Musgrave. Art director, Jim Schubert (AGI).

Front cover -- Statlers in one-horse open sleigh, snow-covered scene. Picture is oval, placed on a red background. Liner notes -- Seasonal message from the Statlers.

Musicians -- Byron Bach, Brenton Banks, George Binkley III, Marvin Chantry, Roy Christensen, Virginia Christensen, Ray Edenton, Carl Gorodetzky, Lennie Haight, Buddy Harman, Jerry Kennedy, Shelly Kurland, Wilfred Lehmann, Charlie McCoy, Bob Moore, Weldon Myrick, Bill Puett, Hargus "Pig" Robbins, Dale Sellers, Jerry Shook, Steven M. Smith, Buddy Spicher, Chris Teal, Samuel Terranova, Bobby Thompson, Gary Vanosdale, Pamela Vanosdale, Pete Wade, Stephanie Woolf, Chip Young.

String & Flute arr. D.Bergen White --

| | |
|---|---|
| I'll Be Home for Christmas | A Christmas Medley |
| Something You Can't Buy | White Christmas |
| I Never Spend a Christmas That I Don't Think of You | Christmas to Me |

**THE ORIGINALS** -- SRM-1-5016 (March 29, 1979)          Sound Stage Studios

Photo of Statlers, Deane & Garvey Winegar. Cover concept, The Statler Brothers. Art direction, Jim Schubert, AGI. Design & illustration, Ross & Harvey, Inc., Chicago.

Front cover -- center photo of Statlers framed by pictures of other originals in earth tones. Original liner notes by the original Statler Brothers, giving details on the music and the guest musicians appearing on this album.

Musicians -- Harold Bradley, Ray Edenton, Dennis Good, Buddy Harman, Gordon Kennedy, Jerry Kennedy, Charlie McCoy, Bob Moore, Weldon Myrick, Bill Puett, Hargus "Pig" Robbins, Don Sheffield, George Tidwell, Pete Wade, & Chip Young.

*The Shelly Kurland Strings* -- George Binkley III, John Catchings, Marvin Chantry, Roy Christensen, Virginia Christensen, Carl Gorodetzky, Lennie Haight, Shelly Kurland, Steve Smith, Sam Terranova, Gary Vanosdale, & Stephanie Woolf.

Also appearing are the following Originals:

Scotty Moore, Mac Wiseman, Carl Perkins, Bashful Brother Oswald, Curly Chalker, Johnny Gimble, Shorty Lavender, Ernest Tubb, Billy Byrd, Bob Wootton, Odell Martin, Don Helms, & Grady Martin.

String, flute, & horn arr. D.Bergen White --

| | |
|---|---|
| How to Be a Country Star | Mr. Autry |
| Where He Always Wanted to Be | Just a Little Talk With Jesus |
| Nothing As Original As You | The Star-Spangled Banner |

**THE BEST OF THE STATLER BROTHERS RIDES AGAIN, Vol. II,** --

SRM1-5024 (1975) Produced by Jerry Kennedy. Liner notes by the Statlers. Cover concept, The Statler Brothers. Design & illustration, Ross & Harvey, Inc., Chicago. Photography, Deane & Garvey Winegar. Art direction, Jim Schubert, AGI.

Cover has pictures of Harold, Phil, Don & Lew riding white horses, dressed in appropriate cowboy gear. The trim on the picture is embossed.

**TENTH ANNIVERSARY** -- SRM1-5027 (July 24, 1980)

Produced by Jerry Kennedy, Sound Stage Studios   Concept, The Statler Brothers. Photography, Deane & Garvey Winegar. Art direction, Jim Schubert.

Front cover -- Statlers in tuxedoes, posed with President Wilson's personal 1920 Pierce-Arrow. Liner notes by the Statlers.

Musicians -- Harold Bradley, Ralph Childs, Ray Edenton, Buddy Harman, Jerry Kennedy, Charlie McCoy, Bob Moore, Weldon Myrick, Wynn Osborne, Bill Puett, Cindy Reynolds, Hargus "Pig" Robbins, Buddy Spicher, Marty Stuart, George Tidwell, Vic Willis, Pete Wade, Bill Wiggins, & Chip Young.

*The Shelly Kurland Strings* -- George Binkley III, John Catchings, Marvin Chantry, Roy Christensen, Virginia Christensen, Carl Gorodetzky, Lennie Haight, Shelly Kurland, Wilfred Lehmann, Rebecca Lynch, Dennis Molchan, Sam Terranova, Gary Vanosdale, Carol Walker, & Stephanie Woolf.

String arr. D.Bergen White --              Charlotte's Web
  Don't Forget Yourself                    We Got Paid by Cash
Produced by Jerry Kennedy & Snuff Garrett -- Charlotte's Web

**YEARS AGO**-- SRM1-6002 (June 18, 1981)                 Sound Stage Studios

Photography, Deane & Garvey Winegar.

Liner notes by the Statlers, front cover picture taken on the stage of their grade school.

Musicians -- Harold Bradley, John Carrigan, Ray Edenton, Buddy Harman, Jerry Kennedy, Charlie McCoy, Bob Moore, Weldon Myrick, Hargus "Pig" Robbins, Pete Wade, & Chip Young.

*The Shelly Kurland Strings* -- George Binkley III, John Catchings, John David Boyle, Roy Christensen, Conni Ellisor, Carl Gorodetzky, Martin Katahn, Shelly Kurland, Dennis Molchan, Julia Tanner, Chris Teal, Sam Terranova, Gary Vanosdale, & Stephanie Woolf.

String arr. D.Bergen White --              You'll Be Back
  Don't Wait on Me                         Love Was All We Had

**THE LEGEND GOES ON . . .** -- SRM1-4048 (June 10, 1982)

Sound Stage Studios. Photography, Ken Kim. Art Direction/Design, Jim Schubert, THP. Lettering, Holly Dickens.

Front cover -- Don, Harold, Phil & Lew seated on a park bench, wearing western-style shirts; plain white background. Liner notes by Barbara Mandrell. The last album Lew DeWitt made with the group.

Musicians -- Harold Bradley, Jerry Carrigan, Ray Edenton, Buddy Harman, Gordon Kennedy, Jerry Kennedy, Charlie McCoy, Bob Moore, Weldon Myrick, Hargus "Pig" Robbins, Denis Solee, Pete Wade, & Chip Young.

*The Nashville String Players* -- George Binkley III, John David Boyle, John Catchings, Marvin Chantry, Roy Christensen, Virginia Christensen, Conni Ellisor, Carl Gorodetzky, Lennie Haight, Martin Katahn, Shelly Kurland, Dennis Molchan,

Julia Tanner, Chris Teal, Sam Terranova, Gary Vanosdale, Pamela Vanosdale &
Stephanie Woolf.
<u>String arr. D.Bergen White</u> --

| I Had Too Much to Dream | A Child of the Fifties |
| I Don't Know Why | What You Are to Me |
| How Do You Like Your Dream So Far | All Over Again |

**TODAY** -- 812-184-1/4 (1983)                                    Sound Stage Studios
    Photography, Bob & Patti Good. Art direction, The Statler Brothers. Design,
Jim Schubert.
    Front cover -- Phil, Don, Harold, Jimmy posed standing, wearing suits & ties,
plain dark background. Liner notes by the Statlers.
    Musicians -- Harold Bradley, David Briggs, Jerry Carrigan, Gene Chrisman,
Ray Edenton, Buddy Harman, Jerry Kennedy, Mike Leech, Sam Levine, Charlie
McCoy, Bob Moore, Weldon Myrick, Hargus "Pig" Robbins, Pete Wade, Tommy
Williams, & Chip Young.
    *The Nashville String Machine* -- George Binkley III, David Boyle, Marvin
Chantry, Roy Christensen, Carl Gorodetzky, Lennie Haight, Dennis Molchan, Walt
Schwede, Chris Teal, Gary Vanosdale, Pamela Vanosdale & Stephanie Woolf.
<u>String arr. D.Bergen White</u> --

| Some Memories Last Forever | Guilty |
| I Never Want to Kiss You Goodbye | Elizabeth |

**ATLANTA BLUE** -- 818-652-1/4 (1984)                            Sound Stage Studios
    Art direction, The Statlers and Ken Kim. Album design and photography, Ken
Kim. Air brushing, Charles McAllen.
    Front cover -- blue jackets, blue shirts, blue background, blue tint. Back cover
-- "The Statlers" logo repeated in dark blue on blue background.
    Musicians -- David Briggs, Jerry Carrigan, Ray Edenton, David Innis, Jerry
Kennedy, Brent King, Mike Leech, Weldon Myrick, Pete Wade, & Chip Young.
    *The Nashville String Machine* -- George Binkley III, Roy Christensen, Virginia
Christensen, Dan Furth, Carl Gorodetzky, Lennie Haight, Larry Harvin, Lee
Larrison, Martha McCrory, Dennis Molchan, Chris Teal, Gary Vanosdale, Pamela
Vanosdale & Stephanie Woolf.
    *The Nashville Hornworks* -- Roger Bissell, Buddy Skipper, George Tidwell.
<u>String & horn  arr. D.Bergen White</u>

**PARDNERS IN RHYME** -- 824-420-1/4 (April, 1985)
    Produced by Jerry Kennedy; Sound Stage Studios and Young'un Sound.
Album graphics, Barnes and Co. Art Direction, Bill Barnes. Photography, Jim
McGuire.
    Front cover -- Harold w/dobro, Don at piano, Jimmy w/electric guitar, Phil at
the typewriter, in room with bay window and hardwood floor. Back cover -- same
room, same angle; the guys laid down their instruments and left. Dedicated to Jerry
Kennedy by the Statlers.

Musicians -- David Briggs, Jerry Carrigan, Ray Edenton, Jerry Kennedy, Mike Leech, Kenny Malone, Weldon Myrick, Eberhard Ramm, Buddy Spicher, Pete Wade, & Chip Young.

*The Nashville String Machine* -- George Binkley III, John Borg, John Catchings, Roy Christensen, Virginia Christensen, Carl Gorodetzky, Lennie Haight, Lee Larrison, Dennis Molchan, Kathryn Plummer, Pamela Sixfin, Chris Teal, Gary Vanosdale, & Stephanie Woolf.

String & horn arr. D.Bergen White

**CHRISTMAS PRESENT** -- 824-785-1/2/4 (Sept. 23,. 1985)     Young'un Sound
Produced by Jerry Kennedy for JK Productions, Inc. Photography, Charles L. Clemmer. Executive Art Direction, The Statlers. Art direction and album design, Ken Kim.

Front cover -- Statlers in overcoats and scarves, holding gaily wrapped Christmas packages. Plain background. Contains lyric sleeve, promotes eight original Statler compositions.

Musicians -- Mike Leech, Henry Strzelecki (b); David Briggs, Bobby Ogden (kb); Jerry Carrigan, Gene Chrisman, Milton Sledge (d); Ray Edenton, Jerry Kennedy, Pete Wade, Chip Young (g); Weldon Myrick (steel g); Bela Fleck (bj); Farrell Morris (percussion).

*The Nashville String Machine* -- George Binkley III, John Borg, Roy Christensen, Virginia Christensen, Connie Collopy, Charles Everett, Carl Gorodetzky, Lee Larrison, Phyllis Mazza, Dennis Molchan, Pamela Sixfin, Mark Tanner, Gary Vanosdale, & Stephanie Woolf.

String arr. D.Bergen White

**FOUR FOR THE SHOW** -- 826-782-1/4 (May, 1986)          Young'un Sound
Produced by Jerry Kennedy for JK Productions, Inc. Photography, Charles L. Clemmer. Executive Art Direction, The Statlers. Art direction and album design, Ken Kim.

Front cover -- Statlers in tuxedoes, seated in empty auditorium with traditional wooden theatre seats. Back cover -- credits given in format resembling traditional theatre marquee.

Musicians -- Mike Leech, (b); David Briggs, Larry Butler (kb); Ray Edenton, Jerry Kennedy, Pete Wade, Chip Young (g); Jerry Carrigan, Gene Chrisman (d); Weldon Myrick (steel g); "Hoot" Hester (f).

*The Nashville String Machine* -- Grace Bahng, George Binkley III, John Borg, Roy Christensen, Virginia Christensen, Charles Everett, Carl Gorodetzky, Lee Larrison, Dennis Molchan, Kathy Plummer, Pamela Sixfin, Chris Teal, Gary Vanosdale, & Stephanie Woolf.

String arr. D.Bergen White

**Note:** Also available as a picture record in a clear plastic jacket, same artwork on
   disc as standard paper jacket. Only Statler album ever made into a picture
   record.

**RADIO GOSPEL FAVORITES** -- 826-710-1/4/2 (Sept. 15,1986)

Produced by Jerry Kennedy for JK Productions, Inc. Photography, Charles L. Clemmer. Executive Art Direction, The Statlers. Art direction and album design, Ken Kim.

Front cover is picture of Statlers in modern radio studio. Back cover is same pose, same studio, as it might have been 30-odd years earlier. Album dedicated to the memory of the Rev. Eugene Jordan.

Musicians -- David Briggs, Larry Butler, Hargus "Pig" Robbins (kb); Ray Edenton, Jerry Kennedy, Pete Wade, Chip Young (g); Jerry Carrigan, Gene Chrisman, Kenny Malone (dm); Mike Leech (b); Charlie McCoy (vb); Buddy Spicher (f); Eberhard Ramm (Fr hr).

*The Nashville String Machine* -- Grace Bahng, George Binkley III, John Borg, John Catchings, Roy Christensen, Virginia Christensen, Charles Everett, Carl Gorodetzky, Lennie Haight, Lee Larrison, Dennis Molchan, Kathy Plummer, Pamela Sixfin, Chris Teal, Gary Vanosdale, & Stephanie Woolf.
String & horn arr. Bergen White.

**MAPLE STREET MEMORIES** -- 832-404-1/2/4 (July 20, 1987)

Produced by Jerry Kennedy for JK Productions, Inc. Young'un Sound

Photography, Charles L. Clemmer. Executive Art Direction, The Statlers. Art direction and album design, Ken Kim.

Front cover -- long shot of Statlers on porch and steps of large, late 19th century home. Back cover -- closeup of Statlers together behind porch rail.

Musicians -- Ray Edenton, Chip Young (g); Jerry Kennedy, Pete Wade (g,db); David Briggs, Billy Ogdin (kb); Gene Chrisman (d); Mike Leech (b); Weldon Myrick (steel g); Bela Fleck (bjo); Buddy Spicher (f).

*The Nashville String Machine* -- Carl Gorodetzky/Concertmaster, George Binkley III, John Borg, John Catchings, Roy Christensen, Virginia Christensen, Jim Grosjean, Lee Larrison, Ted Madsen, Dennis Molchan, Laura Molyneaux, Pamela Sixfin, Gary Vanosdale, & Stephanie Woolf.
String arr. D.Bergen White

**THE STATLERS GREATEST HITS, Vol. III** -- 834-626-1/2/4 (Oct. 3, 1988)

Produced by Jerry Kennedy for JK Productions, Inc. Executive Art Direction, The Statlers. Photography, Charles L. Clemmer. Art direction and album design, Ken Kim.

Front cover is the Brothers seated around a patio table, poolside. Includes three titles previously released only as singles. No musicians listed.

**LIVE . . . AND SOLD OUT** -- 838-231-1/2/4 (Oct. 3, 1989)

Live at Capitol Music Hall, Wheeling, WV

Produced by Jerry Kennedy for JK Productions, Inc. Executive art direction, The Statlers. Photography, Alan Messer. Art direction and design, Ken Kim.

Front cover -- picture taken at same concert.

**The Cowboy Symphony Orchestra** -- Billy "Boopie" James (b); Carroll "Bull" Durham (p); Don "Mousey" Morton (d); Jerry Hensley, Charlie Hamm (g).

This is the last long-play disc issued by Mercury Records. Every release after this date is cassette and compact disc only. There are two long-play discs released by Heartland Music.

## THE VERY BEST OF THE STATLERS -- HL1016 (1984)
Front cover photo, Melodie Gimple.
Front cover is concert picture of group with Jimmy. Side One are titles made with Jimmy, Side Two are titles made with Lew.

## THE STATLER BROTHERS GOSPEL FAVORITES -- HL2012 (1992)
Two-record set, front cover is the Brothers in suits.
No album design credits given.

# CHAPTER 7

# Chart History

The following chart history is compiled from the charts of *Billboard* magazine. First is a history of singles, followed by a history of album releases. Many might wonder why a history of charts? There are many questions that can be answered -- Were there ever more than one single and/or album on the charts at the same time? -- What album was on the charts the longest, and how long was it? -- What album kept making comebacks, and why? -- What was the most popular single? -- And the questions go on and on.

*Billboard* charts are as follows: Hot Country Singles, Hot Country LPs, Hot 100 (singles), and Top LPs (and later on, Tapes). Chart placement on the latter two charts constituted a "crossover" hit.

In the singles history, placement of any single on the Hot 100 is listed below the Hot Country Singles. In the album history, placement on the Top LPs & Tapes chart is listed below the Hot Country LPs. The date is the date the song first hit the charts. The numbers following are the position at which the song was rated for each week it remained on the chart, and the number in brackets is the total number of weeks on the charts.

## CHART HISTORY -- SINGLES

09-25-65    **Flowers on the Wall** (Col.43315) -- 50, 43, 33, 31, 29, 29, 22, 22, 20, 20, 16, 15, 12, 7, 5, 4, 3, 2, 2, 2, 2, 5, 6, 11, 20, 22, 27  [27]

11-13-65    Hot 100 -- 96, 70, 60, 44, 34, 21, 13, 12, 4, 7, 12, 25, 31  [13]

06-18-66    **The Right One** (Col.43624) -- 45, 44, 44, 43, 41, 39, 34, 32, 20, 20, 32  [11]

11-26-66    **That'll Be the Day** (Col.43868) -- 74, 59, 56, 43, 40, 39, 37, 40, 52, 52  [10]

05-13-67    **Ruthless** (Col.44070) -- 57, 47, 37, 26, 20, 14, 11, 11, 10, 10, 11, 23, 32, 37 [14]

09-02-67    **You Can't Have Your Kate & Edith Too** (Col.44245) -- 66, 42, 37, 22, 19, 17, 13, 13, 10, 10, 15, 15, 22, 35 [14]

04-27-68    **Jump for Joy** (Col. 98258) -- 66, 62, 60 [3]

10-19-68    **Sissy** (Col. 98561) -- 75, 75 [2]

01-04-69    **I'm the Boy** (Col. 98556) -- 61, 60, 60 [3]

11-21-70    **Bed of Rose's** (Mer.73141) 71, 61, 49, 39, 35, 21, 14, 13, 10, 10, 89, 80, 10, 9, 9, 9, 18, 23, 35, 42 [20]
01-30-71    Hot 100 Chart -- 68, 65, 63, 59, 58, 58 [6]

04-24-71    **New York City** (Mer.73194) 68, 60, 55, 49, 41, 32, 30, 23, 21, 19, 19, 28, 33 [13]

08-21-71    **Pictures** (Mer.73229) 59, 57, 39, 21, 14, 13, 15, 15, 13, 13, 18, 34, 43, 51 [14]

12-11-71    **You Can't Go Home** (Mer.73253) 73, 62, 55, 54, 36, 31, 31, 24, 23, 31, 31, 32, 59 [13]

03-11-72    **Do You Remember These** (Mer.73275) 51, 36, 22, 16, 4, 4, 2, 2, 2, 2, 9, 13, 23, 29, 33 [15]

08-19-72    **The Class of '57** (Mer.73315) 54, 49, 38, 31, 25, 19, 12, 10, 9, 7, 7, 6, 9, 16, 35 [15]

02-03-73    **Monday Morning Secretary** (Mer.73360) 63, 52, 46, 41, 36, 31, 24, 21, 20, 20, 29 [11]

06-09-73    **Woman without a Home** (Mer.73392) 59, 49, 44, 39, 34, 33, 29, 29, 33 [9]

09-15-73    **Carry Me Back** (Mer. 50219) 64, 52, 42, 37, 33, 32, 30, 29, 28, 26, 36, 52 [12]

01-12-74    **Whatever Happened to Randolph Scott** (Mer.73448) 72, 62, 56, 45, 36, 28, 22, 22, 27, 40, 46 [11]

06-08-74    **Thank You World** (Mer.73485) 93, 87, 82, 72, 52, 47, 42, 38, 35,
            31, 34, 43, 50 [13]

11-09-74    **Susan When She Tried** (Mer.73625) 90, 76, 61, 48, 40, 32, 28, 28,
            23, 19, 18, 15, 26, 56 [14]

03-01-75    **All American Girl** (Mer.73665) 94, 76, 66, 62, 52, 42, 34, 31, 33,
            48, 64 [11]

06-21-75    **I'll Go to My Grave Loving You** (Mer.73687) 97, 94, 84, 69, 54,
            37, 30, 24, 20, 13, 9, 6, 4, 4, 3, 13, 33, 48, 77 [19]
11-01-75    Hot 100 -- 99, 97, 95, 93 [4]

01-03-76    **How Great Thou Art** (Mer.73732) 90, 80, 69, 59, 48, 43, 39, 44
            [8]

04-17-76    **Your Picture in the Paper** (Mer.73785) 77, 65, 49, 38, 30, 24, 19,
            15, 13, 13, 34, 59, 69 [13]

10-02-76    **Thank God I've Got You** (Mer.73846) 68, 49, 31, 24, 18, 12, 10,
            10, 13, 21, 36, 46, 60 [13]

01-15-77    **The Movies** (Mer.73877) 73, 57, 40, 30, 23, 18, 14, 10, 10, 22, 26,
            50, 67 [13]

04-30-77    **I Was There** (Mer.73906) 69, 46, 33, 23, 18, 14, 10, 8, 8, 9, 27, 36,
            52 [13]

08-13-77    **Silver Medals & Sweet Memories** (Mer.55000) 69, 58, 40, 32, 26,
            21, 18, 18, 32, 40, 45, 90 [12]

12-03-77    **Some I Wrote** (Mer.55013) 74, 59, 44, 35, 25, 22, 19, 18, 17, 35,
            55, 64 [12]

03-18-78    **Do You Know You Are My Sunshine** (Mer.55022) 70, 55, 37, 29,
            21, 16, 15, 13, 4, 3, 1, 1, 14, 43, 53, 56, 58 [17]

08-05-78    **Who Am I to Say** (Mer.55037) 47, 37, 24, 17, 12, 8, 7, 5, 3, 3, 5,
            27, 41, 48 [14]

11-18-78    **The Official Historian on Shirley Jean Berrell** (Mer.55048) 80,
            52, 38, 28, 22, 14, 14, 9, 6, 5, 5, 6, 43, 56, 76 [15]

03-31-79    **How to Be a Country Star** (Mer.55057) 55, 43, 30, 25, 18, 12, 8,
            8, 7, 14, 48 [11]

07-07-79    **Here We Are Again** (Mer.55066) 62, 48, 32, 258, 21, 17, 14, 12,
            11, 43, 56, 62, 98  [13]

10-27-79    **Nothing As Original As You** (Mer.57007)  72, 43, 36, 24, 23, 15,
            13, 11, 10, 52  [11]

01-19-80    **Better Than I Did Then** (Mer.57012)70, 49, 31, 26, 20, 13, 12, 10,
            8, 8, 10, 14, 56, 94  [14]

07-12-80    **Charlotte's Web** (Mer.57031)  79, 57, 43, 35, 27, 19, 15, 13, 11, 6,
            5, 9, 25, 55, 77, 97  [16]

11-08-80    **Don't Forget Yourself** (Mer.57037)  68, 50, 39, 31, 28, 25, 19, 16,
            13, 13, 35, 53, 53, 89  [14]

03-28-81    **In the Garden** (Mer.57048)  78, 65, 53, 46, 42, 37, 35, 61, 91  [9]

06-13-81    **Don't Wait on Me** (Mer.57051)  67, 51, 43, 29, 25, 19, 17, 13, 11,
            10, 8, 6, 5, 47, 63, 82, 97  [17]

10-24-81    **Years Ago** (Mer.57059)  65, 50, 37, 30, 27, 22, 20, 16, 14, 13, 12,
            38, 57, 83, 97  [15]

03-13-82    **You'll Be Back** (Mer.76142)  85, 47, 40, 32, 32, 24, 20, 15, 7, 7, 4,
            3, 3, 20, 38, 48, 64, 94  [18]

07-03-82    **Whatever** (Mer.76162)  67, 49, 37, 32, 26, 22, 21,16, 14, 11, 8, 7,
            17, 34, 44, 77  [16]

10-23-82    **A Child of the Fifties** (Mer.76184)  82, 63, 53, 43, 39, 34, 31, 24,
            20, 18, 17, 30, 40, 87, 96  [15]

04-16-83    **Oh Baby Mine** (Mer 811488)  67, 55, 46, 36, 29, 5, 19, 14, 8, 4, 3,
            3, 2, 12, 24, 53, 60, 80, 90  [19]

08-13-83    **Guilty** (Mer 812988)  76, 61, 51, 41, 35, 31, 27, 22, 15, 13, 11, 9,
            26, 40, 59, 76, 97  [17]

12-10-83    **Elizabeth** (Mer 814881)  78, 61, 53, 46, 38, 27, 20 16, 11, 8, 5, 4, 2,
            1, 8, 23, 30, 44, 60, 67, 70, 92  [22]

04-21-84    **Atlanta Blue** (Mer 818700)  65, 51, 43, 39, 31, 27, 21, 18, 13, 10,
            8, 4, 3, 4, 22, 37, 54, 71, 94, 96, 98  [21]

08-18-84    **One Takes the Blame** (Mer 880130)  67, 53, 46, 41, 36, 30, 25, 20,
            17, 13, 10, 8, 8, 24, 33, 43, 55, 75, 79, 84, 86, 90 [22]

12-08-84    **My Only Love** (Mer 880411)  61, 49, 42, 31, 29, 24, 18, 14,11, 6,5,
            3, 1, 5, 6, 40, 59, 73, 92 [19]

04-20-85    **Hello, Mary Lou** (Mer 880685)  64, 47, 41, 35, 28, 23, 19, 12, 10,
            7, 5, 4, 3, 6, 22, 40, 54, 67, 82, 94 [20]

08-24-85    **Too Much on My Heart** (Mer 884016)  67, 55, 43, 37, 32, 27, 18,
            15, 12, 9, 6, 4, 3, 2, 1, 16, 31, 45, 53, 63, 66, 69, 90, 96 [25]

01-11-86    **Sweeter and Sweeter** (Mer 884317)  78, 59, 49, 45, 38, 31, 26, 22,
            17, 14, 11, 9, 8, 11, 31, 45, 70, 79, 93, 96, 100 [21]

05-17-86    **Count on Me** (Mer 884721)  80, 60, 48, 44, 36, 30, 26, 22, 17, 13,
            11, 7, 6, 5, 12, 26, 45, 59, 73, 85, 92, 95, 96, 98 [24]

09-27-86    **Only You** (Mer 888042)  82, 60, 52, 47, 44, 39, 36, 38, 56, 70, 84,
            91 [12]

12-13-86    **Forever** (Mer 888219)  56, 48, 40, 40, 33, 28, 24, 20, 16, 14, 10, 9,
            8, 7, 8, 23, 38, 61, 65, 66, 89 [21]

06-13-87    **I'll Be the One** (Mer 888650)  70, 57, 47, 41, 39, 33, 31, 26, 22, 18,
            16, 14, 12, 10, 22, 38, 50, 59, 68, 79 [20]

10-31-87    **Maple Street Memories** (Mer 888920)  71, 61, 56, 50, 48, 42, 42,
            49, 68, 68, 93, 94, 95 [13]

02-20-88    **The Best I Know How** (Mer 870164)  64, 55, 47, 43, 37, 34, 30,
            27, 24, 20, 17, 15, 25, 40, 54, 59, 70, 80, 81, 88, 94, 94 ,94 [23]

06-11-88    **Am I Crazy** (Mer 870442)  73, 62, 58, 51, 46, 41, 37, 36, 32, 28,
            27, 31, 40, 56, 70, 79, 88, 91, 95 [19]

10-15-88    **Let's Get Started If We're Gonna Break My Heart** (Mer 870681)
            65, 57, 49, 45, 35, 29, 26, 24, 20, 17, 14, 14, 12, 15, 23, 43, 55,
            64, 83, 92, 92, 98 [22]

02-18-89    **Moon Pretty Moon** (Mer 872604)  68, 55, 47, 44, 40, 36, 46, 65,
            86, 98 [10]

05-13-89    **More Than a Name on a Wall** (Mer 874196)  67, 54, 43, 35, 28,
            25, 22, 17, 15, 11, 11, 7, 6, 8, 24, 40, 47, 63, 68, 83 [20]

10-07-89    **Don't Wait on Me** *[Remake of hit 6/13/81]*(Mer 891014)  92, 76,
            68, 67, 96  [5]

11-18-89    **A Hurt I Can't Handle** (Mer 876112)  65, 60, 56, 59, 72, 85, 85
            [7]

07-28-90    **Small, Small World** (Mer 875498)  71, 70, 67, 62, 61, 54, 64   [7]


# CHART HISTORY -- ALBUMS

02-12-66    **Flowers on the Wall** (Col. CS9249)  19, 10, 10, 13, 13, 11, 11, 14,
            20, 27  [10]
02-26-66    Top LP's -- 133, 125, 125  [3]

10-07-67    **The Big Hits** (Col. CS9519)  41, 30, 29, 23, 20, 20, 18, 18, 16, 25,
            25, 24, 24  [13]

01-16-71    **Bed of Rose's** (Mer. 61317)  41, 19, 16, 15, 11, 11, 9, 6, 6, 7, 7, 6,
            5, 7, 8, 14, 14, 12, 13, 27, 27, 25, 30, 28, 31, 32, 30, 29, 37, 37
            [30]
02-27-71    HOT LPs -- 126, 126, 149, 185, 178  [5]

08-21-71    **Pictures of Moments to Remember** (Mer.61349)  37, 32, 26, 23,
            18, 16, 21, 20, 20, 23, 34, 34, 33, 38, 37, 39  [16]

03-18-72    **Innerview** (Mer. 61358)  45, 20, 16, 15, 15, 21, 23, 22, 21, 21, 20,
            19, 16, 14, 12, 12, 28, 28, 35, 42  [20]

09-09-72    **Country Music Then & Now** (Mer. 61367)  41, 33, 27, 25, 22, 19,
            15, 11, 11, 9, 8, 7, 7, 9, 13, 14, 14, 20, 33  [19]

02-10-73    **SB Sing Country Symphonies in E Major** (Mer.61374)  40, 35,
            29, 25, 21, 17, 14, 11, 11, 13, 13, 14, 25, 40  [14]

10-13-73    **Carry Me Back** (Mer.1676)  48, 39, 39, 34, 34, 33, 32, 29, 28, 27,
            23, 20, 19, 17, 11, 11, 18, 20, 27, 41, 39, 49  [22]

08-03-74    **Thank You World** (Mer.1707)  49, 40, 37, 36, 46  [5]

02-01-75    **Sons of the Motherland** (Mer.11019)  36, 32, 36, 35, 33, 32, 29,
            31, 39, 37, 44, 48  [12]

08-09-75  **The Best of the Statler Brothers** (Mer.11037) 41, 32, 20, 15, 10,
          8, 4, 4, 3, 3, 4, 3, 2, 2, 3, 9, 9, 12, 12, 17, 21, 21, 29, 33, 31, 31,
          27, 29, 29, 32, 39, 37, 35, 39 [34]
09-13-75  TOP LPs & TAPE -- 183, 172, 161, 144, 144, 140, 158, 154, 154,
          150 [10]
03-26-77  Re-Entry -- 38, 31, 27, 27, 21, 21, 18, 18, 16, 16, 24, 34 [12]
01-21-78  Re-Entry -- 32, 28, 20, 19, 20 16, 14, 11, 11, 9, 9, 8, 12, 12, 13, 8,
          11, 9, 9, 6, 6, 10, 9, 8, 18, 16, 15, 11, 11, 11, 16, 17, 16, 16, 13,
          12, 15, 14, 14, 16, 16, 20, 19, 26, 22, 22, 28, 24, 22, 22, 20, 22,
          20, 20, 20, 19, 18, 23, 23, 35, 33, 30, 29, 28, 25, 24, 28, 28, 28,
          36, 32, 28, 28, 32, 29, 28, 30, 33, 29, 32, 26, 26, 34, 38, 43, 41,
          46, 44, 43, 38, 50 [91]
12-08-79  Re-Entry -- (8 weeks later) 45, 45, 40, 30, 23, 23, 20, 20, 20, 19,
          28, 25, 36, 41, 43, 41 [17]
04-12-80  Re-Entry -- (2 weeks later) 40, 40, 48, 45 [4]
05-31-80  Re-Entry -- (4 weeks later) 60, 60, 56, 61, 59, 62, 62, 71, 72, 74
          [10]
          **Total Weeks on Chart -- 168**

11-22-75  **Holy Bible - Old Testament** (Mer 11051) 48, 39, 30, 26, 26, 28,
          35, 37, 44 [9]

11-22-75  **Holy Bible - New Testament** (Mer 11052) 38, 32, 26, 25, 23, 23,
          22,30, 41, 44, 49, 41, 41, 46, 49, 49, 47, 45 [18]

04-17-76  **Harold, Lew, Phil & Don** (Mer 11077) 47, 41, 29, 27, 23, 21, 21,
          23, 22, 25, 24, 41, 36, 34, 34, 33, 43 [17]

02-12-77  **The Country America Loves** (Mer 11125) 30, 17 ,11, 10, 13, 20,
          24, 34, 44, 36, 36, 32, 41, 48 [14]

08-13-77  **Short Stories** (Mer 15001) 42, 26 , 24, 23, 21, 21, 25, 25, 33 [9]

04-29-78  **Entertainers . . . On & Off the Record** (Mer 5007) 17, 16, 15, 12,
          10, 8, 7, 5, 5, 6, 5, 8, 14, 8, 8, 7, 7, 8, 8, 9, 10, 8, 11, 10, 11, 10,
          10, 14, 13, 16, 57, 26, 35, 32, 41, 41, 40, 37, 34, 29, 27, 40, 35,
          39, 35, 30, 41, 35, 31, 34, 47, 38, 38, 37, 49 ,49, 45, 45, 45, 41,
          36, 34, 46, 42, 48, 42, 47, 46, 48 [69]

01-06-79  **Holy Bible** (2-record set, Mer 2101) 45, 44, 44, 48, 46 [5]

04-21-79  **The Originals** (Mer15016) 25, 23, 15, 10, 8, 8, 8, 9, 10, 14, 13, 13,
          19, 22, 22, 22, 23, 33, 32, 42, 36, 36 [22]
10-13-79  Re-Entry -- 44, 50, 50, 49, 48 [5]
01-19-80  Re-Entry -- 42, 49 [2]
          **Total Weeks on Chart -- 29**

01-05-80    **Statler Brothers Christmas Card** (Mer 15012) 37, 34 [2]

02-02-80    **The Best of the Statler Bros. Rides Again, Vol. II** (Mer 15024)
            18, 14, 9, 8, 6, 6, 4, 4, 4, 4, 13, 7, 7, 18, 15, 20, 34, 35, 49, 42,
            52, 49, 56, 53, 63, 61, 63, 66, 70, 68 [30]
12-27-80    Re-Entry -- (one week later) 59, 59, 71, 67 [4]

08-16-80    **Tenth Anniversary** (Mer 15027) 34, 32, 30, 16, 15, 15, 14, 13, 14,
            20, 28, 25, 31, 41, 34, 29, 27, 38, 36, 43, 38, 42, 42, 74, 74, 68,
            62 [27]

07-18-81    **Years Ago** (Mer 16002) 28, 19, 13, 13, 9, 9, 10, 16, 12, 18, 24, 41,
            37, 42, 28, 28, 32, 30, 37, 32, 32, 36, 56, 51, 48, 43, 42, 42, 41,
            57, 64, 71, 71, 74, 42, 32, 24, 19, 15, 14, 14, 24, 28, 27, 33, 48,
            51, 50, 54, 53, 52, 63, 75, 74, 75, 75 [58]

07-24-82    **The Legend Goes On** (Mer 14048) 45, 35, 29, 27, 24, 22, 21, 21,
            19, 18, 17, 19, 18, 20, 32, 32, 31, 37, 51, 48, 54, 68 [22]

06-11-83    **Today** (Mer 812-184-1) 49, 42, 32, 32, 31, 26, 18, 15, 15, 14, 11,
            11, 11, 12, 14, 17, 16, 22, 20, 26, 25, 35, 31, 43, 67, 73, 74 [27]
01-28-84    Re-Entry -- 64, 41, 30, 26, 22, 16, 14, 13, 12, 12, 10, 1, 15, 20, 26,
            22, 22, 31, 32, 26, 26, 30, 27, 27, 32, 28, 23, 23, 24, 23, 27, 29,
            26, 30, 28, 31, 43, 50, 55, 68, 70, 72, 71, 73 [44]
08-17-85    Re-Entry -- 63, 63, 59, 59, 60, 66, 66, 70, 68, 67, 70, 70, 71, 67, 73,
            74 [16]
03-01-86    Re-Entry -- 63, 60, 72, 70, 68, 68, 69, 71, 70, 67, 73, 73, 66, 71, 70,
            67, 74, 74 [18]
07-19-86    Re-Entry -- 71, 65, 74, 74, 72, 70, 71, 75 [8]
10-18-86    Re-Entry -- 66, 66, 69 [3]
            **Total Weeks on Chart -- 116**

05-19-84    **Atlanta Blue** (Mer 818-652-1) 26, 20, 16, 14, 12, 11, 11, 10, 11,
            12, 11, 10, 10, 9, 8, 13, 14, 13, 12, 13, 16, 16, 16, 17, 17, 15, 19,
            23, 21, 20, 24, 21, 21, 21, 20, 19, 20, 18, 17, 18, 18, 16, 16, 15,
            15, 20, 19, 23, 20, 19, 22, 23, 24, 27, 34, 32, 31, 32, 32, 27, 27,
            28, 26, 26, 29, 28, 30, 36, 40, 43, 39, 39, 42, 37, 27, 43, 49, 48,
            47, 56, 55, 59, 61, 58, 64, 64, 65, 61, 57, 56, 59, 58, 55, 54, 57,
            59, 57, 56, 61, 65, 67, 69, 62, 62, 59, 64, 58, 54, 49, 71, 65, 59,
            58, 53, 53, 61, 63, 69, 71, 68, 58, 58, 66, 71, 69, 61, 50, 64, 65,
            70, 72, 72, 69, 66 [134]
01-17-87    Re-Entry -- 74, 74 [2]
            **Total Weeks on Chart -- 136**

05-25-85    **Pardners in Rhyme** (Mer 824-420-1)  29, 25, 21, 18, 13, 13, 12,
            11, 10, 8, 10, 8, 10, 9, 9, 9, 9, 7, 6, 5, 5, 3, 3, 1, 2, 3, 5, 5, 10, 11,
            13, 20, 21, 21, 21, 23, 23, 23, 22, 23, 23, 25, 25, 22, 22, 21, 23,
            25, 23, 22, 27, 25, 25, 25, 23, 26, 24, 27, 42, 46, 41, 36, 32, 30,
            30, 28, 27, 25, 45, 27, 27, 30, 44, 42, 38, 33, 32, 33, 48, 45, 47,
            54, 58, 54, 54, 67, 67, 62, 58, 55, 75, 64, 74, 66, 66  [93]
03-14-87    Re-Entry -- 71, 71, 67, 67, 71  [5]
            **Total Weeks on Chart -- 98**

12-21-85    **Christmas Present** (Mer 824-785-1) 49, 45, 45, 42, 42  [5]
12-20-86    Re-Entry -- 66, 49, 49, 58  [4]
            **Total Weeks on Chart -- 9**

06-14-86    **Four for the Show** (Mer 826-782-1)  62, 23, 16, 15, 14, 13, 11, 11,
            8, 8, 8, 8, 9, 9, 9, 8, 8, 9, 9, 7, 8, 12, 18, 37, 28, 28, 44, 46, 46,
            42, 42, 42, 47, 47, 49, 48, 46, 47, 46, 38, 38, 33, 33, 32, 26, 32,
            34, 37, 41, 38, 43, 40, 43, 43, 51, 41, 47, 45, 43, 42, 48, 75  [62]

11-01-86    **Radio Gospel Favorites** (Mer 826-710-1)  56, 51, 39, 36, 36, 33,
            31, 49, 59, 59, 52, 45, 41, 34, 34, 34, 36, 33, 37, 49, 47, 56, 58,
            57, 59, 53, 65, 60, 71, 69  [30]
06-13-87    Re-Entry -- 64, 62, 64, 64, 72, 65, 71, 71, 70, 70  [10]
08-29-87    Re-Entry -- 65  [1]
09-26-87    Re-Entry -- 72, 72, 69  [3]
            **Total Weeks on Chart -- 44**

08-22-87    **Maple Street Memories** (Mer 832-404-1)  31, 18, 11, 11, 12, 12, 9,
            9, 10, 11, 13, 15, 17, 18, 16, 19, 19, 20, 21, 21, 22, 20, 21, 27,
            26, 30, 32, 30, 31, 31, 31, 31, 29, 29, 28, 30, 29, 30, 31, 30, 30,
            31, 32, 32, 35, 32, 30, 31, 36, 31, 31, 38, 41, 45, 46, 45, 47, 49,
            51, 35, 56, 63, 74  [63]

11-05-88    **The Statlers Greatest Hits, Vol. III** (Mer 834626)  44, 33, 31, 26,
            23, 24, 23, 22, 22, 21, 21, 21, 22, 25, 25, 26, 30, 31, 30, 30, 32,
            38, 38, 41, 45, 48, 47, 54, 52, 54, 51, 54, 54, 47, 46, 42, 39, 45,
            38, 36, 33, 35, 35, 37, 40, 38, 38, 39, 47, 44, 51, 50, 58  [53]

11-11-89    **The Statlers -- Live & Sold Out** (Mer 838 231-1)  67, 45, 41, 41,
            41, 43, 42, 42, 42, 43, 40, 40, 41, 46, 44, 51, 50, 50, 54, 60, 75,
            73  [22]

07-28-90    **Music, Memories & You** (Mer 842 518-2)  72, 66, 40, 36, 31, 32,
            32, 38, 40, 41, 44, 46, 55, 54, 61  [15]
11-17-90    Re-Entry -- 63, 65, 64, 64, 61, 56, 64, 57, 60, 64, 73, 71  [12]

08-03-91    **All-American Country** (Mer. 848 370-2/4)  71  [1]

# CHAPTER 8

# Statler Proverbs

The Statlers have, maybe unknowingly, written several proverbs. Webster's Dictionary defines a proverb as "a brief familiar maxim of folk wisdom, usually compressed in form, often involving a bold image and frequently a jingle that catches the memory." Defining further, a maxim is, "a succinct general truth, moral reflection or rule of conduct." The lines given here are from songs they have written, and each meets the above definitions.

There were other lines that I would like to have included here. Some of them hold special meaning for me. But due to an inability to reach an agreement with the publisher's administrator, they have been omitted from this chapter.

1.  You can't trust a memory that's had too much time.
                                                    *"That Haunted Old House"*

2.  A woman will get madder at you for something you don't do to her, than for something that you do.
                                                                          *"Dad"*

3.  Whatever happened to Randolph Scott has happened to the best of me.
                                    *"Whatever Happened to Randolph Scott"*

4.  Time leaves you nothing but memories and tears.
                                                                    *"I'll Be Here"*

5.  You can't find a heart when it's hidden by pride.

*"For Cryin' Out Loud"*

6.  A woman has feelings all her own that only come to surface when she's sleeping all alone.

*"The Best That I Can Do"*

7.  When Elvis died, we all knew that we could, too.

*"A Child of the Fifties"*

8.  It's grief as well as joy that molds terrific men from simple boys.

*"Chet Atkins' Hand"*

9.  Beyond romance there's always a chance that someday you'll be alone.

*"Beyond Romance"*

10. So many times love can be unkind for hearts that can't find their way home.

*"Beyond Romance"*

11. Old memories pass, life goes by too fast, so be there when love comes your way.

*"Beyond Romance"*

12. When life comes down on you too much, out of sorts and out of touch, take it to The One in prayer.

*"Jesus Showed Me So"*

13. Golden things won't turn or tarnish, silver things won't lose their shine; an old sweet memory lasts much longer.

*"I Never Once Got Tired of You"*

14. What I've learned from living is that you can't believe everything you see in your dreams.

*"Everything You See in Your Dreams"*

15. Prayers answered late are still good.

*"I've Never Lived This Long Before"*


16. It may not be a real job, but it keeps our dream alive.

*"What We Love to Do"*


17. Remember life is fragile, so handle it with prayer.

*"He's Always There for You"*


18. "I'm sorry" is never easy to say, and alone is never easy to be.

*"I'm Sorry You Had to Be the One"*


19. Give it your best and if that's not enough, don't lay awake losing rest. Don't even bother to give it at all, if you can't always give it your best.

*"Give It Your Best"*


20. If you don't grow together, sooner or later you'll grow apart.

*"Sweeter and Sweeter"*

---

# You've Been Like a Mother to Me

She's seen me through lots of troubles,
She's stayed up nights so I could sleep.
She's given me more than comfort
She's given me something I can keep.
I love her, and I need her,
And I want to be with her all the time.
I'd fight just to keep her
And I'd die if I thought she wasn't mine.

I love her every morning thank God for her every night
I worship the ground she stands on
And I stand on the ground she'll be alright
When you need me, you know I'll be there
'Cause you've always been there for me.
America, God knows I love you
'Cause you've been like a mother to me.

America, we've been through troubles
And we'll make it again, just wait and see.
America, God knows I love you
'Cause you've been like a mother to me.

America, stand up and show it
That you're proud of the red, white, and blue
You love her, and you know it.
'Cause she's been like a mother to you.

*Don Reid*, September 30, 1974
American Cowboy Music Co., Inc.
Used by permission of
    All Nations Publishing Co., Inc.

# CHAPTER 9

# Happy Birthday, U.S.A.

Gypsy Hill Park, Staunton, Virginia

Taken from the liner notes of the **Sons of the Motherland** album --
"Back in 1970 we started a 4th of July celebration in our hometown of Staunton, Virginia. It was something we wanted to do for our hometown and found it to be a great way to raise money for a lot of the local charities there. Our show each year is free to the public but the charities sell food, crafts, soft drinks, etc., on the grounds. The news of the event spread and now [1977] we have people coming from every state in the country to form crowds of 50,000 each year in our little town of 25,000. It doesn't cost them a cent unless they want to eat a hot dog or let their kids take a pony ride or enjoy any number of events that take place over the two-day event. We always have a guest on our show who comes at absolutely no charge and performs for our hometown gathering. They're not only some of the greatest names in Country Music but some of the greatest friends we have in the world."

Taken from *The Statler Brothers 30th Anniversary Celebration Scrapbook* written by Colin Escott, p. 25 --
"For 25 years the Statler Brothers mounted an outdoor bash on July 4th called 'Happy Birthday USA.' They brought in guests, donated their time, and gave the proceeds to charity. 1994 was the last year they participated. 'The event has grown and gotten so big,' says Harold, 'and we have probably done everything for it and for the community that can be done. It can't get any bigger. It's time to pass it on.' From an initial attendance of 3500, the turnout has grown to almost 100,000.

"The July 4th bash goes hand-in-hand with the Statler Brothers' idea of what it is to be a citizen. Given half a chance, country singers will wrap themselves in the flag, thump their chest and swear allegiance to God, Mom and Home, but the Statlers cut out the bluster and quietly hold fast to the values they were raised on. 'No one has ever accused us of flagwaving in the wrong sense,' says Harold. 'We do it for the corniest reason, because we believe in it.'"

The following is a listing of the Special Guest(s) who appeared each year of the Happy Birthday, U.S.A., celebration, for the 25 years the Statlers were an active part of the festivities.

| | | | |
|---|---|---|---|
| 1970 | No Guest | 1983 | Don Williams |
| 1971 | Carl Perkins & Mac Wiseman | 1984 | Mel Tillis |
| 1972 | Bobbie Roy | 1985 | Helen Cornelius |
| | | 1986 | Mel McDaniel |
| 1973 | Johnny Cash, June Carter, Carl Perkins & The Tennessee Three | 1987 | Sylvia |
| | | 1988 | Reba McEntire |
| 1974 | Bill Anderson | 1989 | No Guest: -- Special Two-hour Statler Feature |
| 1975 | Johnny Russell & Charles McCoy | | |
| 1976 | Tammy Wynette | 1990 | Conway Twitty |
| 1977 | Ronnie Milsap | 1991 | Charley Pride & Neal McCoy |
| 1978 | Johnny Rodriquez | 1992 | Crystal Gayle |
| 1979 | Barbara Mandrell | 1993 | Janie Fricke & Rex Allen, Jr. |
| 1980 | Brenda Lee | | |
| 1981 | No Guest: -- Special Two-Hour Statler Feature | 1994 | No Guest: Special Two-hour Statler Farewell Concert |
| 1982 | Jerry Reed | | |

# CHAPTER 10

# The Statler Brothers and Television

In the late 1980s, the Statlers received an invitation from Jim Owens Productions to host a weekly television show on The Nashville Network. The Statlers had first worked with Jim when they hosted a Music City News Awards show in 1978 that he was producing. The Statlers hosted, or co-hosted, the Music City News Awards show seven years in a row. Then, in 1981, Jim produced their highly rated network television special.

The first television special was entitled "An Evening With the Statler Brothers: A Salute to the Good Times" (1981). Guest stars were Brenda Lee, Barbara Mandrell, Janie Fricke, Conway Twitty, Roy Rogers, and Chet Atkins. It was produced by Jim Owens Productions for Multi-Media Entertainment, directed by Steven A. Womack, filmed on location in Staunton, Virginia, and at the Tennessee Performing Arts Center, Nashville. The retrospective clip of the prom of the Class of '57 was performed by the children of Harold, Phil and Don.

The second special was "Another Evening with the Statler Brothers: Heroes, Legends, and Friends," (1983). Guest stars were Mel Tillis, Reba McEntire, Roy Clark, The Masters V, The Oak Ridge Boys, and Charly McClain. It was produced by Jim Owens Productions & Statler-Grant Productions for Multi-Media Entertainment; directed by Steven A. Womack; and filmed on location in Maggie Valley, North Carolina.

The third special was "Statler Brothers Christmas Present," taped in October and aired in December 1985. Guest stars were Gene Autry, Roger Miller, Merle Haggard, Crystal Gayle, and Harold Lawrence. It was produced by Jim Owens Productions & Statler-Grant Productions for Multi-Media Entertainment, and was directed by Steven A. Womack.

All three of these specials received the Music City News Award for Country TV Special of the Year.

The Statlers appeared on a TNN special dedicated to Minnie Pearl. On that special they performed a song they had written especially for her, entitled "MINNIE, YOU'RE A PEARL." This song has not been recorded for commercial release.

Worried about overexposure, the Statlers had always resisted the idea of a series, and, as Harold says, "We'd seen television suck people in, spit 'em out, and they were never the same afterward." They are a natural for television, though, because they are complete, rounded entertainers with a keen sense of what it takes to mount a show, and, when Jim Owens put the idea to them, they decided that perhaps it wasn't such a bad idea after all. The first show aired October 5, 1991.[1]

Regulars on the program for the first three seasons were Janie Fricke and Rex Allen, Jr. Beginning with the fourth season, Crystal Gayle and Ronna Reeves were regulars. The Bill Walker Orchestra provided the music for each season's shows.

## First Season

October 5, 1991
 Oh Baby Mine
 Carry Me Back
 You, You, You
 Your Cheatin' Heart
 There Is Power in the Blood

October 12, 1991
 The Official Historian on Shirley
  Jean Berrell
 Flowers on the Wall
 Dang Me
 Together Again
 How Great Thou Art

October 19, 1991
 Small, Small World
 More Than a Name on a Wall
 On Top of Old Smokey
 Old Soldiers Never Die
 Just a Little Talk with Jesus

October 26, 1991
 Atlanta Blue
 Don't Wait On Me
 She Thinks I Still Care
 I've Been Everywhere
 One Less Day to Go

November 2, 1991
 Hello, Mary Lou
 My Only Love
 Ballad of Davy Crockett
 Moments to Remember
 A Beautiful Life

November 9, 1991
 I'll Go to My Grave Loving You
 Elizabeth
 Daddy Sang Bass
 All I Have to Offer You Is Me
 In the Sweet Bye and Bye

November 16, 1991
 Bed of Rose's
 Woman without a Home
 Jeepers Creepers
 God Bless America
 I'll Fly Away

November 23, 1991
 Susan When She Tried
 Too Much on My Heart
 Here You Come Again
 I'm Just a Country Boy
 When the Roll Is Called Up Yonder

---

[1]From *The Statler Brothers 30th Anniversary Celebration Scrapbook* by Colin Escott, p. 21. Reprinted by permission of Mercury Nashville.

November 30, 1991
  Do You Know You Are My
    Sunshine
  Forever
  Walk Right In
  Still
  I Believe I'll Live For Him

December 7, 1991
  Do You Remember These
  The Class of '57
  Buttons and Bows
  Now Is the Hour
  Over the Sunset Mountains

December 14, 1991
  Guilty
  Tomorrow Never Comes
  Good-Hearted Woman
  You've Been Like a Mother to Me
  Noah Found Grace in the Eyes of
    the Lord

December 21, 1991
  Thank You World
  How Are Things in Clay,
    Kentucky?
  Running Bear
  Wings of a Dove
  This Ole House

December 28, 1991 --
(Christmas Show)
  Christmas Country Style
  No Reservation at the Inn
  Medley: Here Comes Santa Claus,
    White Christmas, Joy to the
    World, Hark the Herald Angels
    Sing, O' Little Town of
    Bethlehem, Away in a Manger,
    Silent Night, Silver Bells. (with
    Brenda Lee & Forrester Sisters)
  O, Holy Night

January 4, 1992
  Years Ago
  Silver Medals & Sweet Memories
  On the Road Again
  Years
  What a Friend We Have in Jesus

January 11, 1992
  Count On Me
  Charlotte's Web
  Sweet Sixteen
  Back Home Again
  In the Garden

January 18, 1992
  Pictures
  New York City
  Remember Me
  All That I Can Do
  Love Lifted Me

January 25, 1992
  Whatever
  Neighborhood Girl
  Chattanooga Shoeshine Boy
  Goodnight, Irene
  Anywhere Is Home

February 1, 1992
  If I'd Paid More Attention to You
  Some I Wrote
  Pistol-Packin' Momma
  Don't Fence Me In
  Jesus Is the Answer Every Time

February 8, 1992
  I'll Be the One
  Your Picture in the Paper
  Wabash Cannonball
  Alexander's Ragtime Band
  Pass Me Not

February 15, 1992
  Moon Pretty Moon
  What Do I Care

Sioux City Sue
Sentimental Journey
Life's Railway to Heaven

February 22, 1992
Eight More Miles to Louisville
Who Am I to Say
Just to Satisfy You
Lord, I Hope This Day Is Good
The Fourth Man

March 7, 1992
A Child of the Fifties
Don't Forget Yourself
Amanda
The Gambler
Rock of Ages

---

## Second Season
December 12, 1992
A Hurt I Can't Handle
Beyond Romance
Chantilly Lace
Do You Remember These
Precious Memories

December 19, 1992
There Is You
Hat and Boots
Cruisin' Down the River
Someday
The Old Rugged Cross

January 2, 1993
All American Girl
A Lifetime of Loving You in Vain
Don't Take Your Guns to Town
The Battle of New Orleans
Are You Washed in the Blood

January 9, 1993
Memory Lane

Am I Crazy
Henry the VIII
King of the Road
The Eastern Gate

January 16, 1993
I Wonder How the Old Folks Are at
    Home
Same Way Every Time
Cattle Call
Big Bouquet of Roses
May the Good Lord Bless and
    Keep You (with Janie Fricke &
    Rex Allen, Jr.)
On the Jericho Road

January 23, 1993
Dynamite
Thank God I've Got You
Zip-A-Dee-Do-Dah
The Old Lamplighter
He's Always There for You

January 30, 1993
Memphis
Your Place or Mine
Daydreams About Night Things
Thank God I'm a Country Boy
Led Out of Bondage

February 6, 1993
Promise
Maple Street Memories
An Occasional Rose
I Believe in You
Church in the Wildwood

February 13, 1993
To Make a Long Story Short
Fallin' in Love
Singin' in the Rain
Wedding Bells Are Breaking Up
    That Old Gang of Mine
How Great Thou Art

February 20, 1993
  Flowers on the Wall
  Memories Are Made of This (with
    Sounds, Inc.)
  Never Grow Old

February 27, 1993
  I Lost My Heart to You
  The Class of '57
  Tomorrow Never Comes
  Here in the Real World
  Feeling Mighty Fine

March 6, 1993
  Don't Wait on Me
  Monday Morning Secretary
  Rock Around the Clock
  This Ole House
  Everyday Will Be Sunday Bye &
    Bye

March 13, 1993
  You Gave Yourself Away
  My Only Love
  Don't Let the Stars Get in Your Eyes
  Heartaches By the Numbers
  The Brave Apostles Twelve

March 20, 1993
  Do You Know You Are My
    Sunshine
  You Ought to Be in Pictures
  North to Alaska
  Tender Years
  The Old Account

March 27, 1993
  You'll Be Back
  Elizabeth
  Goody, Goody
  I'm an Old Cowhand
  At the Cross

April 3, 1993
  Bed of Rose's
  It Only Hurts for a Little While
  Goin' Steady
  If You Ain't Lovin'
  Hello, Walls (with Janie Fricke &
    Rex Allen, Jr.)
  One Size Fits All

April 10, 1993
  The Movies
  Tumbling Tumbleweeds
  Blueberry Hill
  It's Different Now

April 17, 1993
  I'll Go to My Grave Loving You
  (I'll Even Love You) Better Than I
    Did Then
  The Gambler
  Do You Know You Are My
    Sunshine
  I'm Redeemed

April 24, 1993
  Put It on the Card
  Too Much on My Heart
  Nine to Five
  Elvira
  Amazing Grace

May 1, 1993
  Years Ago
  Nothing As Original As You
  The Fightin' Side of Me
  Fifteen Years Ago
  There's a Man In Here

May 8, 1993
  Chattanooga Shoeshine Boy
  Do You Remember These
  Ain't That a Shame
  Tutti-Frutti
  The Whole World in His Hands

May 15, 1993
  We Ain't Even Started Yet
  More Than a Name on a Wall
  We Won't Be Home Until Then

May 22, 1993
  Thank You for Breaking My Heart
  Love Was All We Had
  The King Is Coming

December 18 or 25, 1993 --
Christmas Show
  The Carols Those Kids Used to Sing
  Silver Bells
  T'was the Night Before Christmas
    Segment -- David Huddleston as
    Santa, Statlers, McGuire Sisters,
    Janie Fricke, Rex Allen, Jr.
    Medley -- Jolly Old St. Nicholas,
    Rudolph,    the    Red-Nosed
    Reindeer, Up on the Housetop,
    Santa Claus Is Coming to Town,
    The Christmas Song
  Who Do You Think
  Brahm's Bethlehem Lullaby
  Carol Medley -- There's a Song in
    the Air, We Three Kings of
    Orient Are, Star of Bethlehem,
    Go Tell It on the Mountain

## Third Season

January 22, 1994
  Hello, Mary Lou
  I've Never Lived This Long Before
  Whispering Hope

January 29, 1994
  Atlanta Blue
  Chet, You're the Reason (with Chet
    Atkins)
  That's All I Want from You
  She Thinks I Still Care
  After the Sunrise

February 5, 1994
  Walking Heartache in Disguise
  He'll Always Have You Again
  Allegheny Moon
  Have I Told You Lately
  Open Your Heart

February 12, 1994
  Dream On
  You Don't Wear Blue So Well
  Winchester Cathedral
  There Goes My Everything
  Jesus Hold My Hand

February 19, 1994
  What We Love to Do
  New York City
  The Prisoner's Song
  Yes, Sir, That's My Baby
  Jesus Showed Me So

February 26, 1994
  Susan When She Tried
  My Past Is Looking Brighter
  I Always Get Lucky with You
  Swingin'
  He'll Pilot Me

March 5, 1994
  All That I Can Do
  No One Will Ever Know
  Goodnight Sweetheart
  Leaning on the Everlasting Arms

March 12, 1994
  Guilty
  Dad
  Blue Moon
  Red Sails in the Sunset
  Little Is Much

March 19, 1994
(Presentation of Gold & Platinum
Albums by Mercury Record Co.)
  Give It Your Best

What Do I Care
It's All in the Game
Oh, Lonesome Me
I'll Have a New Life

March 26, 1994
Oh Baby Mine
You Can't Go Home
Red Roses for a Blue Lady
Goodnight, Irene
His Eye Is on the Sparrow

April 2, 1994 -- Easter Show
Dear Hearts and Gentle People
Gospel Medley -- Statlers, The
    Cathedrals, Vestal Goodman,
    Cathedrals piano player, Bill
    Walker -- Near the Cross, The
    Old Rugged Cross, At the
    Cross, Amazing Grace
Easter Parade

April 9, 1994
There's Magic in the Air**
Before the Magic Turns to Memory
Daddy Sang Bass

April 16, 1994
All the Times
Forever
Five Minutes Before
I Love You for Sentimental
    Reasons
Rock of Ages

April 23, 1994
The Official Historian on Shirley
    Jean Berrell
That Haunted Old House
Sugar Blues
Will the Circle Be Unbroken
When I Take My Vacation in
    Heaven

April 30, 1994
I'll Be the One
For Cryin' Out Loud
Uncle Penn
City of New Orleans
Standing on the Promises

May 7, 1994
Today I Went Back
Woman without a Home
All of Me
The Last Round-Up
Keep on the Firing Line

May 14, 1994
Who Am I to Say
Some I Wrote
Me and Bobby McGee
Take Me Home Country Roads
I Shall Not Be Moved

May 21, 1994
Eight More Miles to Louisville
Silver Medals & Sweet Memories
I Walk the Line
Green Door
Jesus Loves Me

May 28, 1994
Carry Me Back
My Woman, My Woman, My Wife
Today I Started Loving You Again
Farther Along

June 4, 1994
(Let's Just) Take One Night at a
    Time
Beyond Romance
Always
The Naughty Lady of Shady Lane
Lord, I'm Comin' Home

June 11, 1994
Autumn Leaves
More Like Daddy Than Me

I Still Miss Someone
I Never Shall Forget the Day

June 18, 1994
If We Never Had
I Love You So Much It Hurts
Wreck of the Old 97
Last Date (with Floyd Cramer)
The Man Upstairs

---

## Fourth Season
January 28, 1995
Less of Me
Some Memories Last Forever
Singin' the Blues
Battle of New Orleans
I Can Tell You the Time

February 4, 1995
Maggie
Second Thoughts
Everything Is Beautiful
Georgia on My Mind
Revive Us Again

February 11, 1995
I Don't Dance No More
Let's Get Started If We're Gonna
    Break My Heart
When You and I Were Young,
    Maggie
Where the Roses Never Fade

February 18, 1995
Never Ending Song of Love
Mr. Autry
I Won't Take Less (with Crystal
    Gayle & Ronna Reeves)
I've Got That Old Time Religion in
    My Heart

February 25, 1995
You Can't Judge a Book by Its
    Cover
I Wish I Could Be
Margie's at the Lincoln Park Inn
Billy Christian
Me and Jesus (w/Crystal Gayle &
    Ronna Reeves)
Till the Storm Passes By

March 4, 1995
Thank You World
Born to Be with You
This World Is Not My Home

March 11, 1995
Her Heart or Mine
Don't Forget Yourself
Eight More Miles to Louisville
My Old Kentucky Home
Since Jesus Came into My Heart

March 18, 1995
Whatever Happened to Randolph
    Scott
I Had Too Much to Dream
The Vacant Chair
We'll Soon Be Done with Troubles
    and Trials

March 25, 1995
Jealous Eyes
Am I Crazy
Three Bells (with Crystal Gayle &
    Ronna Reeves)
Looking for a City

April 1, 1995
Pictures
I'll Take Care of You
California Here I Come
I Love You, California
Tramp on the Street

April 8, 1995
  Think Of Me
  Your Picture in the Paper
  Ballad of Tom Dooley
  When I Take My Vacation in
      Heaven

April 15, 1995
  Count on Me
  I Don't Know Why
  Mama Tried
  You're Walking on the Fighting
      Side of Me
  Sing Me Back Home
  Hide Thou Me

April 22, 1995
  I'm Not Quite Through Crying
  Here We Are Again
  Tennessee Waltz
  When Your Old Wedding Ring
      Was New
  Glory Land Way

April 29, 1995
  Moon Pretty Moon
  The Star
  Gotta Travel On
  Illinois
  Wonderful Words of Life

May 6, 1995
  There Is You
  (I'll Even Love You) Better Than I
      Did Then
  Only You
  Jesus Living Next to Me**

May 13, 1995
  If I'd Paid More Attention to You
  A Lifetime of Loving You in Vain
  Love Letters
  The Fourth Man

May 20, 1995
  A Child of the Fifties
  How Are Things in Clay, Kentucky?
  In the Sweet Bye and Bye

May 27, 1995
  We Got the Mem'ries
  Hat and Boots
  Deep In the Heart of Texas
  The Eyes of Texas
  Streets of Laredo
  Yellow Rose of Texas
      (w/Crystal & Ronna)
  Life's Railway to Heaven

June 3, 1995
  A Hurt I Can't Handle
  Neighborhood Girl
  Love Me Tender
  Noah Found Grace in the Eyes of
      the Lord

June 10, 1995
  Dynamite
  You Oughta Be Here with Me
  Blue Ridge Mountains of Virginia
  Carry Me Back to Old Virginia
  Turn Your Radio On

June 17, 1995 -- World War II Salute
  Boogie Woogie Bugle Boy
  Mid-Medley -- I'm Walkin' the Floor
      Over You (Harold), I'll Be Seeing
      You (Phil), The White Cliffs of
      Dover (Don), Dream (Jimmy),
      Sentimental Journey (all)
  God Bless America

---

## Fifth Season
January 6, 1996
  We
  Tender Years

She Thinks I Still Care
The Race Is On (w/Ronna Reeves
   & Crystal Gayle)
My Music, My Memories & You
Just a Little While

January 13, 1996
Bye Bye Love
Making Believe
The Blackwood Brothers by the
   Statler Brothers
I Want to Be More Like Jesus
   Everyday (w/James
   Blackwood)

January 20, 1996
I Never Want to Kiss You Goodbye
Will You Be There
Gone
I Wouldn't Take Nothing for My
   Journey Now (w/Vestal
   Goodman)
There Is Power in the Blood

January 27, 1996
I Wonder How the Old Folks Are
   at Home
Mr. & Mississippi
Detour
Cross Over the Bridge (w/Crystal
   Gayle & Ronna Reeves)
When the Yankees Came Home
Rock of Ages

February 3, 1996
'Til the End
Then I Met the Master (w/Jake
   Hess)
Unchained Melody
Goodbye, World, Goodbye

February 10, 1996
Memory Lane
The Last Goodbye

Yours Love
A Beautiful Life

February 17, 1996 -- 100th Show
I'll Go to My Grave Loving You
Fifteen Years Ago
King of the Road
The Statler Brothers Quiz #2
You, You, You
Your Cheatin' Heart
The Old Country Church

February 24, 1996
Take Me Home Country Roads
Holding On
I Can't Stop Loving You
The Other Side of the Cross**

March 2, 1996
Memphis
I Never Once Got Tired of You
Wabash Cannonball
I Guess Things Happen That Way
   (w/Ronna Reeves)
Tennessee Waltz (w/Crystal Gayle
   & Ronna Reeves)
I'm Bound for That City

March 9, 1996
Bed of Rose's
Holding On
I Can't Stop Loving You
I'll Fly Away

March 16, 1996
If It Makes Any Difference
Sugartime
When God Dips His Love in My
   Heart

March 23, 1996
--Rerun--

March 30, 1996
When My Blue Moon Turns to Gold

Falling in Love
The Ballad of Jesse James
There's a Man in Here

April 6, 1996
You Gave Yourself Away
The Best That I Can Do
Sweet Hour of Prayer

April 13, 1996
I Lost My Heart to You
Nothing As Original As You
Pass Me Not

April 20, 1996
Got Leavin' on Her Mind
It Only Hurts for a Little While
Shenandoah
The Missouri Waltz
The Eastern Gate

**These titles were written especially for the television show and have not been recorded by the Statler Brothers for commercial release.

THERE'S MAGIC IN THE AIR
    (Don Reid)
JESUS LIVING NEXT TO ME
    (Langdon Reid)
THE OTHER SIDE OF THE CROSS
    (Don Reid)

On the set. Don, Phil, Harold, and Jimmy work out the final details on a number before taping. This was taken in February 1997, in their sixth season. *The Statler Brothers Show* first aired on The Nashville Network on October 5, 1991. Photo by A. Holtin.

CHAPTER 11

# The Most Awarded Act in the History of Country Music

"The most awarded act in the history of country music . . . Entertainers on and off the record . . . Harold, Phil, Jimmy, and Don . . . the Statler Brothers!" So goes the introduction used at live concerts and on the television show. Never was such an accolade more aptly deserved.

**Grammy Awards**
Best New Country and Western Group - 1965
Best Contemporary Performance by a Group - 1965
Best Country Vocal Performance by a Duo or Group - 1972

**Country Music Association (CMA) Awards**
Vocal Group of the Year -   1972, 1973, 1974, 1975, 1976, 1977, 1979, 1980,
1984

**Academy of Country Music (ACM) Awards**
Group of the Year - 1972, 1978

**Music City News Awards**
Vocal Group of the Year - 1971, 1972, 1973, 1974, 1975, 1976, 1977, 1978,
1979, 1980, 1981, 1982, 1984, 1985, 1986, 1987, 1988, 1989, 1990, 1991,
1992, 1993, 1994, 1996
Entertainer of the Year -- 1983, 1986, 1987
Album of the Year -
1979 - *Entertainers . . . On & Off the Record*
1980 - *The Originals*
1981 - *Tenth Anniversary*
1985 - *Atlanta Blue*
1986 - *Pardners In Rhyme*

**Music City News Awards -- continued**
  Single of the Year -
    1984 - *Elizabeth*
    1986 - *My Only Love*
    1987 - *Too Much on My Heart*
    1990 - *More Than a Name on a Wall*
  Country TV Special of the Year -
    1984 - *An Evening with the Statler Brothers*
    1985 - *Another Evening with the Statler Brothers:*
              *Heroes, Legends & Friends*
    1987 - *Christmas Present*
  Comedy Act of the Year - 1980, 1982, 1983, 1984, 1985
  Songwriter Award -
    1982 - *Don't Wait on Me*, Harold Reid/Don Reid
    1985 - *Elizabeth*, Jimmy Fortune
    1986 - *My Only Love*, Jimmy Fortune
    1987 - *Too Much on My Heart*, Jimmy Fortune
  Country Music Video of the Year
    1985 - *Elizabeth*
    1986 - *My Only Love*
    1988 - *Maple Street Memories*

**American Music Awards**
  Group of the Year - 1979, 1980, 1981

**International Country Music Awards**
  Best International Group - 1976, 1977, 1978, 1979, 1980, 1981

**National Association of Rack Merchandisers (NARM) Awards**
  Best Selling Album By a Country Group
    1978 - *The Best of the Statler Brothers*

**A.C. Nielsen Award**
  Best Syndicated TV Special - 1982 - "An Evening with the Statler Brothers"

**Virginia Broadcasters Association**
  Distinguished Virginian Award - 1986

**Various Other Awards Received**
  "American Spirit of U.S. Air Force" Award - 1990
  Virginia House of Delegates Resolution - 1991
  Virginia State Senate Resolution - 1991

**People's Choice Awards**
  Top Three Finalists for Favorite Group - 1987, 1993

**Plywood Award**
   "Alive at Johnny Mack Brown High School" --
        Lester "Roadhog" Moran & The Cadillac Cowboys

**Gold Albums -- sale of 500,000 units**
          A unit is one record, tape (cassette or 8-track), or compact disc.
   1977 -- *The Best of the Statler Brothers*
   1978 -- *Entertainers . . . On & Off the Record*
   1979 -- *Memories Now & Forever* (Canadian Release)
   1981 -- *The Best of the Statler Brothers Rides Again, Vol. II*
   1981 -- *The Originals*
   1982 -- *Statler Brothers Christmas Card*
   1993 -- *Today*
   1993 -- *Gospel Favorites*
   1993 -- *Holy Bible, New Testament*
   1995 -- *Holy Bible, Old Testament*
   1995 -- *Atlanta Blue*
   1995 -- *Pardners in Rhyme*
   1995 -- *TV Gospel Favorites*
   1995 -- *Tenth Anniversary*

**Platinum Album -- sale of 1,000,000 units**
   1978 -- *The Best of the Statler Brothers*
   1995 -- From the movie, *Pulp Fiction -- Flowers on the Wall*

**Double Platinum Albums**
   1980 -- *The Best of the Statler Brothers*
   1993 -- *The Best of the Statler Brothers*
   1993 -- *Statler Brothers Christmas Card*

**Triple-Platinum Album**
   1995 -- *The Best of the Statler Brothers*

**Number One Chart Placement**
1985 -- Single Releases -- #1 Chart Placement --
        *My Only Love, Too Much on My Heart*
1985 -- Album -- #1 Chart Placement -- *Pardners in Rhyme*

# APPENDIX I

# Chronological Session Listing

| | | | | | |
|---|---|---|---|---|---|
| 04-03-64 | Columbia | 01-13-68 | Cash | 05-17-72 | Cash |
| 07-28-64 | Columbia | 06-03-68 | Columbia | 05-30-72 | Cash |
| 12-18-64 | Cash | 06-04-68 | Columbia | 06-00-72 | Cash |
| 12-19-64 | Cash | 07-30-68 | Cash | 07-27-72 | Cash |
| | | 07-31-68 | Cash | 07-28-72 | Cash |
| 03-12-65 | Cash | 08-29-68 | Cash | 11-01-72 | Mercury |
| 03-13-65 | Columbia | | | 11-02-72 (2) | Mercury |
| 03-13-65 | Cash | 02-24-69 | Cash | 11-03-72 | Mercury |
| 05-12-65 | Cash | 04-22-69 | Columbia | | |
| 06-11-65 | Cash | 04-25-69 (2) | Columbia | 05-21-73 | Mercury |
| 07-28-65 | Cash | 05-07-69 | Columbia | 05-22-73 | Mercury |
| 11-29-65 | Cash | | | 05-23-73 | Mercury |
| 11-30-65 | Columbia | 07-10-70 | Cash | 05-24-73 | Mercury |
| 12-01-65 | Cash | 09-11-70 | Mercury | 10-08-73 | Mercury |
| 12-02-65 | Columbia | 10-19-70 | Mercury | 11-13-73 | Mercury |
| | | 11-10-70 | Mercury | 11-27-73 | Mercury |
| 01-12-66 | Columbia | | | 11-28-73 (2) | Mercury |
| 04-01-66 | Columbia | 04-14-71 | Mercury | 11-29-73 | Mercury |
| 04-29-66 | Columbia | 04-15-71 | Mercury | | |
| | | 04-16-71 (2) | Mercury | 05-15-74 | Mercury |
| 01-11-67 | Cash | 11-16-71 | Mercury | 09-30-74 | Mercury |
| 01-12-67 | Cash | 11-17-71 (2) | Mercury | 10-01-74 | Mercury |
| 02-13-67 | Columbia | 11-18-71 | Mercury | 10-08-74 | Mercury |
| 03-14-67 | Columbia | | | 11-19-74 | Mercury |
| 05-25-67 | Columbia | 01-14-72 | Mercury | 11-20-74 | Mercury |
| 06-22-67 | Columbia | 04-11-72 | Mercury | 11-21-74 | Mercury |
| 08-28-67 | Columbia | 04-12-72 | Mercury | | |
| | | 04-13-72 (2) | Mercury | 04-08-75 | Mercury |
| 01-11-68 | Columbia | 05-15-72 | Cash | 04-09-75 | Mercury |

| | | | | | |
|---|---|---|---|---|---|
| 04-10-75 | Mercury | 02-17-83 | Mercury | 02-06-91 | Mercury |
| 09-23-75 | Mercury | 03-09-83 | Mercury | 02-19-91 | Mercury |
| | | 06-27-83 | Mercury | 02-20-91 | Mercury |
| 01-27-76 | Mercury | | | | |
| 01-28-76 | Mercury | 01-16-84 | Mercury | 02-24-92 | Mercury |
| 01-29-76 | Mercury | 01-17-84 | Mercury | 02-25-92 | Mercury |
| 01-30-76 | Mercury | 01-18-84 | Mercury | 02-06-92 | Mercury |
| 10-19-76 | Mercury | 04-17-84 | Mercury | 02-27-92 | Mercury |
| 10-20-76 | Mercury | | | 04-13-92 | Mercury |
| 10-21-76 | Mercury | 01-14-85 | Mercury | 04-14-92 | Mercury |
| 10-29-76 | Mercury | 01-15-85 | Mercury | 04-15-92 | Mercury |
| | | 01-16-85 | Mercury | 04-16-92 | Mercury |
| 05-24-77 | Mercury | 04-23-85 | Mercury | 04-19-92 | Mercury |
| 05-25-77 | Mercury | 04-24-85 | Mercury | 04-20-92 | Mercury |
| 05-26-77 | Mercury | 05-07-85 | Mercury | | |
| | | 05-08-85 | Mercury | 05-20-93 | Mercury |
| 01-13-78 | Mercury | 06-18-85 | Mercury | 05-21-93 | Mercury |
| 01-16-78 | Mercury | 06-19-85 | Mercury | 06-08-93 | Mercury |
| 01-17-78 (2) | Mercury | | | | |
| 01-18-78 | Mercury | 01-27-86 | Mercury | 05-01-95 | Mercury |
| 02-06-78 | Mercury | 01-28-86 | Mercury | 05-02-95 | Mercury |
| 04-05-78 | Mercury | 02-18-86 | Mercury | 05-03-95 | Mercury |
| 06-27-78 | Mercury | 00-00-86 | Mercury | 05-04-95 | Mercury |
| 09-28-78 | Mercury | 06-16-86 | Mercury | 05-22-95 | Mercury |
| | | 07-16-86 | Mercury | 05-23-95 | Mercury |
| 01-15-79 | Mercury | 11-17-86 | Mercury | 05-24-95 | Mercury |
| 01-16-79 | Mercury | 11-17-86 | Mercury | | |
| 01-17-79 | Mercury | | | | |
| | | 01-14-87 | Mercury | | |
| 01-22-80 | Mercury | | | | |
| 04-29-80 | Mercury | 01-12-88 | Mercury | | |
| 04-30-80 | Mercury | 01-13-88 | Mercury | | |
| 05-01-80 | Mercury | 05-23-88 | Mercury | | |
| | | 05-24-88 | Mercury | | |
| 03-12-81 | Mercury | 05-25-88 | Mercury | | |
| 03-30-81 | Mercury | 11-16-88 | Mercury | | |
| 03-31-81 | Mercury | 11-17-88 | Mercury | | |
| 04-27-81 | Mercury | | | | |
| 04-28-81 | Mercury | 06-23-89 | Live- | | |
| | | | Wheeling, WV | | |
| 03-15-82 | Mercury | | | | |
| 12-07-82 | Mercury | 03-26-90 | Mercury | | |
| | | 11-14-90 | Mercury | | |
| 02-15-83 | Mercury | 12-04-90 | Mercury | | |
| 02-16-83 | Mercury | | | | |

# APPENDIX II

# Pre-Columbia Recordings

In the early 1960s, the Statlers, then known as The Kingsmen, did some recording locally around the Staunton, Virginia, area. This work was as background vocals for local artists. The details are few because the studios no longer exist, and -- to quote a Statler proverb -- "You can't trust a memory that's had too much time." The information shown is from Harold Reid and the label copy. It's been 34 years. I'm pleased Harold can remember this much!

===============================================================
Small studio in Hollins, Virginia                                    1961 or 1962
Harry Snyder (vocal); Harold Reid, Don Reid, Lew DeWitt, Phil Balsley (background vocals); musicians unknown.

1163-45-1005   **THIS OLE HOUSE** (Stuart Hamblen)
               Hamblen Publishing Co.; BMI
               WAYNE-WAY 45-103 -- backed w/SOMEONE LIKE YOU

1163-45-1007   **MAMA WOULD HAVE BEEN SO PROUD**
               (Harry W. Snyder, Harold Reid)
               Bumble Bee Music; BMI
               WAYNE-WAY 45-104 -- backed w/TRADING THE BLUES

**Note:** From the label copy -- Harry Snyder and The Buttermilk Drinkers.
           Wayne-Way Records, 319 W. Main, Waynesboro, Va.
The Statlers do not appear on the flip sides of these 45 singles.
===============================================================
Salem Recording Studio                                               1963
Salem, Virginia
Shirlee Hunter (vocal); Harold Reid, Lew DeWitt, Phil Balsley, Don Reid (background vocals); musicians unknown.

SRP-7100       **BILLY CHRISTIAN** (Thomas Hall)
               Newkeys Music; BMI
               SALEM 535 -- backed w/ ???

**Note:**  From the label copy -- "Shirlee Hunter.  'Salem' Records produced by
McGraw Music Co., Inc.; 111 Main Street, Salem, Virginia."  Don McGraw,
owner, engineer, publisher and distributor.  Mr. McGraw had a music store and
record shop, with a small recording studio in the back.
Source of information on Salem Recording Studio -- Mr. Richard Kiser, Roanoke,
VA.  He was a session musician at Salem in the early sixties, and considered Mr.
McGraw his mentor.
**Note from Harold Reid:**  The "Thomas Hall" is Tom T. Hall.

# APPENDIX III

# Miscellaneous Appearances

The Statlers have appeared in two movies, and several commercials for both radio and TV.

The advertising includes television commercials for Contadina tomato paste and Beechnut chewing gum, both about 1966-67. They also made radio commercials for Dr. Pepper and McDonald's, about 1973-75.

The first movie was *That Tennessee Beat*, (1966), a Robert L. Lippert presentation, released by Twentieth Century Fox, produced and directed by Richard Brill, written by Paul Schneider. The stars were Minnie Pearl, Merle Travis, Sharon DeBord, Dolores Faith, Earl Richards, and Jim Reader. Also appearing were The Statler Brothers, Boots Randolph, the Stony Mountain Cloggers, and Pete Drake (steel guitar player). The two songs featured by the Statlers were FLOWERS ON THE WALL and THE RIGHT ONE.

The second movie was *Smokey & the Bandit II* (1980), a Universal picture produced by Hank Moonjean and directed by Hal Needham. It stared Burt Reynolds, Jackie Gleason, Jerry Reed, Dom DeLuise, and Sally Field. The songs featured are DO YOU KNOW YOU ARE MY SUNSHINE and CHARLOTTE'S WEB. The Statlers appear in the opening scenes.

# Bibliography

Connor, D. Russell. "What Is Discography: Its Goals and Methods." **Studies In Jazz Discography**. New Brunswick, New Jersey: Rutgers University Press, 1971.

Escott, Colin. **The Statler Brothers 30th Anniversary Celebration Scrapbook**. Mercury Nashville, 1994.

Hively, Kay, and Brumley, A.E. Jr. **I'll Fly Away, The Life Story of Albert Brumley, Jr.**; Branson, Missouri: Mountaineer Books, 1990.

Malone, Bill C. **Country Music, U.S.A.: A Fifty-year History.** Austin, Texas: The University of Texas Press, 1968.

Porterfield, Nolan. "Country Music Discography: Esoteric Art and Humanistic Craft." **The Southern Quarterly**, Vol. 22 (3), 1984. pp. 15-29.

Ruppli, Michel. **The Mercury Labels: A Discography in Five Volumes**. Westport, Connecticut: Greenwood Publishing Group, 1993.

Rust, Brian. **Guide to Discography**. Westport, Connecticut: Greenwood Publishing Group, 1980.

Smith, John L. **The Johnny Cash Discography**. Westport, Connecticut: Greenwood Publishing Group, 1985.

--- **The Johnny Cash Discography, 1984-1993.** Westport, Connecticut: Greenwood Publishing Group, 1994.

Stevenson, Gordon. "Discography: Scientific, Analytical, Historical and Systematic." **Library Trends**, (1962). pp.101-135.

Weber, Rev. Jerome F. "Discography: A Plea For Rules," **Recorded Sound**, 57-58, Jan.-Apr. 1975. pp. 380-382.

Wiegland, John P., Editor. **Praise for the Lord** (hymnal), Praise Press, Nashville, Tennessee, 1992.

# Some I Wrote

Some I wrote for money
Some I wrote for fun
Some I wrote and threw away
      and never sang to anyone.

One I wrote for Momma
And a couple still aren't through
I've lost track of all the rest
      but the most I wrote for you.

*Don Reid/Harold Reid*
May 25, 1977
American Cowboy Music Co., Inc.
Used by permission of
  All Nations Publishing Co., Inc.

# Composer Index

*Page Numbers are recording sessions only.*

# Don Reid

All Over Again 82
The All-Girl-All-Gospel Quartet
    116
Angel in Her Face 93
Atlanta Blue 93
Beat the Devil 62
Before the Magic Turns to Memory
    71
The Best That I Can Do 71
The Blackwood Brothers by the
    Statler Brothers 54
The Brave Apostles Twelve 61
A Child of the Fifties 81
Chet, You're the Reason 117
    (DR/Debo Reid/Langdon Reid)
Christmas Eve (Kodia's Theme) 98
    (Debo Reid/DR/*Harold Reid*)
Count On Me 100
Déjà Vu 103
    (DR/*Harold Reid*/Debo Reid)
A Different Song 41, 99
Different Things to Different
    People 69
Don't Forget Yourself 70
Dream On 116
Falling in Love 110
    (DR, Debo Reid)
A Friend's Radio 64
Give It Your Best 95
Grandma 69
Hat & Boots 65
Have a Little Faith 58
Here We Are Again 77
★Holly★Wood★ 94
I Don't Dance No More 85
I Don't Dream Anymore 101
    (DR/Debo Reid)
I Dreamed About You 71
I Never Once Got Tired of You
    (*Harold Reid*/DR/Debo Reid)
    107
I Never Spend a Christmas That I
    Don't Think of You 73

I Was There 66
I Wish I Could Be 50
I'll Be Here 58
I'll Be the One 104
    (DR/Debo Reid)
I'll Go to My Grave Lovin' You 56
I'll Take Care of You 41
If We Never Had 52
Jealous Eyes (Debo Reid/DR) 107
Jesus, Take Another Look at Me
    45
Let It Show 67
Let's Get Started If We're Gonna
    Break My Heart 106
    (*Harold Reid*/DR/Debo Reid)
Lifetime of Loving You in Vain, A
    (DR/Debo Reid/Landgon Reid)
    112
Love Was All We Had 83
Maggie 63
Makin' Rounds 25
Maple Street Mem'ries 105
Monday Morning Secretary 48
More Like Daddy Than Me 100
My Darling Hildegarde 23
New York City 38
Nobody Else 106
Nothing As Original As You 78
One More Summer in Virginia 58
One Takes the Blame 94
Pictures (DR/*Lew DeWitt*) 39
The Rest of My Life 111
Same Way Every Time 112
Silver Medals & Sweet Memories
    68
Sissy 30
So Mary Could Make It Home 57
Some Memories Last Forever 92
Somebody New Will Be Coming
    Along 67
Something I Haven't Done Yet 64
Somewhere in the Night 98
    (Debo Reid/DR)
The Star 66
The Streets of San Francisco 51

## Harold Reid

## Lew DeWitt

## Jimmy Fortune

## Harold Reid &
## Don Reid

## Don Reid & Harold Reid

All American Girl  57
Better Than I Did Then  67
Christmas to Me  74
Christmas Eve (Kodia's Theme)
    (Debo Reid/*DR/HR*)  98
The Class of '57    45
Daddy  41
Do You Know You Are My
    Sunshine  72
Eve  55
Everything You See in Your
    Dreams  111
A Few Old Memories  57
For Momma  99
He Went to the Cross Loving You
    56
I'm Sorry You Had to Be the One
    (*DR/HR*/John Rimel)  97
I've Never Lived This Long Before
    115
If It Makes Any Difference  70
Jesus Is the Answer EveryTime  111
A Letter from Shirley Miller  57
Making Memories  40
My Music, My Memories and You
    107
1953-Dear John-Honky Tonk-Blues
    44
The Official Historian on Shirley
    Jean Berrell  71
The Regular Saturday Night
    Setback Card Game  69
Second Thoughts  39
She's Too Good  55
Something You Can't Buy  75
Song of David  59
Sweeter and Sweeter  95
Left-Handed Woman  54
Think of Me  107
Who Do You Think?  61
Would You Recognize Jesus?  62
You Could Be Coming to Me  66
Your Foolish Game  21

### Harold Reid/Don Reid/Phil Balsley/Lew DeWitt

The Last Goodbye  36

### Phil Balsley/Lew DeWitt/Don Reid/Harold Reid

Saturday Morning Radio Show  44

### Harold Reid/Don Reid/Phil Balsley/Lew DeWitt

Saturday Morning Radio Show #2
    52
Alive at the Johnny Mack Brown
    High School  52
Rainbow Valley Confidential
    Audition Tape  53

### Harold Reid/Don Reid/Jimmy Fortune/Phil Balsley

Mary's Sweet Smile  98

### Arranged and/or adapted by the Statler Brothers

Amazing Grace  95
Are You Washed in the Blood  31
Away in a Manger  73
Beautiful Life, A  29
Brahms' Bethlehem Lullaby  98
Christmas Medley, A   72
In the Garden  70
Jingle Bells  74
Life's Railway to Heaven  85
Love Lifted Me  114
Oh Happy Day  32
Old Rugged Cross, The  113
Pass Me Not  28
Precious Memories  29
Rock of Ages   113
Shenandoah  26
Star-Spangled Banner, The    77
Sweet By and By  91
Tell Me Why  104
There Is Power in the Blood  102
When the Roll Is Called Up Yonder
    107
When You & I Were Young,
    Maggie  39

# The Second Generation

## Kim Reid

The Best I Know How  104
Blessed Be  101
Counting My Memories  77
He Is There  109
He'll Always Have You Again  115
I Had Too Much to Dream  84
I Never Want to Kiss You Goodbye
   90
Is It Your Place or Mine  112
Moon Pretty Moon  105
Old Cheerleaders Cry  79
   (KR/*Harold Reid*)
Take One Night at a Time  94
Who Am I to Say?  70

## Langdon Reid

Chet, You're the Reason  117
   (*Don Reid*/Debo Reid/LR)
He's Always There for You  113
Jesus Living Next to Me  185
A Lifetime of Loving You  112
   (*Don Reid*/Debo Reid/LR)
What We Love to Do  115
   (Wil Reid/LR)

## Wil Reid

Dynamite  110
That Haunted Old House  116
   (WR/*Harold Reid*)
What We Love to Do  115
   (WR/Langdon Reid)

## Debo Reid

Chet, You're the Reason  117
   (*Don Reid*/DR/Langdon Reid)
Christmas Eve (Kodia's Theme)  98
   (DR/*Don Reid/Harold Reid*)
Déjà Vu  103
   (*Harold Reid/Don Reid*/DR)
Fallin' in Love (*Don Reid*/DR)  110
I Don't Dream Anymore  101
   (*Don Reid*/DR)
I Never Once Got Tired of You  107
   (*Harold Reid/Don Reid*/DR)
I'll Be the One (*Don Reid*/DR)  104
Jealous Eyes (DR/*Don Reid*)  107
A Lifetime of Loving You  112
   (*Don Reid*/DR/Langdon Reid)
Let's Get Started If We're Gonna
   Break My Heart  106
   (*Harold Reid/Don Reid*/DR)
Somewhere in the Night  98
   (DR/*Don Reid*)
Walking Heartache in Disguise  108
   (*Harold Reid/Don Reid*/DR)
Will You Be There  100
   (*Don Reid*/DR)

## Kim Reid - Karmen Reid - Kodi Reid

You Don't Wear Blue So Well  97

# Musician and Guest Artist Index

The Statler Brothers are also unique in the recording industry in that their studio musicians remained constant. There was very little turnover in the personnel accompanying them. This listing is divided into categories: Session Musicians, the Cowboy Symphony Orchestra and the All-American Band, the Nashville String Machine and/or The Shelly Kurland Strings, Brass & Woodwind Instruments, Guest Musicians and Guest Artists-Singers (appearing only on a session or two). Guest artists are background vocals, and/or guest appearances.

*[This is the band that travels with the Statlers on tour. They have performed on the TV show, and appeared in videos.]*

### The Cowboy Symphony Orchestra

*(There was a personnel change in January, 1992, and a name change.)*

### The All-American Band

Vanosdale, Gary - viola  43, 47, 49,
   57, 59, 65, 67-68, 70, 72-76, 79,
   81, 83, 85, 90-91, 94-95, 98, 100,
   102-103, 105, 109, 115
Vanosdale, Mary K. - violin  117
Vanosdale, Pamela (Sixfin) - cello
   72, 74-76, 85, 90-91, 94
   (see also Sixfin, Pamela)
Vanderkooi, David - cello  38, 49
Walker, Carol - violin  79
Wilkinson, Kristin - viola, violin
   105, 109, 117
Woolf, Stephanie - violin, viola
   38, 42-43, 47, 49, 57, 59, 65, 67,
   70, 72-76, 79, 81, 83, 85, 91,
   94-95, 98, 100, 102

### Brass & Woodwind Instruments

Bissell, Roger - trombone  60, 62, 94
Childs, Ralph - tuba  81
Cunningham, George - trumpet  60, 62
Good, Dennis - trombone  76
Levine, Sam - saxophone  91
Mullins, Mary Ann - tuba  57
Osiel, Marianne - oboe  103
Puett, Bill - flute, clarinet, tenor sax
   72, 76, 80, 103
Ramm, Eberhard - French horn
   60, 62, 103
Sefsik, Steve - clarinet  42, 65
Sheffield, Don - trumpet
   60, 62, 65, 76
Skipper, James "Buddy" - clarinet  94
Solee, Denis - saxophone, flute  83
Taylor, Bobby G. - oboe
Tidwell, George - trumpet
   44, 65, 76, 80, 94

### Guest Musicians

Atkins, Chet - guitar  117
Bashful Brother Oswald (Pete Kirby)
   - dobro  75
Byrd, Billy - guitar  75
Chalker, H.L. "Curly" - steel guitar  75
Cramer, Floyd - piano  39
Helms, Don - steel guitar  75
Jones, Marshall Louis "Grandpa"-
   banjo  58
Martin, Odell - guitar  75
Moore, Scotty - guitar  75
Perkins, Carl - guitar  19, 20, 75
Scruggs, Earl - banjo  39
Tubb, Ernest - guitar  76
Wiseman, Mac - guitar  75
Wootton, Bob - guitar  75

### Guest Artists - Singers

Foust, Diane Williams   116
Gayle, Crystal  119
King, Doris  116
McCracken, Jean  104
McDorman, Joe  78
Psanos, Cindy Nixon  116
Rae, Diana  104
Smith, Tammy Stephens  116
Suits, Wendy  117
Walker, Jeanine  117

# Song Title Index

**About the Compiler**

ALICE Y. HOLTIN grew up in Florence, Alabama, where she delighted in week-end trips to the Grand Ole Opry in Nashville. She has been a loyal fan of the Statler Brothers for many years, attending their concerts whenever possible. She currently resides with her family in the Arkansas Ozarks, is a former board member of The Little O' Oprey, a music preservation institution, and is a current member of the Association for Recorded Sound Collections (ARSC).

ISBN 0-313-29663-4

90000>

EAN

9 780313 296635

HARDCOVER BAR CODE